CIPS Study Matters

Level 4

Foundation Diploma in Purchasing and Supply

COURSE BOOK

Managing Purchasing and Supply Relationships

© Profex Publishing Limited, 2010

Printed and distributed by the Chartered Institute of Purchasing & Supply

Easton House, Easton on the Hill, Stamford, Lincolnshire PE9 3NZ

Tel: +44 (0) 1780 756 777

Fax: +44 (0) 1780 751 610

Email: info@cips.org

Website: www.cips.org

First edition October 2006
Second edition February 2008
Third edition February 2009
Fourth edition May 2010
Reprinted with minor amendments October 2010

Contents

Preface

Welcome to your new Study Pack.

For each subject you have to study, your Study Pack consists of three elements.

- A **Course Book** (the current volume). This provides detailed coverage of all topics specified in the unit content.

- A small-format volume of **Passnotes**. For each learning objective, these highlight and summarise the key points of knowledge and understanding that should underpin an exam answer. Use your Passnotes in the days and weeks leading up to the exam.

- An extensive range of **online resources**. These include a **Quick Start Guide** (a rapid 40-page overview of the subject), practice questions of exam standard (with full suggested solutions), notes on recent technical developments in the subject area, and recent news items (ideal for enhancing your solutions in the exam). These can all be downloaded from the study resources area at www.cips.org. You will need to log in with your membership details to access this information.

For a full explanation of how to use your new Study Pack, turn now to page xiii. And good luck in your exams!

A note on style

Throughout your Study Packs you will find that we use the masculine form of personal pronouns. This convention is adopted purely for the sake of stylistic convenience – we just don't like saying 'he/she' all the time. Please don't think this reflects any kind of bias or prejudice.

October 2010

The Exam

The format of the paper

The time allowed is three hours. The examination is in two sections.

Section A – case study scenario, with two role play application questions based on the case study, each worth 25 marks.

Section B – questions to test knowledge and understanding. Candidates will be required to answer two questions from a choice of four. As with Section A, questions will be worth 25 marks each.

The unit content

The unit content is reproduced below, together with reference to the chapter in this Course Book where each topic is covered.

Unit characteristics

This unit is designed to enable students to focus on developing and managing effective relationships, old and new, within the supply chain.

Students will be able to review and develop existing relationships and identify opportunities for establishing new relationships that will enhance the performance of the supply chain, while exploring the benefits and risks of establishing such relationships.

By the end of this unit, students will be able to apply a range of tools and techniques to manage relationships and explain how to exploit opportunities in order to maximise the effectiveness of the supply chain.

Statements of practice

On completion of this unit, students will be able to:

* Review the effectiveness of existing relationships and identify potential areas for growth and diversification in the supply chain

* Examine supply chains and appraise key relationships and growth opportunities

* Apply a range of techniques for supplier selection and assessment, for the provision of goods and services

* Appraise procedures to support the outsourcing of services

* Explain the use of a range of interpersonal and communication techniques required to develop personal effectiveness in relationships

* Identify supply chain problems and propose resolutions

* Explain how to monitor and review supply chain relationship effectiveness.

Learning objectives and indicative content

1.0 The context of relationships in supply chain management
(Weighting 30%)

Chapter

1.1 Classify and describe the range of relationships that may exist within supply chains.

- Definition of relationships in the context of supply — 1
- Overview of internal and external relationships — 1

1.2 Evaluate the contribution of appropriate and well managed relationships in achieving co-operation and collaboration between buyers and suppliers.

- The relationship spectrum — 1
- Adversarial — 1
- Arm's length — 1
- Transactional — 1
- Closer tactical — 1
- Single sourced — 1
- Strategic alliance — 1
- Partnership — 1
- Co-destiny — 1

1.3 Evaluate or analyse the challenges in managing effectively the relationships between purchasers and suppliers.

- Supply positioning model — 2
- Supplier preferencing model — 2
- The reasons for changing the way in which a relationship operates — 2
- Managing risk in commercial relationships — 2
- Buyer and supplier behaviour in relationships — 2
- Market management matrix — 2

1.4 Define the natural lifecycle of supply relationships and analyse the position of specific relationships in their lifecycle.

- The concept of the relationship lifecycle — 3
- The stages of the relationship lifecycle — 3
- Linking the relationship lifecycle to the relationship spectrum — 3
- Understanding your position in the relationship lifecycle — 3

1.5 Differentiate between lean and agile supply philosophies on supplier relationships.

- Traditional supply philosophy — 4
- Lean supply philosophy — 4
- Agile supply philosophy — 4

3.0 Managing outsourced relationships
(Weighting 15%)

4.0 Developing and managing relationships with suppliers
(Weighting 30%)

4.1 Identify the causes of conflict in supply relationships and select appropriate methods for their resolution.

•	The positive and negative roles of conflict	10
•	Conflict factors	10
•	Conflict factors related to the types of relationships in the relationship spectrum	10
•	Stakeholder management and conflict	10

4.2 Evaluate the impact of both power and dependency on the management of supplier relationships.

•	Power versus dependency	10
•	Relationship issues resulting from power and dependency	10
•	Managing power and dependency	10

4.3 Analyse the role of transparent communications between purchasers and suppliers in the effective management of supply relationships.

•	Stakeholder communication	10
•	Communication tools and techniques in the context of supplier management	10
•	Transparency: open-book costing	10

4.4 Appraise the use of e-purchasing in supply relationships.

•	E-purchasing and the relationship spectrum	11
•	E-purchasing and supply situations	11
•	Appropriateness of e-tools and their effect on relationships	11
•	Suppliers' perspective of e-purchasing	11
•	Stakeholders' perspective of e-purchasing	11

4.5 Appraise the relationship aspects of international supply contracts.

•	Factors affecting international supply contracts	12
•	Managing risk in international relationships	12
•	Factors affecting performance measurement and ongoing monitoring	12
•	International supplier development	12

4.6 Evaluate a range of techniques to develop stronger relationships between purchasers and suppliers.

•	Supplier development	13
•	Supplier development opportunities	13
•	Supplier development versus supplier relationships	13
•	The stakeholder and supplier development	13

How to Use Your Study Pack

Familiarisation

At this point you should begin to familiarise yourself with the package of benefits you have purchased.

- Go to www.cips.org and log on. Then go to Study and Qualify/Study Resources. Browse through the free content relating to this subject.
- Download the Quick Start Guide and print it out. Open up a ring binder and make the Quick Start Guide your first item in there.
- Now glance briefly through the Course Book (the text you're reading right now!) and the Passnotes.

Organising your study

'Organising' is the key word: unless you are a very exceptional student, you will find a haphazard approach is insufficient, particularly if you are having to combine study with the demands of a full-time job.

A good starting point is to timetable your studies, in broad terms, between now and the date of the examination. How many subjects are you attempting? How many chapters are there in the Course Book for each subject? Now do the sums: how many days/weeks do you have for each chapter to be studied?

Remember:

- Not every week can be regarded as a study week – you may be going on holiday, for example, or there may be weeks when the demands of your job are particularly heavy. If these can be foreseen, you should allow for them in your timetabling.
- You also need a period leading up to the exam in which you will revise and practise what you have learned.

Once you have done the calculations, make a week-by-week timetable for yourself for each paper, allowing for study and revision of the entire unit content between now and the date of the exams.

Getting started

Aim to find a quiet and undisturbed location for your study, and plan as far as possible to use the same period each day. Getting into a routine helps avoid wasting time. Make sure you have all the materials you need before you begin – keep interruptions to a minimum.

Begin by reading through your Quick Start Guide. This should take no more than a couple of hours, even reading slowly. By the time you have finished this you will have a reasonable grounding in the subject area. You will build on this by working through the Course Book.

Using the Course Book

You should refer to the Course Book to the extent that you need it.

*   If you are a newcomer to the subject, you will probably need to read through the Course Book quite thoroughly. This will be the case for most students.
*   If some areas are already familiar to you – either through earlier studies or through your practical work experience – you may choose to skip sections of the Course Book.

The content of the Course Book

This Course Book has been designed to give detailed coverage of every topic in the unit content. As you will see from pages vii–xii, each topic mentioned in the unit content is dealt with in a chapter of the Course Book. For the most part the order of the Course Book follows the order of the unit content closely, though departures from this principle have occasionally been made in the interest of a logical learning order.

Each chapter begins with a reference to the learning objectives and unit content to be covered in the chapter. Each chapter is divided into sections, listed in the introduction to the chapter, and for the most part being actual captions from the unit content.

All of this enables you to monitor your progress through the unit content very easily and provides reassurance that you are tackling every subject that is examinable.

Each chapter contains the following features.

*   Introduction, setting out the main topics to be covered
*   Clear coverage of each topic in a concise and approachable format
*   A chapter summary
*   Self-test questions

The study phase

For each chapter you should begin by glancing at the main headings (listed at the start of the chapter). Then read fairly rapidly through the body of the text to absorb the main points. If it's there in the text, you can be sure it's there for a reason, so try not to skip unless the topic is one you are familiar with already.

Then return to the beginning of the chapter to start a more careful reading. You may want to take brief notes as you go along, but bear in mind that you already have your Quick Start Guide and Passnotes – there is no point in duplicating what you can find there.

Test your recall and understanding of the material by attempting the self-test questions. These are accompanied by cross-references to paragraphs where you can check your answers and refresh your memory.

Practising what you have learned

Once you think you have learned enough about the subject, or about a particular topic within the overall subject area, it's good to practise. Access the study resources at www.cips.org, and download a practice question on the relevant area. Alternatively, download a past exam question. Attempt a solution yourself before looking at our suggested solution or the Senior Assessor's comments.

Make notes of any mistakes you made, or any areas where your answer could be improved. If there is anything you can't understand, you are welcome to email us for clarification (course.books@cips.org).

The revision phase

Your approach to revision should be methodical and you should aim to tackle each main area of the unit content in turn. Begin by re-reading your Quick Start Guide. This gives an overview that will help to focus your more detailed study. Then re-read your notes and/or the separate Passnotes accompanying this Course Book. Then return to question practice. Review your own solutions to the practice questions you have had time to attempt. If there are gaps, try to find time to attempt some more questions, or at least to review the suggested solutions.

Additional reading

Your Study Pack provides you with the key information needed for each module but CIPS strongly advocates reading as widely as possible to augment and reinforce your understanding. CIPS produces an official reading list of books, which can be downloaded from the bookshop area of the CIPS website.

To help you, we have identified one essential textbook for each subject. We recommend that you read this for additional information.

The essential textbook for this unit is *The Relationship-Driven Supply Chain* by Stuart Emmett and Barry Crocker, published by Gower (ISBN: 0–566–08684–0).

CHAPTER 1

Relationships in Context

Learning objectives

1.1 Classify and describe the range of relationships that may exist within supply chains.

- Definition of relationships in the context of supply
- Overview of internal and external relationships

1.2 Evaluate the contribution of appropriate and well managed relationships in achieving co-operation and collaboration between buyers and suppliers.

- The relationship spectrum
- Adversarial
- Arm's length
- Transactional
- Closer tactical
- Single sourced
- Strategic alliance
- Partnership
- Co-destiny

Chapter headings

1 Internal and external relationships

2 The relationship spectrum

3 Transactional relationships

4 Collaborative relationships

5 Relationships and organisational success

Introduction

In this chapter we describe the different types of commercial relationship that exist in the purchasing and supply context.

1 Internal and external relationships

Defining relationships

1.1 This study module is concerned with the commercial relationships that exist between buyers and suppliers. It is appropriate to begin with a few definitions.

1.2 In the Collins Concise Dictionary we find the following definition of 'commercial'.

1. Relating to, engaged in or used for commerce. 2 Profitable; having profit as the main goal

1.3 This conveys an important point about the relationships that we will be studying, namely that they are usually entered into for the purpose of making a profit. However, it is worth noting that some of the organisations with which buyers are concerned are not dominated by a profit motive. For example, this is true of charities and government departments.

1.4 In the same dictionary we find the following definition of 'relationship'.

1. The state of being related ... 3. The friendship, contact, communications etc which exist between people

1.5 Again, this definition brings out an important point about commercial relationships, namely that they are concerned with people, and that contact, communications – and perhaps even friendship – are necessary ingredients.

1.6 Summarising these points, we can say that purchasing and supply relationships involve a degree of closeness between people (usually in different organisations), entered into for the purpose of mutual benefit. As we will see in this chapter, the degree of closeness may be great or slight. And the benefit may not always be monetary – other motivations may also be at work, such as the prestige of working with a particular organisation.

1.7 As buyers, we are mostly interested in relationships with suppliers. A supplier is usually an external organisation providing us with quality goods or services for use in our business, in return for a consideration that will boost its own profits. However, this view of suppliers is not complete.

- As already noted, some suppliers are not motivated by profit. For example, many public sector organisations have a goal of providing the best possible service to their 'customers', and are not attempting to make a profit.

- In some cases, a supplier is not an external organisation. 'Supplier' and 'customer' may both be members of the same organisation. This leads us on to the concept of internal and external relationships (see later in this section).

1.8 It is important to establish effective relationships with suppliers. The nature of an effective supplier relationship will vary with circumstances, and on the relative importance to the buying organisation of the supplier's product or service. However, it is interesting to look at five stages of development in the selection of a supply base, identified in an exercise by the Treasury's Central Unit on Procurement in 1986 (*Procurement Practice and Development*). These are shown in Table 1.1.

Table 1.1 *Selection of a supply base*

Stage	Supply base
Innocence	The organisation uses a large number of suppliers and selects them in a random fashion. There is clear scope for improvement.
Awareness	The organisation still uses a large number of suppliers, but most spending is on just a few of them.
Understanding	The organisation has reduced the number of its suppliers still further, and appreciates the benefits of a good working relationship with suppliers.
Competence	There is a partnership with suppliers for key procurement items. There is multi-sourcing of other (non-key) items.
Excellence	There is a continually-reviewed programme to optimise the supply base so as to achieve strategic objectives.

An overview of internal and external relationships

1.9 The supply chain can be seen as a long sequence of operations and activities, some of them carried out by the organisation itself, and some by suppliers or customers. Within an organisation, operations can be seen from an overall 'macro' perspective, as a single whole operation. It can also be seen as a number of separate operations that have to be carried out to transform the original inputs into the final finished output or service.

1.10 For example, an operation in an advertising agency to prepare a campaign for a client can be seen as a single overall operation, but it can also be seen as a number of 'micro operations', such as TV advertisement production, copy writing and copy editing for magazine advertisements, artwork design and production, media selection, media buying, and so on. Within each of these micro operations, there are other operations. Producing a TV advertisement, for example, involves micro operations such as story boarding and script writing, film production, the shooting of the film, film editing, and so on.

1.11 Each micro operation needs its input of resources, which might include both externally-purchased materials and services and inputs from another department or work group in the organisation. Each micro operation is supplied, both internally and externally.

1.12 The concept of internal supply leads on to the idea that within any organisation there are internal suppliers and internal customers.

1.13 For example, a road haulage company might have operational units for maintenance and servicing of vehicles, loading and driving. One micro process within the overall operation is the repair and servicing of vehicles. The mechanics servicing the vehicles are the internal supplier in the process, and the drivers of the vehicles are the internal customers. Similarly, the team that loads the vehicles is an internal supplier in the loading operation, and the drivers are the internal customers.

1.14 In most respects, an internal customer should be treated as any external customer should be treated. The aim of the organisation should be to deliver a product or service that meets the customer's needs.

1.15 The main difference between an internal and an external customer is that in many cases, the internal customer has no freedom of choice of suppliers, and must use the internal supplier.

1.16   The concept of the internal customer is that within an organisation, internally-delivered goods and services, as well as externally-obtained goods and services, should meet the requirements and expectations of the internal customer. To do this, the needs of the internal customer have to be identified. The needs of the internal customer can only be properly established by having a dialogue with the customer.

1.17   Effective purchasing will therefore make use of cross-functional teams (CFTs), with representatives of the internal customers included within the team.

2   The relationship spectrum

Competitive relationships

2.1   A relationship with a supplier can be either competitive or collaborative.

2.2   In a competitive relationship, the buying organisation seeks to obtain the best price possible from the supplier, for the required quality and delivery standards. The buyer tries to squeeze the supplier's profit margins. A competitive approach can be seen as a win-lose situation, where any gains for the buyer are at the expense of the supplier, and *vice versa*.

2.3   A competitive approach to suppliers should nevertheless be professional and ethical. Even so, it is doubtful whether such an approach is conducive to a long-term relationship with the supplier. There will be no collaboration between buyer and supplier, and no recognition of mutual interests.

2.4   The individual or individuals responsible for buying might argue regularly with the supplier's representatives, and complain regularly about aspects of the products or service supplied (price, promptness of delivery, quality, and so on). In such cases, the relationship will be adversarial.

2.5   Competitive relationships are associated with transactional purchasing. Features of transactional purchasing are as follows.

- Competitive bidding for contracts.
- Many competing suppliers.
- Typically, standard products.
- Wide supply markets.
- No benefit from or need for a high degree of trust between buyer and supplier.
- No supplier power. The cost of switching from one supplier to another is low.

Collaborative relationships

2.6   In a transactional relationship there is a simple exchange between supplier and buyer. The supplier provides goods or services; the buyer provides money in payment. This differs from a collaborative relationship in which the benefits of doing business together arise from ideas of sharing as well as exchanging.

2.7   In a collaborative approach, the buyer organisation seeks to develop a long-term relationship with the supplier. The strategic view is that the buyer organisation and the supplier share common interests, and both can benefit from seeking ways of adding value in the supply chain. There is a win-win situation, where buyer, supplier and end-customer can all benefit.

2.8   The supplier will participate with the buyer in looking for improvements and innovations, secure in the knowledge that any benefits that are achieved will be shared. Buyer and supplier will jointly set targets for improvements in cost and quality, and meet regularly to discuss progress towards achieving these targets. A collaborative relationship is a proactive relationship that has the aim of looking for improvements; it is not a long-term cosy customer-supplier relationship where the *status quo* is allowed to prevail.

2.9   Companies can think constructively and in an innovative way about their relationships with suppliers. You might be expected to show a similar approach in your examination. Here are just three examples of initiatives taken in the automotive industry in recent years.

- Several motor car manufacturers have been involving suppliers in new model design.

- One manufacturer arranged to share a location with one of its suppliers for their manufacturing activities.

- One manufacturer has started to use its suppliers to assemble the cars.

2.10   A customer-supplier relationship will develop naturally over time, through:

- growing trust, as the customer and supplier continue to do business together

- length of time, as the customer and supplier get to know each other better, and gain reassurance from the length of their relationship

- the customer reducing the number of suppliers it uses, possibly down to just the one supplier

- the supplier assigning specific assets to the exclusive use of working on orders for that customer.

Table 1.2 *Collaborative relationships – the benefits*

Benefits of a collaborative relationship to the supplier	Benefits of a collaborative relationship to the buyer
The buyer will appoint a vendor manager to develop the relationship. The supplier will always know who to deal with in the buyer organisation.	The buyer focuses attention on improving the relationship with key suppliers.
The vendor manager will introduce the supplier to the managers in the organisation responsible for buying decisions.	The supplier's awareness of the buyer's requirements will mean that the supplier is more likely to be successful in meeting them.
The supplier will be kept informed of the buyer's forward plans.	The supplier will be actively involved with the buyer in the quality improvement process.
The supplier will gain a much better understanding of the buyer organisation and its needs.	The supplier should develop a high level of trust and confidence in the buyer.
The buyer and supplier will set up joint quality-improvement teams, that both parties will benefit from.	
The supplier is likely to get more business from the buyer, as a preferred supplier.	

Which is better: a competitive or collaborative approach?

2.11 The natural temptation might be to think that a collaborative relationship would be ideal but that in practice, there is all too often an adversarial and competitive relationship with suppliers. This view, however, is not necessarily correct.

2.12 A collaborative approach is not necessarily more suitable than a competitive approach to dealing with suppliers.

- The benefit of a competitive approach is to squeeze the profit margins of the supplier, and in doing so to obtain some of the value that the supplier would otherwise keep for himself.

- Developing a collaborative relationship with a supplier takes time and effort, and it is unrealistic to try creating more collaborative relationships than the buyer can properly handle.

- Collaborative relationships are not worth the time and trouble for non-key items, where a failure in supply would not be damaging.

2.13 The so-called Pareto principle or 80: 20 rule often applies. Here, it would mean that about 20 per cent of a firm's suppliers provide about 80 per cent of the total supplies. The focus of attention for developing collaborative relationships should be on the relatively small number of important suppliers. For items of lesser importance, a competitive relationship might be more appropriate, particularly when the buying organisation has two or more potential suppliers of the item.

2.14 Mark Ralf (in *Strategic Procurement Management in the 1990s: Concepts and Cases*, eds Lamming and Cox), writes: 'The good old-fashioned rottweiler approach to buying must co-exist with a more collaborative approach internally and externally.... Adversarial relationships exist, and rightfully so. What is needed however is a balance between both approaches and a sophisticated understanding of which tactic to use to develop the strategic goals of the organisation. Deciding which relationship is necessary and when is crucial. If this is not done then companies can be sucked into relationships they do not want, and that often generate higher costs, or time consuming activities and behaviour that are dysfunctional.'

Sourcing and relationships policy

2.15 Although competitive relationships are often necessary and desirable, relationships with key suppliers will generally benefit from a collaborative approach. The arguments in favour of integrating the supply chain and developing customer-supplier partnerships along the supply chain might be summarised as follows.

- Supply chains compete, not companies.
- Most opportunities for reducing costs and enhancing value in the supply chain occur at the interface between supply chain partners.
- Adding to the competitiveness of a supply chain calls for a value-added exchange of information between the supply chain partners.
- The integration of the supply chain implies the integration of process in the supply chain.
- Achieving supply chain competitiveness requires a collective determination of strategy by the supply chain partners.

'Cosy relationship' versus a supply partnership

2.16 A proper supply partnership is not a 'cosy relationship' between customer and supplier. A cosy relationship does nothing to bring improvements to the supply chain, whereas a proactive partnership does. Features of a true supply partnership, as distinct from a cosy customer-supplier relationship, are as follows.

- There is a joint and mutual search for greater efficiency and competitiveness.
- There is joint planning for the future by the customer and the supplier.
- They have agreed shared objectives.
- There is an understanding between the customer and the supplier that there should be a joint effort to eliminate waste from the supply chain in order to become more competitive.
- There is openness and transparency between the organisations.
- Each party understands the expectations of the other, and seeks to meet or exceed them.
- The relationship is one of equal partners, and the buyer does not adopt a 'master-servant' attitude.
- They recognise that the relationship might not last for ever, and have a prepared and agreed exit strategy, in the event that the relationship should come to an end.

The relationship spectrum

2.17 We have discussed in general terms the extremes of relationship possibilities, from competitive relationships at one extreme to collaborative relationships at the other. Your syllabus implies a more detailed classification in which these two extremes form the ends of a 'relationship spectrum', with various degrees of closeness in between. This is illustrated in Figure 1.1

Figure 1.1 *The relationship spectrum*

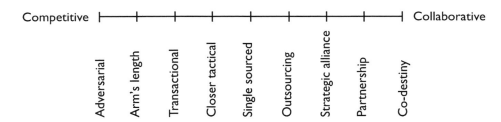

2.18 In Table 1.3 we highlight some of the main features distinguishing each of the relationship types depicted on the diagram.

Table 1.3 *Relationship types and characteristics*

Relationship type	Characteristics
Adversarial relationship	Buyer and supplier are 'opponents', each striving to obtain advantages at the other's expense. There is little trust, communication and cooperation, and there may even be conflict.
Arm's length relationship	This is a distant relationship where the buyer does not need frequent access to the supplier. Purchases are infrequent and of low volume, and the trouble of a closer relationship is not justified.
Transactional relationship	This is very similar to an arm's length relationship, with perhaps a more frequent requirement on the part of the buyer, but still referring to low-value, low-risk supplies.
Closer tactical relationship	This refers to a situation where the trouble of a close, collaborative relationship is not quite justified, but where the buyer is concerned to ensure that he is dealing with a very competent supplier, who perhaps also coordinates the activities of other suppliers.
Single-sourced relationship	In relation to a particular item, or a defined range of items, a buyer grants exclusivity to a single supplier, ie he undertakes not to buy such items from anyone else. This implies a high level of trust between buyer and supplier.
Outsourcing relationship	In order to focus on his organisation's core competencies, a buyer selects an external supplier to provide goods or services previously sourced in-house. Once again, a high level of trust is implied.
Strategic alliance	Two (or more) separate organisations identify areas where they can collaborate to deliver a joint offering. For example, a software developer might form an alliance with a training firm, the trainer providing courses in using the software.
Partnership relationship	Buyer and supplier agree to collaborate closely for the long term, sharing information and ideas for development. There is a very high level of trust and the aim is to find solutions that benefit both parties without detriment to either.
Co-destiny relationship	This is an even closer relationship, in which buyer and supplier link their businesses together for long-term mutual benefit. There is a high level of trust and interdependence.

2.19 Many of these points will be elaborated in the remainder of this chapter and in the chapter following.

3 *Transactional relationships*

When is a transactional relationship appropriate?

3.1 The arguments in favour of long-term collaborative relationships between buyers and suppliers have been advanced time and again in the modern purchasing literature. This can lead to the impression that short-term transactional relationships have no place in a strategic procurement function. As already pointed out above, this is not the case: there are situations where the trouble and expense of developing a long-term collaborative relationship is simply not justified.

3.2 Sometimes this is because of the nature of the product being purchased. If the product has little or no strategic importance to the buyer then a simple transactional model is appropriate. This might apply, for example, to purchases of office stationery.

3.3 Apart from the lack of strategic importance, there is also the consideration that many stationery suppliers exist, all offering similar prices, similar quality and similar delivery performance. No amount of collaboration will enable the supplier to differentiate his offering sufficiently to justify the effort required from the buyer.

3.4 Another case where the transactional model is appropriate is that of items which are purchased only rarely. The process of developing a collaborative relationship involves continuous interaction with the supplier, and this is hardly justified when actual purchases are rare.

3.5 Finally, there may be cases where a transactional relationship is effectively forced on the buyer, even in cases where the product being purchased is of high strategic importance. This can happen if the supplier is much larger than the buyer. In such a case, the buyer may want to work closely with the supplier, but from the supplier's perspective the volume of sales is too small to justify this. We return to this point in the context of supplier preferencing in the next chapter.

3.6 You may be able to think of other cases where a transactional model is appropriate.

Maximising the benefits of transactional relationships

3.7 Of course, just because a transactional model is adopted does not mean that the buyer should relax his efforts to maximise the benefits to his employer. The buyer will still wish to manage the relationship in the most efficient way.

3.8 To do so, he can make use of various modern developments that help to keep down costs and streamline transaction processing. For example, small-value orders may best be handled by use of corporate purchasing cards. Savings may also be available by electronic purchasing. And of course more traditional techniques such as the economic order quantity also have a part to play.

4 Collaborative relationships

The Partnership Sourcing initiative

4.1 In the UK, the government (in the form of the Department of Trade and Industry) and the Confederation of British Industries share an interest in encouraging the development and economic success of British businesses. It was recognised in the 1980s that developing a customer-supplier relationship could generate enormous mutual benefits for both the customer and the supplier. However, the successful development of customer-supplier relationships was all too often hindered by the win-lose attitude towards the purchasing transaction. Either the customer 'won' with a low price or the supplier 'won' with a high price.

4.2   The DTI and the CBI, recognising this problem and the need to do something about it, launched a *Partnership Sourcing* initiative in September 1990. The aim of the initiative was to encourage businesses to recognise the potential benefits from adopting a philosophy of win-win, where both parties in the relationship stand to gain from working together.

4.3   Partnership sourcing is defined by the CBI and DTI as follows:

'Partnership sourcing is a commitment by customers/suppliers, regardless of size, to a long-term relationship based on clear mutually agreed objectives to strive for world class capability and effectiveness.'

4.4   The aim of the initiative was to 'bring about a fundamental change in companies' philosophy leading to the widespread knowledge, understanding and implementation of partnership sourcing in the UK.'

4.5   The CBI and DTI list the principal characteristics of partnership sourcing as:

- top level management commitment
- involvement by all the relevant disciplines/functions
- customer and supplier working together
- a spirit of openness and trust between customer and supplier
- clear joint objectives
- a long-term relationship
- taking a proactive approach to improvement and developing the partnership, not a reactive approach to dealing with problems after they have happened
- a total quality management philosophy
- flexibility.

4.6   Lord Simon, a government minister during the 1990s speaking in 1998, explained the initiative as promoting 'a long-term non-binding relationship in which trading partners, usually a manufacturer and a supplier, work together for their collective long-term advantage, and negotiate prices and specifications as and when necessary.... The government has a continuing policy commitment to encourage all businesses, and especially small and medium-sized enterprises, to adopt the practices which are implicit in partnering.'

4.7   These practices include: 'sharing knowledge, sharing business improvements and sharing risk through what may be a formal or an informal network approach, and also using the supply chain. And the initial nature of the relationship that can be built up in the supply chain to maintain competitiveness ... is going to be increasingly important, in all sizes of business, as the global market place becomes more complex and more competitive.'

4.8   Partnership Sourcing Limited (PSL), a company set up by the government under the Partnership Sourcing initiative, has identified seven types of supplier relationship where partnership sourcing might be particularly beneficial.

- Where the customer has a **high spend** with the supplier.

- Where the customer faces **high risk**, in the sense that the continual supply of the product or service is vital to the buyer's operations, regardless of its market value.

- Where the product supplied is **technically complex**, calling for advanced technical knowledge by the supplier and where the cost of switching to a new supplier would be high.

- **'High hassle'** supplier relationships, where the product supplied is vital to the buyer's operations and is technically complex, such that the relationship requires a lot of time, effort and resources to manage.

- For the supply of a **new product or service**, where a new supplier may be required.

- Where the supply market for the product is **fast-changing**, so that an up-to-date knowledge of technological or legislative changes in the market is essential.

- In a **restricted supply market**, where there are few competent and reliable supplier firms, and closer links with a supplier could improve the security of supply.

Partnering agreement guidelines

4.9   PSL lays down 20 guidelines for a partnership agreement. These are shown in Table 1.4.

Table 1.4 *Guidelines for a partnership agreement*

	Topic	**Guidance**
1	Statement of principle	The title 'Statement of Principle' should be included in any major partnering relationship. For example, 'Partners A and B agree in principle to work together in an open and trusting style ...'
2	Scope	'The scope of the partnering relationship extends to the following materials, components and services ...'
3	Cost	'Each partner will work year on year to ensure that the total acquisition cost of items or services supplied will go down.'
4	Service	'The supplier will work to ensure achievement of customer performance and service levels of not less than ...'
5	Forecasts	'The customer will provide frequent accurate forecasts.'
6	Technology improvement	'Each partner will work to improve the technology ...'
7	Continuous improvement	'Each partner will start a continuous improvement programme in its own business ...'
8	Objectives	'Each partner will agree and set specific agreed annual objectives ...'
9	Hardship	'In the event that any partner gets into difficulty ... it will have the right to approach the other partner(s) requesting relief from hardship.'
10	Cost structure	'For each of the items or services supplied, an agreed open book cost structure will be created ...'

		Topic	Guidance
	11	Training	'The partners will work together to develop appropriate training methods, resources and qualifications for staff …'
	12	Capital investment	'Where expenditure on capital must be undertaken by the supplier to provide services on behalf of the customer, these will be identified at the beginning of the partnership relationship …'
	13	Confidentiality	'It is an absolute obligation of this agreement that any [sensitive] information is not passed to any other third party of any kind.'
	14	Exclusivity	'Where investment is made in intellectual property developed between the parties, supply may not occur under any circumstances to any third party …'
	15	Exit strategy	'The parties agree to the following potential break points in the partnering agreement … When these are reached, any party to this agreement may withdraw without penalty.'
	16	Termination	'In the event that both partners come to a conclusion that the partnering relationship must be dissolved, a notice period of … must be given prior to termination.'
	17	Management	'The partners will ensure that a joint review and management team is established.'
	18	Education and publicity	'Each party will undertake to brief its management and staff frequently.'
	19	Dispute resolution	'The joint review and management team will produce a defined ladder for escalating the resolution of problems to the appropriate level of management.'
	20	Key contacts	'The key contacts in this partnering relationship are x and y.'

Implementing a partnership relationship

4.10   PSL also set out a series of steps to guide a buyer in setting up a partnership relationship. These steps are listed below.

4.11   Which markets and which products and services?

- Identify your supply strategy.
- Identify and rank services for start-up of partnering.
- Develop an action plan.

4.12   Sell the idea.

- Sell to management.
- Sell to the rest of your organisation.
- Sell the idea to potential partners.

4.13 Choose your partners.

- Identify the candidates.
- Review candidates' performance to date.
- Define the criteria for selecting partners.
- Assess their management's interest in developing a partnership relationship.
- Understand their strategy.
- Select partner(s) for a pilot project.

4.14 Define what you want from the partnership relationship.

- Agree the style of relationship.
- Agree tangible relationships.
- Agree to continuous improvement.
- Agree exit strategy.
- Commit to a partnering relationship.

4.15 Make your first partnering relationship work.

- Tell everyone what you are doing.
- Agree monitoring and measuring systems.
- Start work and build joint improvement teams.
- Build the relationship.
- Continuously monitor results against objectives.

4.16 Refine and develop.

- Review and audit.
- Extend the programme.
- Develop new partners for the future.

Joint ventures

4.17 A buyer organisation might decide to form a long-term relationship with a supplier, possibly by setting up a joint venture or partnership. A joint venture might be a jointly-owned company, in which the buyer and the supplier each have an equity stake.

4.18 The reason for a joint venture or partnership might be that new investment is needed to finance an innovation. The supplier and the buyer might be unwilling to finance the whole venture on their own, but might agree to invest jointly, to share the potential benefits and the financial risk. In Central and Eastern Europe, a number of joint ventures have been formed by local companies and Western multinationals, to develop and exploit new consumer markets in those countries. The local company needs the investment finance that the multinational can provide, and the multinational needs the market knowledge and government support that a local firm can provide.

4.19 A joint venture or partnership could be either a temporary arrangement, with a clear end objective or time limit. Alternatively, it might be a long-term relationship without any definite end.

Co-destiny relationships

4.20   A co-destiny relationship is a customer-supplier relationship where the two organisations recognise that their interests are so closely linked that their futures depend on each other. If one succeeds, so will the other.

4.21   In a co-destiny relationship, the associates share:

- goals
- decision-making
- responsibility
- accountability, and
- trust.

4.22   A key feature of this model is sometimes referred to as 'policy deployment' or 'strategy deployment'. This means that priorities and key strategic issues are communicated to all members of the supply chain, however remote, in order to improve joint action.

The impact on supplier management

4.23   Adoption of the co-destiny model has a number of implications for management of suppliers.

4.24   To begin with, the emphasis is on developing a small number of suppliers who are completely trustworthy. The buyer works closely with these, sharing plans and developing jointly agreed processes.

4.25   All information systems may be freely accessed by all members of the supply chain. This implies a very high degree of trust among the partners.

4.26   Rapid response to change is vital, and this is facilitated by decentralisation of decision making among all members of the supply chain.

5   Relationships and organisational success

Achieving lean supply capabilities

5.1   Effective procurement, based on appropriate commercial relationships with carefully chosen suppliers, can be an important factor in overall organisational success. In this section of the chapter we look at some of the strategic contributions that purchasing can make in this area. We begin by examining the concept of lean supply.

5.2   The idea of lean production was first analysed in depth in a book published in 1990. *The Machine that Changed the World: The Triumph of Lean Production*, by Womack, Jones and Roos, is a study of production methods in the motor vehicle industry. The main conclusion of the study is that adoption of modern quality initiatives such as total quality management (TQM) and just in time manufacturing (JIT) has led to the displacement of the old mass production techniques.

5.3   In place of mass production the new model is referred to as lean production. As Saunders expresses it (in *Strategic Purchasing and Supply Chain Management*): 'The main goal of being "lean" is to obtain the same output from half the resources used by older methods – half the number of workers, half the number of design engineers, and half the level of inventory, for example'.

5.4   Implications of this new approach were that high-volume production of standard models was no longer enough to satisfy ever more demanding customers, and that higher levels of quality and shorter time to market in new product development were achievable targets.

5.5   In an important 1992 article, Daniel Jones identified five principles that characterised lean production organisations.

•   As far as possible, tasks and responsibilities are transferred to those who are actually adding value on the production line.

•   Discovering defects and problems immediately, and eliminating their causes, is an important objective of control systems.

•   A comprehensive information system enables everyone to respond quickly.

•   Organisation must be based on empowered work teams.

•   This in turn encourages a strong sense of reciprocal obligation between staff and employing firm.

5.6   The search for lean performance soon spread beyond its origins in manufacturing operations. Service companies realised that the new model was in many respects just as applicable to their markets. Within companies, individual functions began to seek ways of becoming leaner. In particular, the idea gained ground that eliminating waste in purchasing activities, and avoiding duplication of effort throughout the supply chain, could bring important cost and quality benefits. The concept of lean supply was born.

Eliminating waste

5.7   Lean supply is based on the concept of eliminating waste. Waste is any activity that uses resources but adds no value. Examples of waste are excessive inventories, rectifying defective output, unnecessary procedures, which are time-wasting, and so on. Lean supply is associated with the principles of just in time manufacturing and purchasing. JIT is also known as 'lean operations'.

5.8   Japanese car manufacturer Toyota was the first company to develop JIT, and the individual credited with devising JIT in Toyota from the 1940s was Taichi Ohno. JIT was originally called the Toyota Production System. After the end of the world war in 1945, Toyota recognised that it had much to do to catch up with the US automobile manufacturing industry. The company was making losses. In Japan, however, consumer demand for cars was weak, and consumers were very resistant to price increases. Japan also had a bad record for industrial disputes. Toyota itself suffered from major strike action in 1950.

5.9   Ohno identified the so-called 'seven wastes' and worked to eliminate them from operations in Toyota.

- Over-production
- Waste caused by transportation
- Waiting
- Motion – waste caused by physical movement of items
- Over-processing
- Waste caused by inventory
- Defects/corrections.

5.10   The operational requirements for JIT are as follows.

- High quality. Any defects or quality errors in production will reduce throughput and reduce the reliability of internal supply.
- Speed. Throughput in the operation must be fast. Customer orders have to be met by production rather than out of inventory, because there is no inventory.
- Reliability. Production must be reliable, without hold-ups.
- Flexibility. To meet customer orders quickly, production must be flexible. This means that production must be in small batch sizes. Lean production and supply are therefore distinguished from mass production.
- Lower cost. As a result of improving quality and speed of throughput, costs will be reduced.

5.11   A useful definition of JIT is given by Voss, *Just-in-Time Manufacture*, 1987:

'Just-in-time is a disciplined approach to improving overall productivity and eliminating waste. It provides for the cost-effective production and delivery of only the necessary quantity of parts at the right quality, at the right time and place, while using a minimum amount of facilities, equipment, materials and human resources. JIT is dependent on the balance between the supplier's flexibility and the user's flexibility. It is accomplished through the application of elements which require total employee involvement and teamwork. A key philosophy of JIT is simplification.'

5.12   In traditional manufacturing, when there is a production process with several stages, each stage in the process is protected from disruption by means of holding stock. For example, suppose that a process consists of four consecutive stages. In traditional manufacturing, there would be inventories of raw materials and finished goods, and in addition, there would be inventories of part-finished items between Stage 1 and Stage 2, Stage 2 and Stage 3 and Stage 3 and Stage 4. If there is disruption to production at, say, Stage 1, the other stages would not be immediately affected. Stages 2, 3 and 4 would continue to operate, using the inventories of part-finished items already received from Stages 1, 2 and 3. The responsibility for resolving the disruption would fall mainly on the managers of the stage affected, which in this example would be the managers of Stage 1.

5.13   In contrast, in its extreme form, a JIT system seeks to hold zero inventories. In the same four-stage process described above, a disruption at any stage would immediately have an impact on all the other stages. For example, if a disruption occurs at Stage 3, Stage 4 will have to stop working because they have no output from Stage 3. Stages 1 and 2 will also have to stop working, because Stage 2 will only produce when Stage 3 is ready to receive and use its output, and Stage 1 will only resume production when Stage 2 needs more of its output.

5.14   In JIT a disruption at any part of the system becomes a problem for the whole operation to resolve. Supporters of JIT argue that this will improve the speed with which the problem will be resolved, because it is in the interests of everyone to find a solution. Inventories are a 'blanket of obscurity' that hides problems within the system, so that they go unnoticed and unresolved for too long.

5.15   The role of suppliers in JIT is critically important. If a company wishes to apply JIT practices to manufacturing, it will also need to rely on its major suppliers for just-in-time delivery of supplies.

5.16   With **JIT purchasing**, an organisation must establish a close relationship with trusted suppliers for key items. It must then develop an arrangement with those suppliers whereby new deliveries are obtained only when they are needed for production. The supplier must have a flexible production system capable of responding immediately to purchase orders from the purchaser.

5.17   One of the measures taken by Toyota in the 1940s was to establish a suppliers' association, which it used to develop the close supplier relationships that are essential for JIT to be successful. Toyota was able to extend the principle of eliminating waste throughout its supply chain.

5.18   JIT is actually just one of four areas identified in the topic of lean production. The others are as follows.

- **Jidoka**: the use of 'intelligent machines', ie machines that can measure the quality of their own work and will stop if defined parameters are not being met.
- **Heijunka**: the levelling of production to the market demand. This smoothing of production allows for maximisation of the lean supply philosophy.
- **Kaizen**: the philosophy of continuous improvement, which underlies all the activities of lean production.

Chapter summary

- Purchasing and supply relationships involve a degree of closeness between people (usually in different organisations), entered into for the purpose of mutual benefit.

- A buyer has to deal with both external relationships (mainly suppliers) and internal relationships (with his 'internal customers').

- There is a spectrum of possible relationships with suppliers, ranging from competitive at one end to collaborative at the other. Any particular organisation will have relationships at different points of the spectrum with different suppliers.

- Competitive relationships are associated with transactional purchasing. Collaborative relationships are based on long-term strategic purchasing.

- Although much modern thinking has emphasised the benefits of collaborative relationships, there is still a place for competitive, transactional relationships. A task for the buyer is to determine the right type of relationship for each of the items he wishes to purchase.

- Partnership sourcing has been heavily endorsed and promoted in recent years. Other types of relationship at the collaborative end of the spectrum include joint ventures and, at the extreme, co-destiny relationships.

- Appropriate supplier relationships can help to achieve 'lean' ideals, reducing waste along the supply chain to the barest minimum.

Self-test questions

1   Define 'commercial' and 'relationship'. (1.2, 1.4)

2   Explain the five stages in selection of a supply base: innocence, awareness, understanding, competence, excellence. (Table 1.1)

3   List features of transactional purchasing. (2.5)

4   List benefits of collaborative relationships to both buyer and seller. (Table 1.2)

5   In what circumstances may it be inappropriate to seek collaborative relationships? (2.12)

6   List features of a true supply partnership, as opposed to a 'cosy relationship'. (2.16)

7   How may a buyer seek to maximise the benefit of a transactional relationship? (3.8)

8   List the principal requirements for partnership sourcing, as identified by the CBI and DTI. (4.5)

9   PSL identify seven types of supplier relationship where partnership sourcing may be particularly beneficial. What are they? (4.8)

10   What is a co-destiny relationship? (4.20)

11   What are the five principles that characterise lean production organisations, according to Daniel Jones? (5.5)

12   What are the seven wastes identified by Taichi Ohno? (5.9)

13   Explain the terms 'jidoka', 'heijunka', and 'kaizen'. (5.18)

CHAPTER 2

Managing Relationships between Purchasers and Suppliers

Learning objectives

1.3   Evaluate or analyse the challenges in managing effectively the relationships between purchasers and suppliers.

- Supply positioning model
- Supplier preferencing model
- The reasons for changing the way in which a relationship operates
- Managing risk in commercial relationships
- Buyer and supplier behaviour in relationships
- Market management matrix

Chapter headings

1   The supply positioning model

2   The supplier preferencing model

3   The market management matrix

4   Challenges and changes in supply relationships

5   Managing risk in commercial relationships

Introduction

In this chapter we describe how buyers can manage the challenges arising in their relationships with suppliers.

1   The supply positioning model

Introduction

1.1   A supply positioning model is a tool for determining what kind of supply relationships we should seek in relation to the various items we purchase for our organisation. The aim is to distinguish between the criticality of the different items purchased and to use this information in establishing suitable relations with the organisations that supply us with each item.

1.2 Many academics and consultants have attempted to develop such models. For example, in your earlier studies you may have come across such familiar examples as the Kraljic matrix. However, the guidance published by CIPS in relation to this subject appears to refer to just one such model, developed by members of the consultancy PMMS. We therefore begin our discussion with that model.

The PMMS supply positioning model

1.3 Like many similar models, the PMMS version maps the different items purchased onto a two-dimensional grid. For each item we determine:

- the level of risk we run in using that item (measured along the horizontal axis of the grid)
- the cost of the item (measured along the vertical axis of the grid)

1.4 The basic idea is that for items that are critical in terms of their risk, or in terms of the amount of spend, we must adopt a type of relationship that secures supply. By identifying items that are critical we ensure that management time and effort is directed most effectively.

1.5 In terms of risk, Table 2.1 lists some of the factors that might be considered in relation to each item to be purchased.

Table 2.1 *Factors relevant to the risk of supply*

Ability of current supplier
Lead time for delivery
Technological developments
Issues of corporate social responsibility
Complexity of the item (eg in terms of its specification or manufacturing process)
Competition in the supply market
Length and complexity of the supply chain
Length of product lifecyles in the industry sector
Criticality of the item in terms of our business processes

1.6 In terms of the cost of an item (the vertical axis in the model), everything is relative: what is a high cost for one organisation may be a trivial amount for a larger organisation.

1.7 The model is drawn up in the shape of a two-by-two grid: see Figure 2.1. As with many of the theoretical models illustrated in this text, this leads to a pattern of four distinct areas in the grid; top left, top right, bottom right, bottom left. For want of a better word, we refer to these areas throughout the text as 'quadrants', even though this term should strictly refer to a quarter of a circle.

Figure 2.1 *The PMMS supply positioning model*

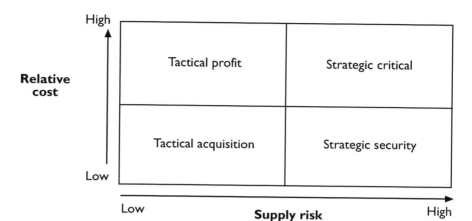

Analysing the four quadrants

1.8 Note the terms used in this model. Those with high supply risk are referred to as strategic; those with low supply risk are referred to as tactical.

1.9 **Strategic security** items are those with high supply risk and relatively low cost. It is vital to ensure security of supply, and the low cost of the items makes it relatively easy to do this. For example, if necessary we can hold large stocks without too damaging an effect on costs. For the medium to long term, our objective should be to reduce the risks relating to supply: finding additional suppliers or developing closer relationships with existing suppliers.

1.10 **Tactical acquisition** items are those with low supply risk and relatively low cost. Often there will be very many items falling into this category, which can become a burden to purchasing staff unless care is taken to streamline purchasing routines. It is likely that there are a large number of suppliers, and at the same time a large number of users within the buying organisation. The issue of dealing effectively with low-value purchases is dealt with in more detail in the *Purchasing Contexts* syllabus (also at Level 4), but typical methods that may be used include purchasing cards, call-off orders against a framework agreement, online ordering through approved supplier catalogues etc. In terms of the relationship spectrum (see previous chapter) we are probably looking at the transactional or competitive end of the spectrum.

1.11 For both of the above categories, the low value reduces the buyer's bargaining power. To overcome this, the buyer should aggregate such purchases as much as possible. In the case of strategic security items, it may be possible to tempt the supplier into a better deal if the buyer can offer to increase the range of items he purchases from that supplier.

1.12 **Tactical profit** items are costly but subject only to slight supply risk. Finding a source of supply presents little problem (there are probably many suppliers available), but the opportunity for improving profit must be taken. This arises from the relatively high cost of the items: even a small percentage saving can add significantly to the bottom-line profit. This suggests that buyers should continually shop around among potential suppliers and regularly get quotes before the next purchase. It would be a mistake, for these items, to enter a long-term supply agreement with a single supplier: this would rule out possible savings as factors change in the competitive environment.

1.13 **Strategic critical** items are the most important of all. The supply risk is great, and the cost of these items is high. It is vital to ensure security of supply at a good price, and this suggests a need for long-term collaborative relationships with a very small number of suppliers.

1.14 It is a costly and time-consuming exercise to carry out a supply positioning analysis. It can only be justified by the results it delivers. These are summarised in Table 2.2.

Table 2.2 *The outcomes of a supply positioning exercise*

Outcome	Explanation
Better understanding of relative importance of items to be bought	The exercise forces buyers to think very carefully about two important aspects of each item they buy: its supply risk and its relative cost.
Better understanding of required relationship strategies	The nature of the item in terms of its supply risk and its relative cost helps the buyer to determine the most appropriate type of supply relationship.
Better understanding of stock requirements	Items of low cost are relatively inexpensive to hold in stock, and if they are items with high supply risk (ie strategic security items) this suggests a deliberate policy of stockholding (contrary to modern thinking in most cases, but indicated by the results of the analysis).

Kraljic's matrix

1.15 The PMMS supply positioning model is extremely similar to a matrix that has long been familiar in the academic literature: the Kraljic matrix or **procurement positioning grid** developed by Peter Kraljic (1973). Kraljic's matrix is a tool of analysis that seeks to map the importance to the organisation of the item being purchased against the complexity of the market that supplies it. The vertical axis (measuring the importance of the item) is usually related to the amount of the organisation's annual spend on the item in question: high spend implies high importance.

Figure 2.2 *Kraljic's grid*

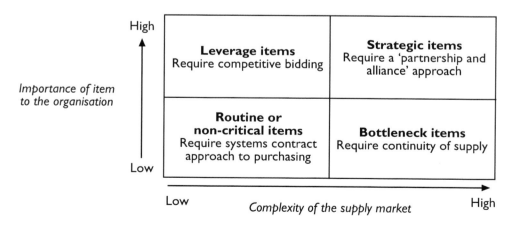

1.16 The approach that the organisation should then take to sourcing an item is decided by where the item is positioned on the grid.

- If an item falls within the low spend/low risk category as a routine item the approach may be to use IT management of the spend. This may be achieved by permitting the supplier to manage the inventory and re-stocking against an annually negotiated agreement, eg as with stationery supplies. Purchasing management is achieved by monitoring the spend against regular reports provided, as agreed with the supplier.

- If an item falls within the high-dependency bottleneck section the objective is one of strategic security. Approaches could be carrying a higher level of stock than would otherwise be the case or developing a closer relationship with suppliers than the value of the item would otherwise indicate. The purchasing objective is to ensure continuity of supply.

- The leverage section indicates a more traditional approach where a number of suppliers exist in a market and can be judged by commercial criteria such as price, quality and delivery. The objective is to secure supply but it is not one where a long-term relationship of importance is envisaged.

- The strategic section of the grid examines the implications of high risk and high value items where the approach could be a more long-term sustainable relationship that will bring benefits through closer supply chain, IT and management processes.

1.17 The horizontal axis demonstrates the risk an organisation is exposing itself to in terms of the degree of difficulty in sourcing a particular product or component or the vulnerability of the supplier to fulfil their obligations. The vertical axis examines profit potential and is used to indicate the extent to which the potential of supply can contribute to profitability.

1.18 Profit potential may be realised by cost reductions, value analysis or efficiency gains. For items in the strategic quadrant we can consider supplier relationships over the longer term by developing supply chain solutions to areas of cost and waste. This can add to profit potential by joint product/service development opportunities and a more integrated approach to information technology and knowledge management.

1.19 Applying the matrix would give different results for different organisations, and even for the same organisation over time. For instance, the sourcing of steel has moved from an adversarial relationship for many organisations when there was a situation of global over supply to a more strategic relationship as organisations react to the impact of Chinese demand on the supply market. In other words, for many organisations steel has moved from being a leverage item to being a strategic item.

1.20 Applying Kraljic's matrix to a particular context is a fairly straightforward process that can prove highly effective. However, it does have some weaknesses.

- It ignores the fact that not all the risk of the supply comes from within the relationship between customer and supplier. External environmental factors, especially competition and the PESTLE factors, can impact greatly.

- It applies to products/services rather than to suppliers. A supplier of non-critical items may also be the supplier of strategic ones, for instance. Applying the grid to suppliers rather than goods or services is often used when contemplating a supplier reduction programme. Treating a strategic supplier as a non-critical one, for instance, simply because it supplies both types of product would be a clear mistake.

- While the buyer may perceive an item to be a leverage one, this is only perceived on the other side of the relationship by the supplier if the buyer's spend is significant. In other words, the relative sizes and perceptions of the parties should also be taken into account. This leads us on to the next tool of analysis: the supplier preferencing model.

1.21 You should compare the two supply positioning models and their implications for purchasers using the following equivalences.

- Kraljic leverage items = PMMS tactical profit items
- Kraljic routine items = PMMS tactical acquisition items
- Kraljic bottleneck items = PMMS strategic security items
- Kraljic strategic items = PMMS strategic critical items

2   *The supplier preferencing model*

The supplier's perspective

2.1   The supply positioning models above of course illustrate the buyer's perspective on the items to be purchased. This will often differ significantly from the supplier's perspective: what is very important to the buyer may be relatively unimportant to a particular supplier.

2.2   Once again, CIPS guidance indicates that we are to approach this issue by reference to a PMMS model, and once again we will be looking at a two-by-two matrix. In this case, the vertical axis measures how attractive it is to the supplier to deal with the buyer; while the horizontal axis measures the monetary value of the business that might be available from the buyer.

The PMMS supplier preferencing model

2.3   The horizontal axis is self-explanatory, but the attractiveness of the buying organisation (measured on the vertical axis) is less obvious. There are various factors that might make a supplier keen to do business with a buying organisation.

- A buying organisation might be in some way glamorous or high profile. Suppliers will want to deal with such an organisation merely for the sake of boasting to other customers or potential customers about who is on their client list. By contrast, some organisations are inherently unattractive to deal with, and suppliers will give preference to other potential customers unless they are looking to use spare capacity. This might be the case, for example, if the buyer has a poor reputation on corporate social responsibility.

- A buying organisation with a reputation for fair dealing, or with a record of prompt payment to suppliers, will naturally be attractive. Similarly, a buying organisation will be attractive if it has a reputation of engaging closely with suppliers, keeping them well informed, and perhaps working with them on new product development.

- Whatever the current attractiveness of a buying organisation, things may change in the future. For example, changes of personnel may lead to changes in the methods of dealing with suppliers. Changes in the competitive environment may make a buying organisation more, or less, successful than it used to be, which can also change its level of attractiveness.

2.4   In summary, the factors that create and maintain a buyer's 'good/attractive customer status' include: clear and comprehensive specification of requirement; clear terms and conditions of purchase; positive reputation (eg for ethical values, integrity and fair dealing); high value of spend; preference for long-term contracts; invoices paid on time in full; transparent and efficient purchasing processes; positive communication with suppliers; strong CSR, environmental and ethical policies (protecting the supplier's reputation).

2.5   Put the other way around, the picture might look as in Table 2.3

Table 2.3 *Becoming less attractive to suppliers*

Buyers may become less attractive to suppliers if they:	Penalties of poor relationship management may take the form of:
Often make late/incomplete payments	Refusal of high-quality suppliers to deal with them or enter long-term agreements
Negotiate very unfavourable terms	
Often query, change or dispute order details and contract terms	Loss of supply, if suppliers find better customers (possibly competitors)
Use excessive bureaucracy	Lower priority for suppliers, leading to poor performance, information-sharing etc
Deal unethically (eg soliciting bribes)	
Have a poor reputation re ethics, labour conditions, product safety	Higher prices, or less favourable credit terms, to compensate suppliers for costs of doing business
Are excessively litigious (suing for damages for minor infringements)	More law suits, if suppliers reflect customer's litigious approach

2.6   Once again, we have four quadrants: see Figure 2.3.

Figure 2.3 *The PMMS supplier preferencing model*

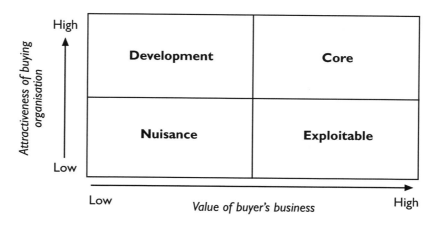

2.7 In the bottom left quadrant, we have buyers who are neither inherently attractive to the supplier, nor particularly valuable in terms of volume business. The PMMS model labels these unfortunate organisations as **nuisance customers**. (Much of the terminology used in these models is disparaging, but bear in mind that the terms are just intended as a convenient shorthand.) Many suppliers have a policy of reviewing their customer base regularly with a view to terminating contracts with customers who are not 'paying their way'. The situation usually is that the customer takes more effort and cost to service than the value of the business justifies. From the supplier's perspective, the option of termination – or alternatively, hiking prices by a substantial amount – may be the best solution.

2.8 Staying with the relatively unattractive buying organisations, the bottom right quadrant contains **exploitable customers**. They are exploitable in the sense that they offer large volumes of business, which compensates for any lack of inherent attractiveness. It may be this very fact that causes the customer to be unattractive: if the buyers believe they are a major customer, they may exploit this with aggressive behaviour. In such an environment the supplier is grateful enough to do what is required of him under the supply contract, but will not go out of his way to provide extras. And any extras that are demanded will be charged at additional cost.

2.9 In the top left quadrant we have **development customers**. These are customers who do not – or at least do not yet – offer large volumes of business, but who for other reasons are attractive to the supplier. The supplier may see potential for growth in the customer overall, or at least in the volume of business that the customer can offer. It will pay the supplier to court the customer by 'going the extra mile' in fulfilling obligations. This could mean providing extra services for little or no additional cost in order to win favour with the customer, or perhaps accommodating changes in schedules or order levels without complaint. If all goes well, the supplier hopes to push this customer into the top right corner of the grid.

2.10 The top right is occupied by **core customers**. These are the organisations attractive in their own right, and offering valuable levels of business to the supplier. Naturally, the supplier will do all that is possible to stay in favour with these organisations – they are his core business and he will want to maintain close relations. The supplier will want to be aware at the earliest possible stage of any looming threat to the business, and for this reason will keep in regular contact with the customer.

2.11 As in the supply positioning models, examined earlier, the supplier preferencing model is not static. The supplier would ideally like to be moving all his customers into the top right quadrant and will work towards doing so. On the other hand, downward progress is possible too. We have already seen that some customers in the bottom left quadrant face possible eviction. Equally, a core customer could move down into the exploitable quadrant if for some reason its inherent attractiveness declined (perhaps because of association with a financial scandal, or because of public concerns over corporate social responsibility issues).

2.12 Buyers can learn a great deal by trying to view relationships from the perspective of their suppliers. It should not be difficult to guess where in the grid a buyer stands: the general attitude of the supplier's sales staff should give plenty of clues. If the sales staff are helpful, and proactive in involving the buyer closely, the signs are good. On the other hand, if sales staff rarely bother to make contact, or show indifference, then a buyer can conclude that he is in the bottom two quadrants.

2.13   It is not necessarily a bad thing for the buyer to be in this situation. For example, a medium-sized firm sourcing its stationery from one of the large number of online catalogues has no particular need to be regarded by the supplier as a core customer. The situation is not particularly sensitive, and the items to be purchased from this supplier are not critical. But if a supplier is the source of critical and valuable items the buyer should work towards becoming a valuable customer. Regular contact with the supplier will be important in establishing what the buyer can do to achieve this.

3   The market management matrix

Supply positioning and supplier preferencing combined

3.1   The PMMS supply positioning model classifies our purchases into four different categories. The supplier preferencing model identifies four different attitudes that our suppliers may have towards us. If we combine the two models there are potentially 16 different situations that may face the buyer. As an example, a supplier who regards us as core business may be providing us with any of the four different categories of supplies. Similarly, a supplier who regards us as a nuisance customer may be providing us with any of the four categories.

3.2   By combining the two models we get the market management matrix– again, the work of the PMMS consultancy. It is very difficult to illustrate, but in Figure 2.4 we attempt it.

Figure 2.4 *The market management matrix*

Development customers		Core customers	
Tactical profit	Strategic critical	Tactical profit	Strategic critical
Tactical acquisition	Strategic security	Tactical acquisition	Strategic security
Nuisance customers		Exploitable customers	
Tactical profit	Strategic critical	Tactical profit	Strategic critical
Tactical acquisition	Strategic security	Tactical acquisition	Strategic security

3.3   It has been claimed that this model helps buyers to analyse the markets in which they operate and to choose appropriate supply relationships for all their different purchases.

3.4   As an example, suppose that we are considering a purchase that falls into the 'strategic critical' quadrant of our supply positioning model. This is an item vital to our commercial success and we are very concerned to ensure reliable and high quality supply. We should feel very exposed if the supplier currently providing us with this item regards us as a nuisance customer. We would much prefer to be dealing with a supplier for whom we fall in the 'core' or 'development' quadrants of the supplier preferencing model.

Applying the models

3.5 These models are only useful if we use them to examine the different categories of purchases and the implications they have for our relations with suppliers. Here are a couple of examples.

3.6 **Tactical acquisition** items (low supply risk, low value) may sound like the least of our problems. In practice, though, these items are invariably numerous and have the potential to cause major workload. Many organisations attempt to deal with this by placing greater trust in their own staff (in user departments) and in their suppliers. They streamline purchasing procedures (eg by issuing purchasing cards to staff in user departments), and they set up arrangements with suppliers (eg framework agreements) that allow trouble-free ordering. If this works well, then the problem is solved; if the suppliers do not perform, the nature of the market is that we can take our business elsewhere.

3.7 **Tactical profit** items (low supply risk, high value) give scope for great benefits to both buyer and supplier because of their financial value. This suggests a need for tough negotiation with several suppliers, possibly by means of a tendering exercise or online auction.

4 *Challenges and changes in supply relationships*

Introduction

4.1 In this section we look in turn at each of the relationships specified in learning objective 1.2 (see the relationship spectrum in Chapter 1 above) and examine each one in a little more depth, focusing on the new insight provided by the models described earlier in this chapter.

Adversarial relationships

4.2 Modern thinking has moved away from the use of adversarial relationships and much of the academic literature nowadays focuses on alternative approaches. Despite this, most buyers recognise that the adversarial approach still exists and, in the right circumstances, offers the most suitable way of dealing with suppliers.

4.3 The nature of such a relationship is that buyer and supplier attempt to get the best possible deal for their respective organisations, even if the gains they achieve are matched by losses for the other party. For tactical profit items, as we mentioned in the previous section, this may well be an appropriate method of dealing. Although the supply relationship may continue indefinitely, if it is working well, the buyer does not regard it as a long-term relationship and does not cultivate the supplier as he might do in a more strategic relationship.

4.4 The relationship will be characterised by a minimal amount of trust, information exchange, and flexibility in dealing with requirements. While each party may assure the other of the importance of the relationship, the reality is different and either buyer or supplier may terminate at short notice if a better opportunity arises elsewhere. Both buyer and supplier will attempt to make the maximum out of the deal and neither will be motivated to 'go the extra mile' or provide additional services.

Arm's length relationships

4.5　This is similar to the adversarial relationship, but implies less direct contact between buyer and supplier. Purchases may be infrequent, and will normally relate to tactical acquisition and tactical profit items. Buyers will again attempt to get the maximum possible benefit for their organisation, and neither buyer nor supplier will be motivated to provide anything for nothing.

4.6　The arm's length tag suggests that there is little need for regular contact between buyer and supplier. Once the buyer has done enough to set the deal in motion he will only need to contact the supplier in exceptional circumstances. There is no need for regular meetings.

4.7　These relationships are envisaged to be for the short term, because the buyer will be looking for opportunities to do a better deal if possible. The nature of the market is such that new suppliers can be found at short notice if necessary.

Transactional relationships

4.8　These relationships typically apply to items in the tactical acquisition quadrant of the supply positioning model (low supply risk, low value). The buyer's objective is simply to obtain these items with as little trouble and at as little cost as possible.

4.9　Both buyer and supplier will be aware that the deal could be of long-term duration, provided it works well for both. To achieve this, they will normally work closely together to set up a smooth arrangement, then will simply let it run into the future. Buyers may not be motivated to repeat a tendering exercise if the existing supplier is performing well (though in the public sector this may not be an option). Both parties are motivated to trust each other and perform their side of the bargain.

4.10　The buyer's behaviour must reflect the nature of the relationship. An adversarial approach is not appropriate here, but at the same time the buyer wants the deal to proceed with minimum intervention. This means that it will not involve the regular communication and personal contact essential to a more strategic relationship.

Closer tactical relationship

4.11　We are still in the bottom half of the supply positioning model: dealing with low-risk items, either tactical acquisition or tactical profit. The chosen supplier may be one of the various suppliers with whom the buyer has transactional relationships. The task for the buyer is to identify one such supplier who performs particularly well, and to engage more closely. In some cases the chosen supplier may take responsibility for a wider range of purchase items, perhaps coordinating other suppliers in a tiering arrangement.

4.12　This arrangement implies a need for closer communication. The buyer will need to be sure that other suppliers, now effectively relegated to a second tier position, are aware of the situation. Any suggestion of adversarial treatment would be out of place in this kind of relationship.

4.13　In terms of the supply positioning model, the items suitable for this treatment could come from any one of the four quadrants.

4.14   To make this work, both parties will need to invest significant time and effort. The objective of the buyer is to get the supplier to do more, in terms of coordinating activities, while not paying more for his supplies than he was previously. There may be a need to pay the supplier some kind of handling fee, which from the buyer's point of view must be recouped by means of the savings achieved from the new relationship.

4.15   Such relationships will typically be for the long term, and both parties will work hard to achieve continuous improvement as the deal progresses. There is risk in putting so much business in the hands of one supplier, and the buyer will only be motivated to do this if trust is present.

Single-sourced relationship

4.16   These relationships typically apply in the low-cost half of the supply positioning model (tactical acquisition or strategic security items). The buyer hopes to gain greater commitment and preferential treatment from the supplier by offering the supplier exclusivity.

4.17   This is of course a risky procedure. If the single supplier fails, the buyer is exposed. For this reason, many organisations who experimented with single sourcing eventually resorted instead to dual sourcing so as to have a backup source of supply.

4.18   In a single source relationship the buyer must trust the supplier, because there will inevitably be a temptation towards complacency. When the supplier believes he has the business wrapped up under a long-term agreement he may not be motivated to apply his best efforts to it. The buyer must be confident in the supplier's commitment before entering such a deal.

Outsourced relationships

4.19   A buyer will not usually outsource in areas which deliver competitive advantage. This means that an outsourcing relationship will not usually apply in the strategic critical quadrant of the supply positioning model. However, outsourcing is usually regarded as a strategic move, which suggests that this may apply in the strategic security quadrant. Certainly it would not apply in the tactical profit quadrant: this is an area where buyers want to take advantage of changing opportunities, whereas an outsourcing agreement is inevitably for the long term.

4.20   This kind of relationship is appropriate when the buyer believes that a supplier can do something better than his own organisation can achieve. He expects to achieve cost savings or improved efficiency or both, as well as enjoying the freedom from managing the service in-house.

4.21   Owing to the long-term and strategic nature of the decision, buyers must proceed very carefully, with full investigation of the existing arrangement and proposed new arrangement. Once the deal is done it is important to monitor performance closely so as to ensure that the expected benefits are being realised.

Strategic alliances

4.22   This kind of relationship will apply in the strategic critical quadrant of the supply positioning model. A buyer wishes to ally himself with a supplier because he believes that they can work together to achieve long-term mutual benefit. The alliance may cover a geographical area, a market segment, or a defined part of the product portfolio.

4.23   Like all strategic relationships, an alliance of this kind is based on a high level of trust and mutual commitment.

4.24   The CIPS guidance for this module points out a further aspect of strategic alliances: namely, the possibility that a buyer may become a victim of this kind of relationship. CIPS cite the case of a buyer purchasing software recommended by a consultancy. The buyer must ask himself why that particular software was recommended: was it because the consultancy and the software supplier are working together in a strategic alliance, or is the software genuinely the best solution to the buyer's need?

Partnership relationship

4.25   Again, this is a long-term relationship in which buyer and supplier work together to achieve mutual benefits. Each party is committed to continuous improvement, and elimination of waste in the supply chain. The relationship is designed to achieve rewards that will be shared by both parties.

4.26   Partnership relationships will apply only to items in the strategic critical quadrant of the supply positioning model. The crucial importance of these items to the buying organisation makes it essential to secure efficient supply at a good price. The items concerned are so critical that supply failure could cause major damage to the buying organisation's operations.

4.27   Such relationships are characterised by a high level of trust and constant communication between the parties. Often there will be a regime of cost transparency, in which the buyer is aware of the supplier's cost structures and the supplier is aware of his share in the buyer's financial set-up.

4.28   Both buyer and supplier must be confident that the relationship is genuinely for the long term. It would be very damaging for mutual trust if it transpired that the buyer, say, was exploring other opportunities in the supply market. For this reason, the relationship must be a focused one, in which each party works to the benefit of the other, without exploring opportunistic benefits elsewhere.

4.29   It may be difficult for a buyer to identify a suitable partner if starting from scratch, but in many cases such relationships evolve gradually over the years. A supplier who performs to a very high standard in a more limited relationship may eventually be invited to engage in closer collaboration.

Co-destiny relationships

4.30   There is an even closer link between buyer and supplier, and once again this would apply only to items in the strategic critical quadrant of the supply positioning model.

4.31   It is difficult to distinguish this from the partnership relationship, and for the purposes of this analysis the above comments apply again.

5   *Managing risk in commercial relationships*

Evaluation of suppliers

5.1   When an organisation is making a non-routine decision about which supplier to select for making a purchase order, the decision will be based on an assessment or evaluation of the alternative suppliers. It is important to do this systematically in order to minimise the risk of choosing an inappropriate supplier.

- When the supplier is already known to the organisation, from previous dealings, the supplier can be evaluated on the basis of its track record. An evaluation of an existing or known supplier is called **vendor rating**.
- When the supplier is not known to the organisation already, there is a need to judge the capabilities of potential suppliers in a different way, and on the basis of different information.

5.2   The extent or depth of any evaluation will depend on the volume and the value of the supply contract. Greater care should be taken with larger and more valuable contracts.

5.3   The evaluation of a potential supplier who has not yet had dealings with the organisation is likely to be based on the following factors.

- The financial stability of the supplier. The supplier might be asked to provide a copy of its most recent financial accounts. A purchaser generally prefers a supplier who is financially stable and with good operational cashflows. In contrast, there can be embarrassments when a supplier is financially unstable and is in urgent need of cash.
- The commercial capabilities of the supplier. Commercial capabilities might be assessed in terms of:

    (i)   technical capabilities

    (ii)   production capacity

    (iii)   just-in-time delivery capability

    (iv)   ability to use electronic data interchange (EDI) with the purchaser

    (v)   new investment plans.

- The apparent management skills of the supplier. If the supplier appears to have good management capabilities, it should be likely to provide a good service.
- Other factors might be checked, such as how long the supplier firm has been established, whether the supplier trades with competitor firms, and whether it searches the market and, if so, how and how often.

5.4   A purchaser might arrange a **site visit** to a potential supplier. Before making a site visit, the purchaser should prepare a list of items to look for and questions to ask. During the visit, this checklist should be used to make sure that nothing is omitted. The checklist might also have boxes for the purchaser to give a score or rating (very good, good, fair etc) to the supplier for each of a number of key factors. An overall assessment can then be made on the basis of these scores or ratings, and the overall rating of each supplier visited can be compared.

Risk management

5.5   Careful evaluation of suppliers is a necessary part of minimising risk in the supply chain. However, the guidance for this module issued by CIPS outlines a more detailed risk management process, consisting of five stages.

- Identify sources of potential risk
- For each possible risk event, determine its likelihood and its impact
- Assess the overall impact of all risk factors
- Investigate risk reduction
- Plan, control and reduce risk

5.6   **Sources of risk** may be predictable or unpredictable. For example, it should be possible to plan for staff shortages during peak holiday time because this is predictable. On the other hand, if two or three key personnel leave the organisation unexpectedly to pursue other opportunities we may be caught unawares.

5.7   Some sources of risk arise within the organisation (like the staff shortages just mentioned). Others are external to the organisation (eg a movement in currency exchange rates or interest rates). To identify sources of risk it is clear that past experience is a good starting point. But in appropriate cases this should be supplemented by research into particular sources of risk.

5.8   The **likelihood and impact** of each possible risk should be determined. If a risk is judged to be of low likelihood, and low impact even if it occurs, then there is not much point in worrying about it. But where the risk is very likely, or could have a damaging impact even if it is unlikely to happen, it will be appropriate to take action in advance.

5.9   The **overall impact** of several risk factors may be greater than their individual impacts. To cater for this, the buyer should tabulate all possible risks and attach a weighting factor to each, based on their likelihood and potential impact. By adding up all the weightings the buyer can assess the overall risk.

5.10   To **investigate risk reduction** the buyer should consider the various possible things that could go wrong with a purchase and think of ways to reduce the risks. One possibility is to take direct action aimed at reducing the risk. Another is to transfer the risk to someone else by means of an appropriate term in the purchase contract. A final possibility is to take out appropriate insurance.

5.11   To **plan, control and reduce** risk is a task that should be assigned specifically to persons with appropriate responsibility. The task is carried out by careful monitoring of plans to ensure that actual outcomes are shaping up as they should. Use of technology is important in this area (eg in collating progress reports from suppliers, flagging when designated action is due to be taken etc).

Chapter summary

- A supply positioning model is a tool for determining what kind of supply relationships we should seek in relation to the various items we purchase for our organisation.

- The PMMS supply positioning model is a two-by-two matrix analysing supply risk along the horizontal axis and relative cost along the vertical axis. The Kraljic matrix is very similar.

- The four quadrants of the PMMS model are: top left – strategic security; top right – strategic critical; bottom left – tactical acquisition; bottom right – tactical profit.

- The supplier preferencing model is a tool for determining how a supplier views us as a customer. It is a two-by-two matrix, with a vertical axis measuring 'attractiveness of buying organisation' and a horizontal axis measuring 'value of buyer's business'.

- The four quadrants of the supplier preferencing model are: top left – development; top right – core; bottom left – nuisance; bottom right – exploitable.

- The market management matrix attempts to combine the supply positioning model with the supplier preferencing model.

- The spectrum of supplier relationships ranges from adversarial, through arm's length, transactional, closer tactical, single-sourced, outsourced, strategic alliances, and partnership to co-destiny relationships.

- Management of risk in commercial relationships begins with systematic evaluation of suppliers.

- CIPS outline a five-stage risk management process: identify sources of potential risk; for each risk, determine likelihood and impact; assess overall impact of risk factors; investigate risk reduction; plan, control and reduce risk.

Self-test questions

1 List factors relevant to the risk of supply. (Table 2.1)

2 In the supply positioning model, what term is given to items of high cost and high supply risk? (Figure 2.1)

3 In which quadrant of the supply positioning model do tactical acquisition items appear? (Figure 2.1)

4 What is measured on the horizontal axis of the supplier preferencing model? And on the vertical axis? (Figure 2.3)

5 In what quadrant of the supplier preferencing model do development customers appear? (Figure 2.3)

6 How does the market management matrix combine the supply positioning model and the supplier preferencing model? (3.1)

7 What features characterise an adversarial relationship? (4.4)

8 Transactional relationships typically apply to what types of supply? (4.8)

9 Explain the risks to the buyer of adopting a single-sourced relationship. (4.17, 4.18)

10 Partnership relationships typically apply to what types of supply? (4.26)

11 What factors will be taken into account when evaluating a potential new supplier? (5.3)

CHAPTER 3

The Relationship Lifecycle

Learning objectives

1.4 Define the natural lifecycle of supply relationships and analyse the position of specific relationships in their lifecycle.

- The concept of the relationship lifecycle
- The stages of the relationship lifecycle
- Linking the relationship lifecycle to the relationship spectrum
- Understanding your position in the relationship lifecycle

4.9 Review the circumstances in which supply relationships end, and select appropriate methods for their termination and, where appropriate, determine ways of retrieving and retaining the relationship.

- Resolving disputes
- Using the contract to terminate a relationship
- Maintaining a supply relationship post-conflict
- Ways of retrieving and retaining the relationships

Chapter headings

1 The concept of the relationship lifecycle

2 The stages of the relationship lifecycle

3 Other aspects of the lifecycle model

4 Termination of supply relationships

Introduction

In this chapter we describe the distinct stages through which supply relationships typically progress.

1 The concept of the relationship lifecycle

Historical development of the concept

1.1 In the 1970s, an aspect of management theory and practice that attracted much attention was the concept of the product lifecycle. A typical product had a predictable lifecycle pattern, from introduction to the market, to market growth, market maturity and then market decline. A task of management was to achieve the maximum profitability from the product over its lifecycle, for example by charging a high price for the product during its introduction and growth phases until competition eventually forces down the general market price.

1.2 In the 1980s, there was much greater focus on the customer. Instead of treating each sale as a single transaction for making profit, companies began to think of a customer as someone who might make a series of purchase orders over time. Rather than maximise profits from each separate sale transaction, companies began to think in terms of maximising profits over a series of transactions with the customer. Customer satisfaction and customer service became important issues. 'The customer is king', but if the customer is satisfied by the service provided, he will come back for more business. This led on to the concept of the customer lifecycle, as distinct from the product lifecycle. Even so, the focus was on selling.

1.3 In the 1990s, the focus of attention switched again, from the customer to the customer-supplier relationship. Instead of thinking in terms of maximising profits from a customer over a long-term relationship, the key question became how to maximise the benefits for both the customer and the supplier over a long-term relationship, through a partnership of collaboration. The aim should be to maximise the benefits for both the customer and the supplier over a **relationship lifecycle**.

Example

1.4 A component for a cooker costs £10. The lifecycle of the cooker is six years, during which it should be very reliable. After six years, the cooker will have declining utility. After ten years, it will be useless. The component has no other use except as a part of this particular cooker.

- If the supplier of the component took a product lifecycle approach, it would try to maximise its profits over the lifecycle of the cooker, probably by trying to obtain the highest price possible for the component from the cooker manufacturer.

- If the supplier took a customer lifecycle approach, it would think about the possibility of new orders from the customer, for the same or a similar component. If the prospect of new orders is good, the supplier is unlikely to charge the highest price possible for the initial order, but will think longer term. A lower price now will probably result in higher profits in the longer term, through replacement orders. In such a relationship, the customer and supplier might agree on a continuous replenishment strategy, or if the customer operates JIT purchasing, the supplier might agree to manage the inventory for the component.

- With a relationship lifecycle approach, there would be close collaboration between the component supplier and the cooker manufacturer. The customer and supplier would work together to maximise their joint benefits. This collaboration will lead not just to repeat orders for the supplier, but to new business in the future through sharing a common strategy, for example in the development of new or enhanced products.

1.5 When a customer and a supplier do business together, they must communicate with each other. Companies can communicate in any of the following ways.

- One or the other company exchanges data. An **exchange of data** might be to place an order.

- With supply chain management, customer and supplier integrate the use of information. Each has its own computer system, but they share information between their computer systems. Each 'partner' supplies the other with information it has gathered.

- At the highest level of collaboration, customer and supplier share a process for approving and confirming the information in their systems. To a large extent, they have a common information system.

1.6 In a relationship lifecycle approach to customer-supplier relationships, the partners should think in terms of collaborating at a high level for shared information. This collaboration, and the long-term nature of the relationship, mean that a high level of trust builds up between the partners, helping them to move ever closer (provided the commercial case for doing so remains). The driving forces for building on trust are increased quality and innovation, and reduced risk for both parties.

1.7 Elements of a relationship lifecycle, that distinguish it from a customer lifecycle, are as follows.

- The relationship is information-based, and information is shared.

- Both partners focus on the competitive advantage that can be provided by the supply chain.

- Both partners are continually seeking to re-define the relationship, with focus being given to potential future products and the future needs of each partner.

1.8 With a relationship lifecycle approach, there will be close collaboration between customer and supplier, particularly in the areas of:

- conceiving of and designing new products
- new product launches
- pricing a new product
- promoting a new product
- forecasting future sales demand and future customer needs.

2 The stages of the relationship lifecycle

The Kettering model

2.1 Various authorities have attempted to distinguish between stages in the relationship lifecycle. However, once again the CIPS guidance issued for this module indicates that a particular model is intended. Frustratingly, this is a particularly complicated model comprising no fewer than 25 stages, some of which relate just to the buyer, others to the seller, and still others to buyer and seller combined.

2.2 When the model was published, under the name of the **Kettering Relationship Lifecycle Model**, in *Supply Management* magazine (issue of 6 July 2006) it provoked a hostile response from at least one reader. In the issue of 3 August 2006 a letter from a reader was published containing the following comments.

I read the feature with a mixture of incredulity and déjà vu ... This model takes this [breaking down a process into its stages] to ludicrous extremes.

2.3 Presumably the model is likely to feature in your examination, so it is important that you should study the paragraphs that follow. However, as with all of your CIPS studies, you should adopt a critical and sceptical stance. It is legitimate to question the features of all the models you encounter. This is particularly the case when a model appears more elaborate and academic than you are accustomed to seeing in your normal professional work.

The 25 stages of the model

2.4   With that note of warning behind us, we now give brief notes on each of the 25 stages in the model. The stages are classified in three main segments: initiation (comprising Stages 1–10, and being the beginning of serious discussions between buyer and seller); agreement (comprising Stages 11–16, and dealing with the process by which buyer and seller conclude the terms of an agreement); and delivery (comprising Stages 17–25, and marking the phase during which the supply agreement is in force).

2.5   **Stage 1: seller develops offering**. A supplier will use market research and other tools of analysis to determine potential customers for his existing products and potential demand for new products.

2.6   **Stage 2: seller there to be found**. The supplier makes himself known to the market by listings in directories, online databases, and use of his own website etc. In some cases he may interrogate his website to establish who has visited and what they looked at. This may lead to establishing a sales visit.

2.7   **Stage 3: buyer has need**. Within the buyer organisation, a purchaser or a member of a user department identifies a need.

2.8   **Stage 4: seller creates need**. It is not clear from the model whether this is an alternative to Stage 3 or an addition to it. It refers to the process whereby a supplier convinces a buyer that a need exists which his products are able to satisfy.

2.9   **Stage 5: buyer specifies**. With the need established (Stage 3, Stage 4 or both), the buyer must specify his requirement exactly. This may mean collaboration between buyers and technical specialists.

2.10   **Stage 6: conditioning by seller**. The seller attempts to impose his view of the need, of how it can be satisfied by his products, and of the importance of buying sooner rather than later. He will make it clear that his offering is in some way special so as to inflate its value. He will use persuasive techniques to hurry the buyer along (discounts for early purchase etc).

2.11   **Stage 7: seller sells**. The seller aims to convince the decision makers in the buying organisation that they should buy his products. The seller may be talking to the purchasing department, but equally he may seek to sway user departments.

2.12   **Stage 8: buyer searches**. With his need identified and specified, the buyer searches for possible suppliers. Ideally, he will be able to identify more than one possible supplier so that offerings can be compared. In the meantime, he hopes that decision makers in the user departments are not already committed to one particular – and persuasive – supplier.

2.13   **Stage 9: conditioning by buyer**. In response to Stage 6 above, the buyer aims to impose his view of the situation. He will say or imply that he has no flexibility to increase his initial offer, and that he has other potential suppliers who can provide the same or a better offering.

2.14 **Stage 10: serious discussion.** With target suppliers identified, and less likely candidates eliminated, the buyer discusses the business case for the purchase within his own organisation. His aim is to get a commitment to purchasing, within agreed parameters relating to price, delivery etc.

2.15 This concludes the first segment of the model: initiation. Stages 11–16 below are the second segment: agreement.

2.16 **Stage 11: buyer enquiry.** In most cases, the buyer will seek quotes from potential suppliers on the basis of the specification created in Stage 5 above. (This will not always be the case, particularly if the buyer has a partnership relationship with a particular supplier.)

2.17 **Stage 12: seller quotation.** Ideally, this will arrive in response to the buyer's enquiry. However, it is common for suppliers to send in quotations to decision makers outside the purchasing function, and without having been solicited, in the hope of achieving a sale.

2.18 **Stage 13: negotiation.** This is the subject of an entire module at Level 4 of the CIPS qualification. In a nutshell, buyer and supplier deploy the information they have gained so far, together with the wisdom of their accumulated experience, to haggle with each other over key terms in a possible supply agreement.

2.19 **Stage 14: headline agreement.** In some cases the outcome of initial negotiation is a headline agreement, summarising the main points of an eventual agreement, but with a view to further discussion on detail later.

2.20 **Stage 15: detail agreement.** Eventually, perhaps after further negotiation, the parties are ready to commit to a supply agreement. The details of this should ideally be committed to writing.

2.21 **Stage 16: implementation.** Both buyer and supplier take the necessary actions to bring the agreement into force.

2.22 This concludes the second segment of the model: agreement. The remaining stages relate to the third segment: delivery.

2.23 **Stage 17: initial delivery.** In the early period of the agreement there may be unexpected difficulties to overcome, but these should be minimal if proper planning has been undertaken and a sound, detailed agreement put down on paper.

2.24 **Stage 18: refining.** As the relationship progresses, it may be appropriate to adjust the agreement to reflect greater knowledge of requirements on both sides. There may also be opportunity to inject improvements into the way the agreement was first envisaged.

2.25 **Stage 19: ongoing delivery.** Once the agreement is properly underway the supplier maintains delivery of the required goods, and the buyer maintains his side of the bargain in terms of receipt and payment. This stage could last for years, if the goods are required for everyday operations of the buyer, or alternatively could be a one-off delivery of a capital item.

2.26 **Stage 20: continuous improvement**. If the agreement is for a lengthy period, there will be opportunities to improve performance. However, the buyer must beware of frequently requesting improvements from the supplier which were not contemplated in the original agreement, unless he is prepared to pay for them.

2.27 **Stage 21: business development**. The supplier has by now won a customer, and will seek to exploit the old saying 'Your best new customer is an existing customer'. In other words, he will seek to increase the business he does with the buying organisation, making use of the internal contacts he has now acquired.

2.28 **Stage 22: extension**. This occurs where both parties are satisfied with the agreement and wish to continue it beyond the original contract period.

2.29 **Stage 23: completion**. This may occur either because the buyer's requirement has now been met in full, or because one party to the agreement wishes to terminate (perhaps because of dissatisfaction with the performance of the other party).

2.30 **Stage 24: latent termination**. This is the situation where the parties keep up a relationship despite the fact that the supplier is no longer selling. Both parties see the value of maintaining contact so that next time a requirement arises they can do profitable business together.

2.31 **Stage 25: final termination**. This refers to the (relatively rare) situation when the two parties decide they will never do business together again.

3 Other aspects of the lifecycle model

Linking the lifecycle model to the relationship spectrum

3.1 It may well have occurred to you that not all relationships go through all the stages outlined above. The model appears to aim at being comprehensive in listing all possible stages in a relationship, but in particular cases some of the stages may be modified or bypassed altogether.

3.2 Arguably the model applies most closely to the left hand side of the relationship spectrum (adversarial relationships etc). This is because the early stages of the model refer to a situation where buyer and supplier may have little initial familiarity with each other, or in fact may know nothing at all about each other.

3.3 At the right hand side of the spectrum we are considering relationships which have probably taken much time to build up. If we are in a partnership relationship with a supplier, we have most likely known the organisation for years. Much of the initiation segment of the model is therefore irrelevant, or it took place in some shape or form years ago.

3.4 Even in the case of a partnership relationship the model, if it has any worth at all, should highlight some stages that are relevant. For example, in the delivery segment it will still be possible to talk about continuous improvement and ongoing delivery.

3.5   The message from this section is that if you are asked a question about the lifecycle model you should consider carefully what type of relationship is being discussed. Don't rush to assume that all stages in the model are applicable to all relationships.

Understanding your position in the relationship lifecycle

3.6   The relationship lifecycle described in this chapter may strike you as a somewhat academic tool, but it is intended to assist buyers in their professional work. In order to apply it to a real-life supply relationship, a buyer would need to know the stage that the relationship has currently reached.

3.7   This is usually a fairly simple matter. To convince yourself of this, just think briefly about a number of suppliers you are currently in contact with. You should be able to identify without any difficulty which of the 25 stages of the lifecycle you are currently occupying.

3.8   There is also an opportunity for forward planning. By considering where we currently are in the cycle we can foresee what the upcoming stages are and react appropriately.

3.9   By considering the lifecycle stages we can derive useful information. For example, if we are in the 'business development' stage (Stage 21) we should be aware that the supplier may be talking to others in the organisation in the hope of gaining extra business. This may be unwelcome news to the purchasing function, because it raises the possibility of user departments committing the organisation's resources without specialist purchasing involvement.

3.10   As another example, suppose we judge that with a particular supplier we are in the 'initial delivery' stage (Stage 17). It is clear from what has been said about this stage that we should be reviewing our agreement with the supplier and considering any refinements that may be appropriate for Stage 18.

4   *Termination of supply relationships*

Why do supply relationships terminate?

4.1   The reasons for the decline and termination of a relationship could be any of the following.

*   The buyer has changed the type of products it makes or the markets it sells to, and no longer needs the products or services provided by the supplier. A relationship lifecycle might possibly last no longer than the lifecycle of the single product that the organisation buys from that supplier, or the lifecycle of the product made by the buying organisation.

*   The supplier makes a strategic shift into other supply markets, and is no longer willing to make the products the buyer wants.

*   Problems arise with the relationship, because it has become too 'cosy' and no longer achieves the continuous improvements that it once did, because competitive efforts are relaxed. The relationship might also become bureaucratised and inflexible.

- A new supplier enters the market offering a product or service on terms that the existing supplier cannot match. This might happen, for example, because the supply market has become more global, and a new foreign supplier has entered the market. The buyer might therefore seek to establish a new relationship with the new supplier.

- There is a dispute about the quality of goods supplied, leading to a rift between customer and supplier. Examples occasionally make the news headlines, such as the dispute in 2000-2001 between the Ford Motor Company and Firestone, supplier of the tyres for its Explorer model in the US, about the extent to which the tyres alone were to blame for a series of road accidents (and the ensuing litigation).

4.2   Other detailed reasons could be given, but in summary we can classify the main reasons for termination under the following three headings.

- In the simplest case, both parties conclude that they have fulfilled the objectives they wished to achieve when entering the relationship. The relationship has served its purpose and now comes to a natural end.

- Sometimes a relationship is damaged by disputes between the parties. We look at conflict in supply relationships in Chapter 10 of this text and suggest ways in which it may be handled constructively. In some cases, however, this will not be possible and the supply relationship may end in acrimony.

- Finally, a relationship may end because one party is convinced that the other party has behaved badly.

4.3   There are many possible scenarios to illustrate this last possibility. For example, a buyer may decline a supplier's proposal for an improved method of working together, but may use the idea for developing his relationship with another supplier. When the original supplier finds out, he is likely to be very aggrieved. Similarly, a supplier may make a direct approach to a buyer's customer, offering to supply direct. When the buyer finds out that the supplier is trying to bypass him in this way he in turn is likely to be aggrieved. These are just two (fairly extreme) examples of how a relationship may turn sour because of inappropriate behaviour by one of the parties.

4.4   More generally, a buyer may feel aggrieved if he believes that the supplier is not meeting the terms of the contract, or is giving preference to other customers (perhaps competitors of the buyer), or imposes unexpected price rises, or suffers a decline in quality.

4.5   Similarly, a supplier may feel aggrieved if the buyer is slow to pay for his supplies, or if the promised volumes of business fail to appear, or if the buyer makes frequent changes to scheduling or specifications.

4.6   Either party may feel aggrieved as a result of poor communications, abuse of intellectual property, or different interpretations of the contract. In all these situations, the conflict resolution techniques of Chapter 10 may offer a means of **retrieving and retaining** the relationship; but if these fail, termination is the likely result.

Using the contract to terminate the relationship

4.7   Invariably, a supply relationship will be embodied in a legal contract. When a buyer thinks of terminating a relationship he must refer carefully to any relevant terms contained in the contract.

4.8   If the reason for termination is a breach of contract by the supplier (eg failure to provide goods of the specified quality) the situation will probably be covered by a specific clause in the contract. It is likely that the buyer will be entitled to repudiate the contract, which means that he regards it as no longer being in existence. The contract may also contain clauses relating to the damages that may be claimed by the buyer in this case (eg it may contain a liquidated damages clause).

4.9   The contract may also contain a clause about the use of arbitration or mediation in the event of dispute. If this is so, the buyer must ensure that he complies with any obligation to follow a dispute resolution procedure. Failure to do so will put him in breach of contract.

4.10   Finally, the contract may contain a *force majeure* clause. This covers the situation where the contract proves impossible to fulfil because of events outside the control of the parties. Again, the buyer must study the clause carefully to check whether it covers the particular circumstances of the case.

Maintaining a supply relationship post-conflict

4.11   Depending on the circumstances in which the relationship terminated, it may be appropriate to keep lines of communication open. This is unlikely to be the case if the relationship ended in acrimony, but even then a buyer must be completely professional in his attitude to the supply market. It is never appropriate to use the kind of rude or abusive behaviour that will prevent good interpersonal relations in future.

4.12   In Section 2 of this chapter we described the stages in the relationship lifecycle. Stage 24 was labelled 'latent termination'. We described this as 'the situation where the parties keep up a relationship despite the fact that the supplier is no longer selling. Both parties see the value of maintaining contact so that next time a requirement arises they can do profitable business together'.

4.13   The need for keeping communications open is particularly important when the relationship has terminated simply because both parties have achieved their objectives. This suggests that the parties can work together effectively and profitably, which makes it likely that more business will arise in the future.

4.14   Apart from the possibility of future business, there is also the consideration that buyers wish to stay up to date with developments in the supply market. The more contacts they preserve, the better they are able to do this.

Chapter summary

- The relationship lifecycle is the concept that relationships between buyer and supplier may move through various discrete stages. It implies that relationships are for the long term.

- The Kettering model is an ambitious attempt to list all the possible stages (25 stages in total!) through which a relationship may progress. These are divided into three stages: initiation; agreement; and delivery.

- Not all relationships go through all the possible stages of the Kettering model.

- By considering the stages in the model, we can attempt to identify whereabouts we are in our relationship with any particular supplier.

- All relationships terminate eventually. This may be because objectives have been fulfilled, or because disputes have damaged the relationship, or because one party believes the other has behaved badly.

- If the time has come to terminate a relationship, the buyer must pay careful attention to relevant clauses in the supply contract.

- It will often be appropriate to maintain contact with the supplier even after the relationship has ended.

Self-test questions

1 List elements of a relationship lifecycle that distinguish it from a customer lifecycle. (1.7)

2 What are the three main segments of the Kettering Model? (2.4)

3 What is meant by Stage 6 of the Kettering Model (conditioning by seller)? (2.10)

4 What is meant by Stage 14 of the Kettering Model (headline agreement)? (2.19)

5 What is meant by Stage 24 of the Kettering Model (latent termination)? (2.30)

6 Give practical examples of how the Kettering Model can help buyers in their work. (3.9, 3.10)

7 List reasons why supply relationships may terminate. (4.1, 4.2)

8 What is a *force majeure* clause in a supply contract? (4.10)

CHAPTER 4

Modern Concepts in Supply Relationships

Learning objectives

1.5 Differentiate between lean and agile supply philosophies on supplier relationships.

- Traditional supply philosophy
- Lean supply philosophy
- Agile supply philosophy

1.6 Analyse and explain the corporate social responsibility (CSR) and ethical, technological, legal and environmental constraints on relationship development.

- Component parts of CSR
- The case for CSR
- The case against CSR
- CSR and supplier development

Chapter headings

1 Traditional vs lean and agile philosophies

2 Lean and agile supply

3 Corporate social responsibility

4 Ethical and environmental issues in purchasing

Introduction

The nature of supply relationships has undergone many changes in recent decades. In this chapter we look at a number of modern concepts and developments that have contributed to this.

1 Traditional vs lean and agile philosophies

Target costing

1.1 An increase in the proportion of external spending by manufacturers means that many such companies can be described as 'low value added' firms. In other words, the price paid by the eventual consumer is largely made up of costs charged by suppliers to the manufacturer. The manufacturer himself adds relatively little value.

I.2 The implication of this is clear. To achieve competitive prices such companies must focus on their costs, which increasingly arise outside the boundaries of the firm. Purchasing's contribution in reducing costs right along the supply chain, while maintaining and improving quality, is vital.

I.3 One technique that is relevant here is that of **target costing**. This is an approach pioneered by Japanese firms which differs considerably from the earlier Western approach to setting prices.

- The traditional model builds up the cost of a product by analysing its components step by step. A profit margin is then added on and the result is the selling price of the product. With luck, this will be a price that the market can stand; if it is not, the product will be unsuccessful.

- Target costing starts at the other end. The manufacturer first estimates the selling price that the market will be willing to pay for a product with specific features. He then works backward to calculate the production cost that must be achieved in order to provide a reasonable profit.

I.4 The difference between these approaches is crucial.

- The traditional approach accepts costs as given, and calculates a selling price that must be achieved. We must then hope that the market will be willing to pay.

- Target costing starts with what the customer will pay, and then attacks costs so that they are reduced to the required level.

I.5 Target costing is hardly feasible without close cooperation between members of the supply chain. Each member must work closely with the others to identify opportunities for cost reductions and progressively seek to drive costs and prices downwards.

I.6 Two aspects of supplier relations are particularly important in this respect: working together to remove duplication of effort, and cost transparency.

I.7 Removing **duplication** means reducing elements within the supply chain which do not add value but do add to costs. Some of these are identified by Richard Lamming in 'The Future of Purchasing: Developing Lean Supply', printed in *Strategic Procurement Management in the 1990s: Concepts and Cases* – a book which is a mine of new ideas on strategic issues in purchasing. Here are some examples of practices that do not add value but do add to costs.

- Production of invoices, produced for compliance reasons only, to satisfy accountants, tax authorities, etc

- Expediting, which would be unnecessary and therefore non-existent in a perfect supply chain

- Inspection, which like expediting is a tacit acceptance of inadequacy

I.8 **Cost transparency** means that suppliers should be ready to talk frankly with customers about cost structures. The supplier can benefit from this because greater information frequently means that the customer can suggest improvements for the supplier to exploit.

Agile supply

1.9 A focus of lean supply (as discussed in Chapter 1) is on the customer-supplier partnership in the supply chain. The dominant driver is to achieve a highly-integrated and down-sized supply chain. The benefits will be lower costs (or added value) through more productive working relationships between the buyer and supplier.

1.10 However, the major risk with reliance on a single supplier in a close partnership is that supply could be fragile and break down unexpectedly. For example, in 1995, the failure of one supplier to deliver a component for a power steering system resulted in Ford having to shut down temporarily six of its plants.

1.11 Around 1990, there was a widely-held view that a company should have a second supply source, or even operate a 3–2–1 practice, whereby a lead supplier is given half the business and two other suppliers are given a sufficient volume of business to maintain their interest. Since 1990, many supplier relationships have been developed strategically, and having alternative suppliers for the same product is no longer a strategic option. Where a company has a close strategic relationship with a supplier, there must at least be agility in the supply chain.

1.12 Agility is proficiency at dealing adequately with change or unexpected events, such as recovering from a situation where a supplier has failed. Unplanned events in the supply chain could be caused by staff shortages, breakdowns, delayed deliveries or a need to expedite an order to a customer who has an urgent requirement for supply.

1.13 With agile supply, the focus of strategy is on getting speed and flexibility into the supply chain. Achieving agility calls for:

- streamlining the physical flow of parts from suppliers
- streamlining the bilateral flow of information through electronic data interchange
- adaptability in responding to changing needs of the market.

1.14 If there is an agile supply chain, the supply chain management will be integrated with planning and execution systems, so that:

- customers will know when their order is going to be shipped
- there is a high ratio of products shipped to labour
- information flows instantaneously through the supply chain, both ways.

1.15 Companies must be able to react to customers who expect immediate replies to their requests for assistance or information. Even more of a challenge for companies is the growing expectation of many customers to have '48 hour delivery' to any point in the world.

2 *Lean and agile supply*

The CIPS Position on Practice paper

2.1 CIPS have published an influential and authoritative guide to lean and agile supply philosophies: *Lean and Agile Purchasing and Supply Management*. According to this paper, there are five key principles to lean thinking.

- Specify what creates value as seen from the customer's perspective.
- Identify all steps across the value stream.
- Make those actions that create that value flow.
- Only make what is pulled by the customer just in time.
- Strive for perfection by continually removing successive layers of waste.

2.2 One odd (no doubt unintentional) feature of the CIPS paper is its insistence that all activities of an organisation are either non-value adding (ie those that do not directly contribute to the satisfaction of customers) or necessary non-value adding (ie those that have to be done in order to comply with legislation). This seems to omit the category of value adding activities: those that do directly contribute to the satisfaction of customers.

2.3 At all events, the point of the distinction is to emphasise that value adding activities should be the focus of the organisation's efforts. Buyers, along with everyone else in the organisation, should try to reduce non-value adding activities. This is a key aim of lean/agile organisations. We have already seen how such organisations aim to eliminate the seven kinds of waste identified by Taichi Ohno. Table 4.1 identifies the types of waste that may occur, grouped into Ohno's seven categories.

Table 4.1 *Taichi Ohno's seven wastes*

Waste caused by ...	**Comments**
Over-production	Producing output which customers are not yet demanding leads to stockholding costs and possibly scrap. This refers both to finished goods for external customers, and to work in progress for the next stage in the production process
Transportation	Moving materials between different locations adds cost. This may refer to moving materials from their source to our production facility, or to moving materials within the production facility. Either way, effective planning can minimise the unnecessary transportation.
Waiting	Delays in processing mean that more time is taken than is really needed. This is quite common in the traditional manufacturing process, but lean supply aims to eliminate it.
Motion	Unnecessary motion violates sound ergonomic principles and can cause waste of time and possibly injury to staff.
Over-processing	This can happen when unnecessarily sophisticated equipment is used to produce relatively simple goods, adding to their cost.
Inventory	Lean supply aims to eliminate the use of buffer stocks because stockholding costs do not add value, and because holding stocks can mask inefficiencies in the production process.
Defects/corrections	Clearly the costs of rework and scrap do not add value, but do reduce the bottom-line profit.

2.4 The CIPS paper identifies the origins of the lean model in the motor industry. 'Sourcing strategies [led] to a smaller number of suppliers that could then be more effectively managed.' However, CIPS also point out the danger of reducing the supply base too drastically, eg by a policy of single sourcing. An effective risk management process is needed to identify the dangers here.

2.5 Similar remarks apply to the practice of outsourcing. This too has been favoured by organisations seeking to become lean, but in some cases has led to the loss of core competencies.

2.6 The CIPS paper also cites the definition of agile as 'quick and nimble', as opposed to lean, which means 'having no surplus flesh or bulk'. Others have distinguished between lean and agile in terms of manufacturing companies and their methods of supplying customers.

- Lean manufacturing refers to the situation where goods are produced only when 'pulled' by a customer, and to the standard of quality required by the customer.

- Agile manufacturing goes one step further by means of 'late customisation'. This is familiar to anyone who has ordered a computer from the Dell website: Dell allows the online customer to specify exactly what components are required in the computer system and then manufactures it exactly to the customer specification. This can be done very rapidly, because all of the component parts are finished to a high degree and ready for incorporation in the finished product.

Distinguishing lean and agile from traditional manufacturing

2.7 In the case of manufacturing companies, the traditional production model incorporated a number of features rejected by more modern lean and agile philosophies.

2.8 The traditional model allowed only modest choice of features in finished goods, because it was not economic to produce the many different combinations of features that would be possible. In lean and agile supply, the product is not actually finished until the customer orders it, and the customer's specification can be matched as in the example of Dell cited above.

2.9 Again in the traditional model, there was emphasis on 'economic batch quantities'. This meant that machines would be set up to produce certain minimum quantities, below which production was not regarded as economic. The problem with this approach is that the organisation may be producing far more items than are actually required by customers, internal or external. This technique too is avoided in lean and agile organisations.

2.10 Lean and agile thinking also rejects the need for substantial stockholdings, common in a traditional manufacturing environment. The term 'buffer stock' was often used to describe stock held 'just in case' it was needed. In lean and agile thinking, the focus is on ensuring that the need for stock is avoided.

Features of lean supply

2.11 We return to the five distinguishing features of lean supply identified in the CIPS Position on Practice paper.

- Specify what creates value as seen from the customer's perspective.
- Identify all steps across the value stream.
- Make those actions that create that value flow.
- Only make what is pulled by the customer just in time.
- Strive for perfection by continually removing successive layers of waste.

2.12   The first point relates to the 'customer's perspective'. This implies a need for close relations with the customer to ensure that his perception of value is embodied in what the supplier is offering. It is not safe to assume that the customer has the same perception of value as the supplier.

2.13   In the second point, the key term is 'value stream'. In a traditional supply chain, there will be many activities and processes that do not add value. In a lean or agile chain, the aim is to eliminate these, leaving just a stream of value adding activities.

2.14   Once we have identified the value adding activities, we need to consider how to link them so as to deliver the total value to the end customer. That is what is meant by the third point.

2.15   The fourth point is a distinguishing feature of lean and agile philosophies. As we have already seen, the traditional model of manufacturing often leads to production in advance of customer requirements (whether this refers to internal or external customers). Lean and agile production avoids this.

2.16   The final point refers to the avoidance of waste. This was discussed in detail above in connection with the analysis of seven types of waste identified by Taichi Ohno.

2.17   The CIPS paper also identifies specific techniques that are typical of a lean environment. For example, lean companies make great use of the internet in order to streamline processes, at the same time as reducing costs. E-procurement is a common tool in agile companies. So too is the use of purchasing cards, with responsibility for purchasing devolved away from the purchasing departments and into the hands of end users – of course, with appropriate limits in place, and often in conjunction with suppliers and catalogues pre-approved by purchasing professionals.

The impact of lean supply on supply relationships

2.18   Lean supply is based on long-term partnerships with a downsized supply base. Lamming argues that the elimination of duplication of effort and capability in the supply chain can only be achieved 'by recognition of mutual dependence and common interest between customer and supplier – beyond the principle of operational collaboration'. Lamming also describes the features of lean customer-supplier relationships: see Table 4.2.

2.19   Some critics, however, also point out that lean supply can have a negative effect on supply relationships. New & Ramsay, for example, note that excessive leanness can create rigidity, with insufficient slack in the system to take account of fluctuations in demand and disruptions to supply – potentially creating problems and disputes. The costs of becoming lean may also discourage small suppliers from participating in the supply chain.

Features of agile supply

2.20   The CIPS Position on Practice paper already referred to describes agile supply as 'using market knowledge and a responsive supply network to exploit profitable opportunities in the marketplace'. This links in with the point already made about late customisation. An organisation with 'agility' is able to see opportunities for product modification at any time that the market appears ready for it. In this sense, product lifecycles may be very short indeed, because the organisation's offering is changing constantly in response to market demand. This is similar to the way in which late customisation is applied.

Table 4.2. *Customer-supplier relationships in lean supply*

Factor	Lean supply characteristics
Nature of competition	Global operation, local presence
	Based on contribution to product technology
	Dependent upon alliances/collaboration
Basis of sourcing decisions	Early involvement of established suppliers
	Joint efforts: target costing, value analysis
	Single and dual sourcing
	Suppliers providing global benefits
	Re-sourcing only as a last resort
Exchange of information between supplier and customer	True transparency (eg on costs etc)
	Two-way discussion of costs/volumes
	Exchange of technical/commercial info
	Electronic data interchange
Management of capacity	*Kanban* system: signal demand in real time
	Regional strategic investments discussed
	Synchronised capacity
	Flexibility to operate with fluctuations
Delivery practice	True just in time (JIT)
Dealing with price changes	Price reductions based on cost reduction from order onwards: joint efforts
Attitude to quality	Supplier vetting becomes redundant
	Mutual agreement on quality targets
	Continual interaction/improvement (*kaizen*)
	Perfect quality as a goal

2.21   Whereas lean thinking attempts to remove stock from the supply chain, as being a source of waste, agile thinking is more ready to accept stock, provided the reasons for holding it are sound. For example, the CIPS paper cites the example of a supplier who was asked by its customers to hold stock to enable response on very short lead times. This is an example where stock is not a source of cost, but a source of value enhancement for the customer.

2.22   Stock is also accepted by agile companies who practise late customisation. Typically, the stocks held will mostly be in the form of work in progress, waiting to be converted into finished goods in response to customer orders.

2.23   Students sometimes come away with the idea that agile supply is a development of lean supply, but with additional features. A truer perspective is given by Professor Andrew Cox, again cited in the CIPS paper: Cox believes that the lean philosophy is most powerful when the winning criteria are cost and quality, whereas agility is paramount where service and customer value enhancement are key.

2.24   Where lean supply is based on long-term partnerships with a few suppliers, agile supply is based on a looser, more fluid, easily-reconfigured and often ICT-integrated (or 'virtual') supply network. This enables rapid, short-term, mutually-beneficial alliances to be formed and disbanded as required to seize opportunities.

3   *Corporate social responsibility*

Social responsibilities of organisations

3.1   Ethical issues are increasingly a concern to organisations as public opinion emphasises the need for large enterprises to be good 'corporate citizens'. There are important issues which face an individual organisation as it formulates strategies and policies about how it interacts with its various stakeholders, including strategies concerning relationships with suppliers.

3.2   Some of these matters will be covered by legislative and regulatory requirements, and/or professional codes of practice.

- Legislative requirements include, for example, an employer's duty to provide a safe and healthy workplace (Health and Safety at Work Act) and the various legal protections afforded to employees by successive Employment Acts.

- Regulatory requirements include, for example, those laid down by specific industry regulators such as Ofcom for the communications industry, the Competition Commission (regulating merger and acquisition activity), and the Advertising Standards Authority (regulating media advertising).

- Professional codes of practice include, for example, the ethical codes published by such bodies as the Chartered Institute of Purchasing and Supply and the Institute of Chartered Accountants in England and Wales. Members of these bodies are obliged to comply with the rules they lay down.

3.3   Some organisations may have a 'compliance based' approach to ethics which strives merely to uphold these minimal requirements. However, the term 'corporate social responsibility' (CSR) covers policies which the organisation adopts for the good and wellbeing of stakeholders, taking a more proactive 'integrity based' approach.

3.4   Although corporate objectives may primarily be financial, particularly in the private business sector, many firms now also set social responsibility objectives, in relation to matters such as the following.

- Sustainability issues: the conservation and perpetuation of the world's limited natural resources (eg by limiting greenhouse gas emissions)

- Environmental issues: the reduction of environment pollution, waste management, the avoidance of environmental disfigurement, land reclamation, promoting recycling, energy conservation and so on

- Ethical trading, business relationships and development: consumer protection, improvement of working (and social) conditions for employees and subcontractors (particularly in developing nations), avoidance of exploitation, debt minimisation, contribution to local communities and so on.

Why should an organisation set CSR objectives?

3.5   Milton Friedman and Elaine Sternberg have argued the view that 'the social responsibility of business is profit maximisation': to give a return on shareholders' investment. Spending funds on objectives not related to shareholder expectations is irresponsible: regard for shareholder wealth is a healthy discipline for management, providing accountability for decisions. The public interest is served by profit maximisation, because the State levies taxes.

3.6 'Consequently,' argued Friedman, 'the only justification for social responsibility is enlightened self interest' on the part of a business organisation. So how does CSR serve the interest of the firm?

3.7 Law, regulation and Codes of Practice impose certain social responsibilities on organisations (eg in relation to health and safety, employment protection, consumer rights and environmental care). There are financial and operational penalties for failure to comply (eg 'polluter pays' taxes).

- Voluntary measures (which may in any case only pre-empt legal and regulatory requirements) may enhance corporate image and build a positive brand.
- Above-statutory provisions for employees and suppliers may be necessary to attract, retain and motivate them to provide quality service and commitment – particularly in competition with other employers/purchasers.
- Increasing consumer awareness of social responsibility issues creates a market demand for CSR (and the threat of boycott for irresponsible firms)

3.8 However, business also needs to remember the 'enlightened' part of the equation! Profit maximisation does not, by itself, always lead to ethical behaviour – as examples of environmental and human exploitation show. (High-profile past examples include: environmental degradation caused by Shell oil refineries in Nigeria; child labour used by Nike and other Western clothing manufacturers; fraudulent reporting by Enron...)

3.9 In addition, Henry Mintzberg notes that a business's relationship with society is not purely economic: a business is an open social system which makes a variety of non-economic exchanges with the society in which it operates (people, information/knowledge, image), and creates a variety of non-economic impacts. Social responsibility helps to create a social climate and infrastructure in which the business can prosper in the long term.

The CIPS commitment to corporate social responsibility (CSR)

3.10 The CIPS president for 2005, Ian Taylor, made CSR the theme of his year of office. The importance of the topic for CIPS members is underlined by the amount of material published by the Institute on its website. In particular, the Institute has published a comprehensive White Paper, *Corporate Social Responsibility*. The discussion below is a summarised version of the White Paper.

3.11 According to CIPS, CSR is important to all organisations for the following reasons.

- Enhancing stakeholder value
- Helping to increase reputation
- Ensuring increased knowledge of supply, enabling minimum risks from suppliers

3.12 The White Paper highlights concerns such as the use of child labour and sweatshops in the supply chains of many organisations. These are argued to have had an adverse impact on share prices, brand equity, staff morale and media profiles.

3.13 The Institute specifically encourages members to consider the long-term implications of their actions and to question objectives that may unintentionally have negative socioeconomic consequences.

Definitions of CSR

3.14 The White Paper cites a number of attempts to define or explain CSR.

- CSR places a company's social and environmental impacts in the context of its obligations to society. It promotes the integration of stakeholder issues into business operations. CSR makes company values come alive (values such as accountability, transparency, ethics, respect, integrity and humanity).

- CSR is concerned with treating the stakeholders of the firm ethically or in a responsible manner.

- CSR is about how companies manage the business processes to produce an overall positive impact on society.

- The commitment of business to contribute to sustainable economic development, working with their employees, the local community and society at large to improve their quality of life, in ways that are good for business and good for development.

Key areas of CSR for purchasing professionals

3.15 The White Paper identifies the following key areas of CSR.

- Environmental responsibility
- Human rights
- Equal opportunities
- Diversity
- Corporate governance
- Sustainability
- Impact on society
- Ethics and ethical trading
- Biodiversity

3.16 **Environmental responsibility** is not just desirable for moral and ethical reasons, but is also increasingly addressed by legal regulations (for example, the EU Environment Liability Directive).

3.17 **Human rights** refers to such issues as child labour, working conditions, wages and exploitation. Organisations are increasingly aware that they can influence such issues, not just in their home countries but also in areas of the world from which they source supplies. Buyers should be aware of the International Labour Organisation's four core 'rights' relating to people at work.

- Freedom of association (in effect, recognition of workers' rights to form trade unions)

- Elimination of slave labour

- Elimination of child labour

- Elimination of discrimination in employment

3.18 **Equal opportunities** have been the subject of legislation in the UK since at least 1976; any discrimination on the basis of sex, disability, religion/benefits, sexual orientation and age is forbidden. Purchasing professionals must be aware of the need for equal opportunities both in terms of the products and services produced, and in terms of the supply base (the issue of diversity, see next paragraph).

3.19 **Diversity** of suppliers means the structuring of the supply base in such a way as not to discriminate against minorities. Many organisations in both the public and private sectors are adopting supplier diversity programmes, which foster economic growth. But you should note that buyers who deliberately extend their supply base (eg to include suppliers from ethnic minorities) are going against the modern trend towards slimming the supply base. There is a difficult balancing act here.

3.20 **Corporate governance** has come to prominence in the wake of some well publicised company failures. Terms and conditions agreed with suppliers may cover such areas as limiting the organisation's exposure to unnecessary risk, putting in place measures to control the circumstances under which risk will be borne, and positioning the organisation with regard to ethical matters such as CSR.

3.21 **Sustainability** means living in ways that do not compromise the wellbeing of future generations. Purchasing professionals can help in this area by ensuring appropriate policies both within their own organisations, and by encouraging similar practices among their suppliers.

3.22 **Impact on society** is an increasingly important area of concern for purchasing professionals and for top corporate management. The White Paper distinguishes between the forward linkages and backward linkages that can affect an organisation's impact on society.

- In its backward linkages an organisation should be concerned about the conditions and wages provided by their suppliers, particularly those in third world countries.

- In its forward linkages an organisation should be concerned about how, further down the supply chain, their products are disposed of or recycled.

3.23 **Ethical trading** has increasingly come into prominence in recent years. How can organisations reconcile their obligations to shareholders – above all, their obligation to achieve the maximum possible profit and capital growth – with broader standards of ethical behaviour? For example, is it permissible for an organisation to keep labour costs down by exploiting poorly paid workers in third-world countries?

3.24 The overwhelming opinion in most modern organisations is that the answer to this question is 'No'. Responsible companies believe that their obligations to maximise profits should not be fulfilled at the price of unfair exploitation. It is interesting to look at why this opinion has become the prevalent one.

3.25 One reason is simply the increasing thought that has gone into the issue. When companies were locally based, such problems were either non-existent or at least less pressing. Now that the world economy is increasingly dominated by multinational corporations the issue can no longer be ducked.

3.26 Arising from this, corporations are influenced by the sheer strength of public opinion. Members of the public, though they may well hold shares in companies, do not have day-to-day responsibilities for profit-maximising strategies. Free from this constraint, they look with repugnance on activities that seem to violate basic human rights. Responsible organisations have to take account of public opinion, because ultimately it is members of the public who pay for their products.

3.27 **Biodiversity** has been defined as 'the total variety of life on Earth'. In principle, most people support the idea of preserving diversity of habitats, genetic profiles and species. It is a responsibility of organisations to minimise any adverse impact on these areas.

Corporate governance

3.28 One aspect of corporate social responsibility has been much in the news in recent years. This is the topic of corporate governance, which refers to the ways in which organisations police their own activities. In the UK, this was the subject of the Cadbury Committee, established in 1991 in the wake of various company scandals.

3.29 More recently, the news headlines have concerned companies on the other side of the Atlantic, such as the Enron and Worldcom scandals. This led US legislators to enact the Sarbanes Oxley Act in 2002 (often referred to for short as SOX). The common theme with all of these corporate disasters, on both sides of the Atlantic, was a failure by the companies concerned to regulate their own affairs properly. Often, it was found that certain dominant individuals within the company exercised undue influence, without being subject to adequate checks and restraints on their actions.

3.30 Both the Cadbury Committee and SOX aim to strengthen the internal regulatory regime of corporate bodies so as to avoid a repeat of these scandals. Measures that can help include the appointment of independent non-executive directors, the establishment of audit committees within companies, and the establishment of strong internal controls which the directors are required to evaluate and certify. These requirements may be backed up by enhanced civil and criminal penalties for breaches of the law.

Is there a case against CSR?

3.31 Earlier in this chapter we mentioned the arguments of Friedman and Sternberg, which tend to cast doubt on the merit of CSR as an organisational objective. Playing Devil's advocate, we could easily put forward arguments to suggest that companies should focus entirely on profit maximisation; where this conflicts with CSR principles, it is the task of society, not company directors, to set things right.

3.32 As an example, we could point out that use of recycled materials, or materials from sustainable sources, is often more expensive than the alternatives. Use of third world labour can save money for a company. And similar examples could be multiplied.

3.33 In many cases these arguments can be countered on their own terms, ie on the basis that they are incorrect in their cost assumptions. For example, by working closely with suppliers, a buyer may be able to use recycled materials without any increase in cost. But ultimately the arguments take place within a moral framework: society, in the form of legislators and opinion formers, has simply decided that certain practices are undesirable, even if in some cases they might save money.

3.34 Against this background, it is not really an option for buyers to ignore the requirements of legislation and ethical codes. This is the reason why ethical considerations are a constraint on the formation of supplier relationships: buyers must observe certain leading principles even if they could save money by flouting them.

4 Ethical and environmental issues in purchasing

Why are buyers interested in ethics?

4.1 Ethical issues, and in many cases environmental issues, are important in purchasing.

- Both customers and suppliers expect to see ethical behaviour from an organisation. If a customer or a supplier has doubts about the honesty and 'rightness' of an organisation's business practices, there will be a lack of trust, and absence of trust will affect the relationship with that customer or supplier. Customers might refuse to buy from the organisation. When the customers are consumers, there could even be the possibility of an organised boycott of the organisation's products.

- Concern for the environment is just one aspect of ethical business policies.

4.2 Unethical behaviour is unlikely to be beneficial in the long term. Although a short-term profit advantage might be gained from 'sharp practice' or lack of concern for the environment, there are greater long-term benefits from being, and being seen to be, strictly ethical. Even the appearance of bad behaviour, even if it is an unfounded rumour, can damage a firm.

4.3 Nowadays, policies on ethical behaviour are considered an essential element in strategic management, and some companies have an ethical policy that they publish and make known to all their staff.

4.4 Examples of consumers boycotting the products of a company accused of unethical behaviour are numerous.

- From 2000, there was a movement to boycott Esso petrol stations because of the environmental policies of the producers of Esso, the Exxon Corporation.

- In December 2001, Triumph International, a producer of luxury lingerie, faced a boycott of its products by consumers angry at a supply decision taken by the company to use a factory in Burma, a country noted for very low wages, a record of human rights abuses and the use of child slave labour.

- In December 2001, public relations firm QBO published details of a survey showing that two-thirds of consumers aged in their thirties and forties had at some time boycotted the products or services of at least one company. Of those who had stopped buying from a company, 95 per cent never returned to buy again from that company, but only 10 per cent made any fuss when they ceased buying. Nearly half of the respondents surveyed thought that British firms were now more unethical than they were a decade ago.

Professional codes of practice

4.5 Buyers are more exposed to temptation than most professionals. They control large sums of organisational funds. They are engaged in decisions between one supplier and another, all such suppliers having an interest in influencing the buyer's decision. It is difficult to determine wholly objective criteria for deciding between rival suppliers, and non-objective criteria may enter by the back door. This places great responsibility on the buyer's shoulders.

4.6   National and international bodies representing purchasing professionals have published codes of practice setting out (usually in fairly broad terms) what activities are considered unethical and giving general guidance on the ethical performance expected of members. A starting point in studying this area is a consideration of the ethical code published by the Chartered Institute of Purchasing and Supply.

4.7   The code makes it clear that seeking membership of the Institute is in itself an undertaking to abide by ethical standards. Failure to do so may be punishable by disciplinary process.

4.8   Not surprisingly, the guidance emphasises the overriding principle that members should not use a position of authority for personal gain. Equally, members have a responsibility to uphold the standing of the Institute by their behaviour both inside and outside their employing organisations.

4.9   Specific guidance is also offered in the following areas.

   •   Members must declare any personal interest which might impinge on their work activities, or which might appear to do so in the eyes of others.

   •   Members must respect confidentiality of information and must not use information received for personal gain. The information they provide should be true and fair.

   •   Members should avoid any arrangements which might prevent fair competition.

   •   Except for small-value items, business gifts should not be accepted.

   •   Only modest hospitality should be accepted. Members should not accept hospitality which might influence a business decision, or which might appear to do so.

   •   Any doubt on these last two points should be discussed with the individual's superior.

4.10   In the United States, the Institute for Supply Management (ISM) goes into somewhat greater detail on what is considered unethical. Members are required to avoid 'sharp practice' and the Association cites a number of examples, summarised in Table 4.3. (These are quoted in *Purchasing and Supply Management* by Dobler and Burt, in a chapter with a wealth of detail on strategic and operational aspects of purchasing ethics.)

Ethical issues in dealings with suppliers

4.11   To ensure compliance with this kind of professional guidance management have a duty to take certain actions that will promote appropriate behaviour.

4.12   A very common first step is to prepare written standards of conduct to which staff are expected to adhere. This is an almost universal practice in large businesses. It applies not just to purchasing staff, but to others in the business who may be subject to unethical influences. David Farmer refers to United States surveys suggesting that such written policies play an important role in raising and maintaining standards.

Table 4.3 *Examples of 'sharp practice'*

- A buyer talks in terms of large quantities to encourage a price quote on that basis. However, the order is then placed for a smaller amount which does not justify the low price thus developed.

- A large number of bids are solicited in the hope that the buyer will be able to take advantage of a quotation error.

- Bids are solicited from unqualified suppliers whom the buyer would not patronise in any case. These bids are then played against the bids of responsible suppliers in order to gain a price or other advantage.

- A market is misrepresented by a buyer who places in competition the prices of seconds, odd lots, or distress merchandise.

- An attempt is made to influence a seller by leaving copies of bids, or other confidential correspondence, where a supplier can see them.

- A concession may be forced by dealing only with 'hungry' suppliers. The current philosophy is that a purchase order should create a mutual advantage with a price that is fair and reasonable.

- Obscure contract terms of benefit to the buyer's firm are buried in the small type of contract articles.

- A buyer may take advantage of a vendor who is short of cash and who may seek only to cover his out-of-pocket costs. (However, such a situation poses a dilemma, since the vendor may be saved from borrowing at a disadvantage and may look upon such an order as a blessing.)

4.13 To ensure that the written policies are followed in practice, management should ensure that they are publicised widely and monitored systematically. Many buying organisations ensure also that their suppliers have access to their internal rules, as it is suppliers who may be most aware of abuse. Above all, management should foster an ethos of responsible and ethical behaviour, in which abuses are held to be intolerable rather than quietly accepted.

4.14 This step should be supported by the provision of appropriate training.

4.15 Measures that management can put in place to avoid possible abuse include the following.

- Rotation of buyers to avoid any particular buyer becoming too 'cosy' with any particular supplier

- Controls over single sourcing deals to ensure that they are in the best interest of the organisation and not merely entered into for personal gain

- Controls over the authority levels of individual buyers

- Encouraging suppliers to use a known hotline number to report any wrongdoing in confidence

- Encouraging employees to report ethical breaches without fear of reprisal

4.16 We now round up a few instances where professional integrity may be compromised unless buyers are vigilant.

4.17   One area is the provision of information to suppliers. Table 4.3 identifies the practice of deliberately inflating estimates of order sizes in order to obtain a price that would not be offered if the true usage patterns were admitted. Modern practice on partnership and co-makership between buyer and supplier make such abuses even less acceptable than they were before.

4.18   Another problem is where a supplier or potential supplier makes a genuine error in a quotation or an invoice. To what extent is the buyer entitled to take advantage of this?

4.19   Several different versions of this scenario can be envisaged.

- Suppose the potential supplier wins the contract, and then discovers that the costings on which he based his quoted price are flawed? Many buyers would feel entitled to hold the supplier to his quote. However, the issue is not simple: in the extreme case the buyer may have to reckon on the supplier simply not being able to complete the contract on the agreed basis because to do so would lead to his bankruptcy.

- A slightly simpler case arises when the supplier mistakenly submits an invoice for less than the full amount he is entitled to. Should the buyer simply pay the reduced amount without comment? Most purchasing professionals would argue that, at least in the case where a long-term agreement is concerned, it is necessary to point out the error in order to safeguard mutual trust.

4.20   Another issue is that of late payment. In many cases the exact terms of payment are not spelled out in the contract and serious dispute may arise. In other cases the payment terms are well understood on both sides, and yet the buying firm fails to make payment on time. This can be very damaging to future relations, and amounts to a lie on the part of the buyer if it is done deliberately. As so often, though, the issue can be blurred: many large organisations have control systems which are prone to cause delays in payments being made even where deliberate intent is absent.

4.21   Finally, we mention the practice of seeking quotations from suppliers where there is no intention to purchase. Often this is done as a check on the competitiveness of existing suppliers. However, the effect is that potential suppliers are being tempted by an illusory hope of work to provide free services to the buying firm. Another aspect of this, cited in Table 4.3, is the use of such quotations to obtain concessions from suppliers who genuinely are in line to receive the contract. In either case, there must be serious question marks about the ethics of this practice.

Environmental issues in purchasing

4.22   Recent decades have seen an unprecedented upswing in public concern over environmental issues. Pollution of the world's waters, damage to the atmosphere, and exhaustion of mineral and other resources, have all attracted the attention of pressure groups and the wider public. In many cases the blame has been laid at the door of large corporations, allegedly pursuing short-term profits at the expense of long-term damage to the environment.

4.23   These pressures have led many organisations to take direct action. Often the stimulus comes from organisations whose objectives are clearly wider than profit maximisation. For example, it is clear that local government authorities, though they are charged with observing tight financial disciplines, have wider obligations to the public.

4.24 Once any organisation takes on an environmental stance, it is likely that such attitudes will begin to spread along the supply chain. Similar commitments will be demanded from that organisation's suppliers, who in turn will pass on the philosophy to their own suppliers. A momentum towards better environmental policies is then underway.

4.25 This kind of reasoning does not begin and end in the purchasing department. On the contrary, it is often an overall corporate policy that leads to change and development. Even so, purchasing staff have an important role to play in giving effect to the environmental objectives.

4.26 Areas of environmental concern in which purchasing staff have a role to play are summarised by Malcolm Saunders in *Strategic Purchasing and Supply Chain Management*: see Table 4.4.

Table 4.4 *Environmental concerns relevant to purchasing staff*

• Recovery, recycling and reusing of materials and waste products
• Safe disposal of waste products that cannot be recycled
• Supplier selection policies to support firms that conform to environmental standards with regard to air, water and noise pollution
• Supplier and product selection policies that reflect concern for conservation and renewal of resources
• Safe testing of products and materials
• Concern for noise, spray, dirt and vibration in the operation of transportation facilities

Establishing an environmental policy

4.27 As usual in the task of defining a policy, the first step is to determine objectives. There are several reasons why purchasing functions might want to pursue environmental policies.

- In some cases, there are cost savings to be achieved. For example, energy savings are both environmentally responsible and also economical. The same can be said of measures to eliminate excess packaging.

- Many countries have incorporated environmental concerns into legislation which organisations must comply with. Conforming with such rules is obviously essential, and failure to do so can lead to heavy fines.

- Finally, some companies have made a virtue of their environmental concern and used it to boost sales. In the UK, the Body Shop chain is often quoted as an example of this.

4.28 The problems of defining an environmental policy start early. For example, it is not always clear whether Product X is more or less friendly to the environment than Product Y. Scientists often present conflicting views, and even if a scientific view is widely held it may turn out to be flawed as new research results are published.

4.29 A comprehensive effort must be made to assemble information from every possible source, remembering that not all sources are completely free from prejudice. For example, a trade association may be inclined to provide information which favours the products of its members. And the information produced by pressure groups must also be viewed with caution.

4.30 An essential prerequisite for an environmental policy is the support of senior management. This should not be in doubt if purchasing's initiative is merely fitting in with corporate policies. However, if there is no overall corporate policy on environmental issues then purchasing's efforts to institute a departmental policy may be hampered.

4.31 The next step is to lay down guidelines on measures that can be instituted within the organisation. To some extent this may require negotiation with other functions. For example, purchasing may wish to minimise packaging, but this may conflict with the ideas of marketing staff. With tact and goodwill on both sides such ideas can be reconciled, but if this proves difficult the result may be stalemate. This illustrates again the importance of commitment from top management.

4.32 Finally, purchasing staff need to decide their attitude to suppliers. What action will be taken, if any, in respect of existing suppliers whose products are damaging the environment? What criteria will be established in respect of new suppliers? How will suppliers be monitored for compliance with new guidelines?

4.33 Whatever policy is finally agreed in these respects it is likely to be ineffective unless it is put in writing and communicated to all concerned.

Detailed elements of an environmental buying policy

4.34 The first element in an environmental buying policy should be uncontroversial. This is a commitment to avoid buying products that are damaging to the environment if alternative products are available with similar price and quality.

4.35 A major obstacle in the past to adoption of environmental policies has been that 'green' products have typically been more expensive than their 'non-green' equivalents. The last few years have seen radical changes in this situation and in many cases actual savings are to be made in choosing the green alternative.

4.36 However, if such alternatives are not available, or not easily accessible, the position is more difficult. Options that should be explored include consultation with the supplier with a view to reducing the damaging environmental impact, and consultation with production managers to see whether the product can be dispensed with.

4.37 An important feature of most environmental policies is cooperation with suppliers, which fits in neatly with modern ideas on partnership relations. Suppliers should be encouraged to adopt a policy similar to that of the buying organisation so that good practice eventually permeates the supply chain. In appropriate cases, it may make sense to offer suppliers technical help in order to achieve environmental objectives. Whether or not such help is charged for will depend on the particular circumstances.

4.38 A common step in this process is to send suppliers a questionnaire enquiring about their policies and practices in relation to environmental issues. Responses should be analysed carefully and any perceived shortcomings should be constructively discussed.

4.39 Once suppliers have given the required undertakings it is necessary to monitor their performance in this respect as in any other area. A seller's compliance with the UK environmental standard BS 7750 and/or with the European Union Eco-Management and Audit Standard (EMAS) is *prima facie* evidence that good practice has been built into their systems, but this does not dispense with the need for periodic visits by buying staff to the supplier's premises.

4.40 Finally, a word of warning is in order in relation to health and safety. Human beings are also part of the environment! Buying products which are dangerous in themselves, or which are manufactured in processes which place workers in danger, clearly runs counter to ideas on environmental concern. It is usually simple enough to monitor definitely hazardous substances and products. Less easy is to distinguish products that are made by a hazardous process or that are dangerous to dispose of.

Ethical and environmental issues and the choice of suppliers

4.41 When a firm is selecting a supplier, it should give some consideration to the ethical behaviour and environmental policies of the respective suppliers. Ethical and environmental issues could affect either the choice of supplier, or the terms on which a company arranges an agreement with a supplier. Issues that might be considered when selecting a supplier include the following:

- Scarce resources. Is the supplier using scarce resources responsibly?

- Pollution. Is the supplier responsible for pollution, or what measures does the supplier take to prevent pollution?

- Energy efficiency. Is the supplier energy efficient? What measures has the supplier taken to reduce its consumption of energy?

- Who owns the supplier organisation? Are there any ethical concerns about the ownership of the company?

- Does the supplier pay its employees a proper wage?

- Does the supplier have ethical employment and working practices?

- Do the suppliers themselves use any suppliers about which there are ethical or environmental concerns?

- Does the supplier have any history of operating unethically or illegally?

- Does the supplier discriminate in any way on the grounds of race, gender, religion, age or any other basis other than competence?

Chapter summary

- Target costing is a feature common in 'lean' organisations. Selling prices are set by reference to what the market will stand, and costs are then driven down to a level that leaves a satisfactory profit.

- Cost transparency means that suppliers should be ready to talk frankly to customers about cost structures.

- Agile supply is based on getting speed and flexibility into the supply chain.

- A possible distinction between lean and agile manufacturing is that the former refers to a situation where goods are produced only when 'pulled' by a customer, whereas the latter is based on 'late customisation'. It is not the case that agile supply is the same as lean supply but with some added features bolted on.

- Corporate social responsibility is to some extent enforced by legislation and codes of conduct. However, many organisations voluntarily go beyond what is strictly required of them.

- According to CIPS, CSR is important to organisations for three reasons: enhancing stakeholder value; helping to increase reputation; ensuring increased knowledge of supply and hence minimising supply risk. The CIPS White Paper on CSR identifies nine key areas: environmental responsibility; human rights; equal opportunities; diversity; corporate governance; sustainability; impact on society; ethics and ethical trading; biodiversity.

- Buyers are concerned with ethical issues because in the long term unethical behaviour is against the best interests of their organisations. Managers should ensure that written policies on ethics are observed in practice.

- Buyers have an opportunity to spread awareness of environmental issues along the supply chain by challenging their suppliers to observe best practice.

Self-test questions

1   Explain the technique of target costing. (1.3)

2   According to CIPS, what are the five key principles of lean thinking? (2.1)

3   Give examples of waste, categorised in the seven types identified by Ohno. (Table 4.1)

4   Which type of production is more tolerant of stock holding – lean or agile? (2.21)

5   Give examples of legislative requirements, regulatory requirements and professional codes of practice covering CSR requirements. (3.2)

6   For what three reasons, according to CIPS, is CSR important to all organisations? (3.11)

7   What nine main areas of CSR are identified in the CIPS White Paper? (3.15)

8   What is the Sarbanes Oxley Act concerned with? (3.29)

9   List some of the requirements of the CIPS ethical code. (4.9)

10   What measures can managers adopt to avoid unethical dealings with suppliers? (4.15)

11   For what reasons might a purchasing function wish to establish an environmental policy? (4.27)

CHAPTER 5

Stakeholders and Organisational Culture

Learning objectives

1.7 Evaluate the relationship between internal and external stakeholders in the supply chain and propose ways of maintaining objectivity within the relationships.

- Ways of maintaining objectivity in relationships
- Services versus manufacturing supply chain relationships
- Technical specialists versus purchasing specialists

1.8 Assess the importance of culture and relationship values within supply networks.

- Organisational culture
- Relationship values and behaviours
- Managing buyer and supplier perspectives on values and behaviours

2.1 Formulate objectives for relationships with suppliers.

- The impact of internal and external stakeholders on supplier selection
- The impact of internal suppliers on supplier selection

Chapter headings

1 Internal and external stakeholders

2 Technical specialists and purchasing specialists

3 Culture and relationship values within supply networks

Introduction

The syllabus in this area is something of a hodge podge of different topics only very loosely related, if at all. In this chapter we simply work through them one by one.

1 Internal and external stakeholders

Stakeholders' expectations

1.1 A very useful way of looking at an organisation's environment is by analysing its stakeholders. These are the people and organisations who literally 'have a stake' in what the organisation chooses to do, or not to do. The fact that their expectations are wide-ranging and important is demonstrated in Figure 5.1.

Figure 5.1 *The position of stakeholders in the environment*

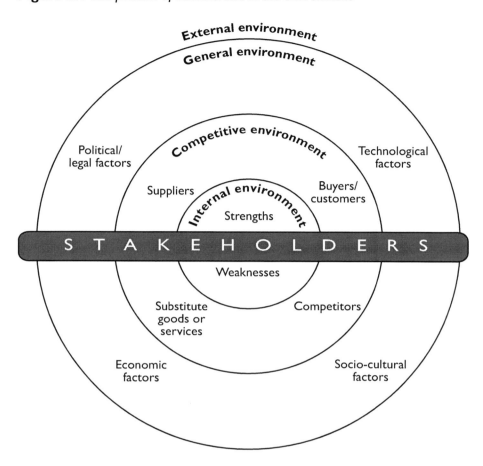

Adapted from Dobson and Starkey (1993) and Boddy (2002)

1.2   What Figure 5.1 shows is that stakeholders comprise both people within the organisation and those outside it, ie from both the internal and the external environment. Typically, a commercial organisation will have the stakeholders, and their related expectations, as shown in Table 5.1.

1.3   Identifying an organisation's stakeholders, and their expectations, is part of the strategic analysis process, often termed stakeholder analysis. It can be as simple or as complicated a process as the organisation chooses. But the result of stakeholder analysis is often a set of conflicting demands or expectations, most often between owners' demands for a good return on their investment, and employees' expectations of job security. As the organisation cannot hope to meet them all, what should it do?

1.4   The answer again depends on the organisation. Some will try to balance the expectations of their stakeholders, so profit maximisation will be sacrificed, to a degree, in favour of job security. Most profit-making organisations, however, will not seek a balance, as the whole reason for their existence is the maximisation of profit. Instead, by conducting stakeholder analysis they will simply have made themselves more aware of those stakeholders who, for the moment, will have their expectations met by the organisation, and those who will be disappointed.

Table 5.1 *Stakeholders and their expectations*

'EXTERNAL' STAKEHOLDERS	Typical expectations from organisation
Government	Best practice in employment Adherence to laws Environmental awareness Receipt of tax revenue Acceptable use of grants
Suppliers	Continued relationship Fair dealing Timely payments Involvement/partnership
Customers	Competitive pricing Quality and availability After-sale service Fair dealing
Lenders	Return on investment – interest Good security for loan Timely payments
Society as a whole	Adherence to laws Environmental awareness
Employees	Good security of job Timely payments Best practice in employment Interesting work Opportunity for development
Owners	Return on investment – dividends, and capital growth Good security of investment

1.5 Stakeholder expectations are quite fluid, as is the degree to which the stakeholders actually have an interest in the organisation. Over time, the balance that the organisation is trying to achieve with its strategy for stakeholders will shift. This means that stakeholder analysis needs to be an ongoing process.

Stakeholder mapping

1.6 This may be used to assess how to manage each stakeholder group.

Figure 5.2 *Satisfying stakeholder groups*

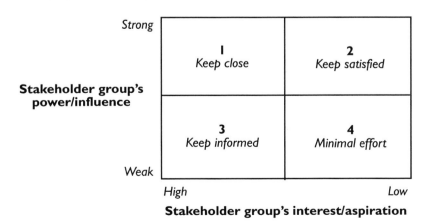

1.7 The terms within the quadrants describe the approach to management. For example, Quadrant I stakeholders have the most power and influence over the organisation and are clearly interested in what the organisation does (major shareholders may be located in this quadrant). Management must have a close working relationship with these stakeholders to ensure that they do not use their strong power and influence against the organisation.

The influence of stakeholders

1.8 There are two main reasons why managers must consider the influence of stakeholders when setting organisational objectives.

- Managers must accept that stakeholders can affect the success of a strategy. For example, customers may not buy products, staff may leave, shareholders may sell their shares etc.

- Managers must ensure that they take into account the interests of stakeholders when making decisions. For example staff may not want to be relocated to another town or may be demotivated if a centralised structure is adopted.

1.9 Focusing more closely on purchasing (as opposed to the organisation as a whole), it is possible to list many groups that have an interest in purchasing decisions (eg decisions on which supplier to choose). In the external environment the most obvious stakeholders are customers and suppliers. Internally, any or all of the following departments might wish to influence purchasing decisions.

- Production
- Quality control
- Research and development
- Warehousing and distribution
- Finance
- Sales and marketing

1.10 In a service environment the list of stakeholders might be even more extensive. For example, the external stakeholders in a local government authority would include all users of community services, ratepayers, local businesses, the Office of Government Commerce, central government, etc.

The impact of stakeholder requirements on purchasing

1.11 In many cases, the purchasing department will be directly affected by the requirements of stakeholders. For example, the requirement of an **external customer** for timely delivery of a quality product is an important driver for a buyer within the organisation. He must help to achieve timely delivery by ensuring that inputs to the production process are available when required. He must help to achieve quality in the finished product by ensuring quality in the input resources.

1.12 Examples could be multiplied. An external customer with uneven demand for its own products will similarly place uneven demands on its suppliers. Customers facing pressures to reduce costs will apply similar pressure to their suppliers. Customers facing pressures to increase the quality of their products will pass on the pressure to their suppliers.

1.13 **External suppliers** are also, naturally, an important influence on buyers. A buyer must make sure that his suppliers are kept fully informed of specifications, schedules, reporting requirements etc. More generally, suppliers must be aware of the kind of relationship that the buyer is seeking and the implications of that for their own performance.

1.14 Suppliers have legitimate requirements that they can expect buyers to satisfy. For example, they are entitled to be paid according to the terms of their contract. It is not necessarily easy for the buyer to ensure this personally, but Finance must be made to understand that prompt payment is a contractual term.

1.15 Suppliers are also entitled to ongoing negotiation with their customers. It is legitimate for them to seek additional business and to seek ways of making the business profitable to themselves. Naturally, this does not mean that they are entitled to impose terms on an unwilling buyer, but buyers should understand that a supplier is not behaving improperly by doing this. Failure by the buyer to accommodate reasonable dialogue with his suppliers can obviously damage relationships.

1.16 Suppliers may of course stretch the boundaries beyond what is acceptable to the buyer. For example, the supplier may demand a certain level of trust, and resent too many checks by the buyer. In such a case, the buyer must obviously insist on carrying out the checks he considers necessary, while being aware that unnecessary checking can damage a relationship. Similarly, the supplier may look for exclusivity in his dealings with the buyer (ie a single sourcing deal), or he may want the buyer to recommend him to other potential customers. In all such cases, the buyer must arrive at an appropriate balance: accommodating the supplier may strengthen relations, but may go further than the buyer is comfortable with.

Internal stakeholders

1.17 So far we have mainly considered external stakeholders. However, a buyer must equally be aware of parties within his own organisation who have a stake in the purchasing process. We will first of all develop the above discussion to encompass internal suppliers, then move on to consider two groups specified in your syllabus: technical specialists and purchasing specialists.

1.18 The concept of **internal suppliers** and internal customers is well developed in the purchasing literature. In a particular organisation, Department A may perform functions or produce goods which are necessary for the activities of Department B. In this case, Department A is an internal supplier of Department B, and B is the internal customer.

1.19 This situation poses difficult questions.

- Is B obliged to buy from A, or might B be allowed to source its requirement from an external supplier?

- If B does buy from A, is it appropriate that B should reward A by some form of payment?

1.20 To make this more definite, suppose that in a particular organisation there is a well developed IT department, offering services to the purchasing function and other internal departments. Is it in any circumstances allowable for purchasing to source their IT requirements from an outside provider, or are they obliged to use the internal resource? And how should other departments be charged, or the IT department rewarded, for the work done? (In the following paragraphs we refer to the IT department by way of example only; the discussion applies equally to any 'internal supplier' department.)

1.21 With regard to the first question, there will normally be rules laid down in company policy. For example, a particular organisation may require all IT services to be provided by the internal IT department: user departments have no choice. At the other end of the spectrum, user departments may have complete freedom to contract with external providers: the internal IT department must just compete effectively to win 'contracts' from user departments.

1.22 Somewhere along this spectrum there are intermediate policies. For example, there may be a company rule that user departments must be serviced by the internal IT department unless the internal resources are overloaded, or unless the user department can find a better price externally.

1.23 This leads us on to the second question: the 'price' of providing the IT services. Some companies (particularly small companies) make no attempt to charge user departments for the use of IT services. They simply regard the costs of the IT department as an overhead cost to be deducted in total from profits. A disadvantage of this method is that there is no particular incentive for the IT department to manage its costs effectively.

1.24 To overcome this difficulty, many companies attempt to exercise control by imposing commercial disciplines over the IT department and the user departments. The IT department is required to charge out its services to user departments on some basis calculated to recover the costs of running the department (and perhaps to make a 'profit' as well). The prices charged by the IT department are referred to as 'transfer prices'.

1.25 This gives user departments an incentive to use the IT department wisely. Without this discipline they might be inclined to waste IT time with frivolous requirements, but this is less likely to happen if they are 'paying' for the IT services. Payment in this case means that the manager of the user department suffers a dent in his departmental budget; by the same token, the IT department enjoys a notional 'revenue' to help cover its operating costs.

1.26 The level of the charges imposed by the IT department may be laid down at Head Office level, or may be negotiated with user departments: it depends on company policy in individual cases.

1.27 These questions are not easy to resolve. By insisting that all IT requirements are carried out internally, the organisation potentially saves itself the cost of using external suppliers. Moreover, there is an argument that the internal department is 'on our side' and motivated to do the work particularly well. On the downside, we may be forced to employ too many IT staff so that we can cope with peaks of demand; these may then be under-utilised at other times. And in addition, the IT department may suffer from complacency, with the possible quality problems that stem from that.

1.28 The issue of transfer pricing is also difficult. For one thing, a transfer pricing system can lead to endless negotiation (perhaps bickering) between departments. User departments will be arguing for a low price; the IT department will want a premium price. Deciding what is fair will be difficult. User departments who perceive the internal service as overpriced will agitate to be allowed to source externally. Moreover, this kind of system can divert attention away from opportunities to make external sales of the IT department's services.

1.29 The whole area of internal supply can bedevil relations with external suppliers. For example, if a user department requests quotations from outside suppliers, but then places the work with an internal department, the external suppliers will naturally question the process. They may lose interest in quoting when next they are asked.

2 Technical specialists and purchasing specialists

Terminology

2.1 Your syllabus makes a distinction between technical specialists and purchasing specialists. The guidance for this unit issued by CIPS makes a distinction between technical specialists and non-technical specialists. We might therefore be inclined to think that 'non-technical specialists' and purchasing specialists are one and the same thing. However, the CIPS guidance defines non-technical specialists as personnel in Finance, Logistics etc; whereas technical specialists are personnel such as engineers, software designers and architects.

2.2 In this section we follow the syllabus wording exactly, because CIPS have stated that the exams will be based on the syllabus, not on the guidance material. We therefore interpret this syllabus caption as referring to the relationship between purchasing staff on the one hand and technical specialists on the other. However, for safety's sake we refer briefly to a couple of points related to non-purchasing, non-specialists as well.

2.3 The distinction between technical and non-technical specialists is that the former group are regarded as expert in areas which enable them to advise on or even specify a requirement. For example, a designer may be in a better position than anyone – possibly even than purchasing staff – to specify a component required for a newly designed object. Contrast this with, say, a finance specialist. Finance have a legitimate stake in purchasing activities, but it is clearly of a different nature.

The potential for conflict

2.4 The paragraph above highlights the possibility of conflict between a technical specialist and a buyer. The specialist may insist that a particular supplier is used because (a) he produces goods or services of the highest quality, and/or (b) he is known to the specialist from previous dealings and is therefore trusted. The buyer, on the other hand, may see an opportunity to invite other potential suppliers, in the hope that they can provide a better deal: even higher quality, or lower cost, or more reliable service or whatever.

2.5   In the public sector the buyer's position is strong. In most cases, competitive tendering is a legal obligation, and it is not open to the specialist to (in effect) award the contract to a favoured source. In the private sector there is no such obligation, and the situation must be resolved by appropriate discussion and negotiation between specialist and buyer.

2.6   Designers and engineers have the primary responsibility for the nature and content of a company's products and the processes of their manufacture. But the discussion above has emphasised the element of choice that runs through many design and engineering processes. There is no single right way to design and manufacture a product, and once the question is of choosing between alternatives, purchasing staff have a vital role to play.

2.7   Purchasing must develop close relations with a number of other functions, including design and engineering. The nature of the relationship is well expressed by Gary J Zenz in *Purchasing and the Management of Materials*.

Engineering must not be so exacting that its demands override price and market considerations, and purchasing must not stress price to the point where it interferes with sound engineering requirements. Engineering has the responsibility for setting specifications and has the final say. Purchasing can ask for and suggest changes but cannot make changes.

2.8   What this means is that amongst the possible materials that might be used there is a spectrum of choice, and purchasing staff are in the best possible position to advise on the cost effects of different choices. Further, where engineering choices are in question – eg the degree of tolerance to be specified – purchasing again has a role to play. A supplier who is required to work to a very strict tolerance will undoubtedly charge more than if loose tolerances apply. The extent of the pricing differential is a matter for purchasing staff to assess, so that a reasoned balance can be arrived at.

2.9   Another area of possible conflict is **standardisation**. Purchasers typically favour the use of a relatively small number of more or less standardised parts. Designers and engineers, for example, tend to see good cause for ordering 'specials': items of a non-standard type, which however may be very similar to standard parts regularly purchased by the organisation. They may do this because of a wish for innovation and technological improvement.

2.10   Once again, the role of buyers is important. They must not be so wedded to their own ideas of convenience purchasing as to overlook cases where standardisation is inappropriate. They must be able to balance quality and cost issues sensitively, and to discuss these factors in language that makes sense to designers.

2.11   Purchasing's involvement is usually formalised in the processes for ensuring standardisation. Only purchasing staff have an overview of the extent of 'special' specifications emanating from different departments. Purchasing staff are aware, and nobody else is, when requisitions are made for nearly identical materials; it is up to buyers to act when this happens and to argue the merits of standardising.

2.12 In some organisations this formalisation is evidenced in an approved list of standard parts. All departments are encouraged to specify as far as possible on the basis of the approved list, and departures from this principle will be scrutinised and possibly challenged.

2.13 Purchasing have the leading responsibility for preparation and maintenance of the list. They must stay in touch with information from a variety of sources: for example, they must stay abreast of new product development by suppliers, and they must be aware of any problems relating to the standard parts reported by production or marketing staff.

Techniques for collaboration

2.14 Handling this kind of potential conflict calls for skilled management by buyers. Here are some techniques that may help.

- In some organisations, a specialist may be seconded to the purchasing department to assist in arriving at sourcing decisions that meet the objectives of all parties.

- In some organisations, the use of cross-functional teams in project work helps to ensure that all legitimate claims are heard.

- Other organisations favour a **lead buyer approach**. This involves delegating defined purchasing responsibilities onto a designated individual within a user department. For example, a member of the manufacturing department is given responsibility for certain purchasing activities.

- Another possibility is the **business partnering approach**. This is where a member of the purchasing team works within a different functional area, typically one in which there is a large external spend. The business partner – ie the purchasing specialist – liaises closely with members of the other function, acting in effect as a representative of the purchasing department. It is his task to identify situations where the involvement of the purchasing function can add value.

Non-technical specialists

2.15 Just a brief note, as promised, on the relations between buyers and non-technical specialists. These may include business managers with responsibility for particular areas of the organisation, or for particular projects. The category may also include members of functions such as finance or logistics. Finally, the impact of end users in various departments may be considered.

2.16 In the case of business managers, an important problem is the high degree of delegated authority they may enjoy. This can lead to situations in which purchasing staff find that they have been bypassed: they are required to authorise and process purchases that have already been made by the manager. To avoid this situation, buyers must strike up a close relationship with relevant managers from an early stage, so that they are aware of important buying decisions before these have actually been made.

2.17 The work of the logistics function is closely aligned with that of purchasing. Each impacts frequently and directly on the other. This can lead to problems unless each keeps the other thoroughly informed, particularly when changes of plan are in question (eg revised delivery schedules from suppliers).

2.18 We have already remarked, earlier in this chapter, on the need for good communications between buyers and finance staff. This is particularly important to ensure that the buyer can carry out his contractual obligations to the supplier, including payment in full and on time.

2.19   With regard to end users, good communication with buyers is again essential. For one thing, end users are often in an excellent position to help in defining the specification for the good or service required. After all, they are the people who will be using it. For another, it can provoke needless and unwelcome resistance from users if they have not 'bought in' to the purchase decision because they were not consulted about it.

3   Culture and relationship values within supply networks

Organisational culture

3.1   Organisation culture has been defined as 'a pattern of beliefs and expectations shared by the organisation's members, and which produce norms which powerfully shape the behaviour of individuals and groups in the organisation' (*Schwartz and Davies*). It has been summed up as 'the way we do things around here'.

3.2   Organisation culture may be expressed through:

- Behaviour: informal norms (such as familiarity or formality with colleagues); rules and standards of behaviour formulated as part of the disciplinary or ethical codes of the organisation; standard procedures and channels of communication (a powerful influence in conformist bureaucratic organisations); 'short-cuts' developed in practice and so on.

- Artefacts: dress codes, office décor, symbols (eg logos), corporate marketing (mythology) and indeed all work outputs (since these reflect the organisation's values). Things such as office size, access to facilities and company cars may take on a symbolic value, reflecting status or power, say. Organisational politics (processes by which individuals and groups gain and use power in the organisation) often dictate which artefacts become valued and sought-after, and what they 'mean'.

- Rituals: business formalities, ceremonies (eg performance awards, retirement functions)

- Beliefs and values: mottos (such as 'The customer is king'; 'Get it right first time'); attitudes to matters such as quality, risk, technology, employee relations; the importance of values such as seniority, empowerment, teamworking etc.

3.3   An organisation's culture is often shaped by its history. Since cultures develop over time and are not easy to change, they often reflect the values of the era in which the organisation was founded (hence the persistence of 'old-fashioned' bureaucratic cultures) and/or of the organisation's founder. Myths and stories about the 'heroic' early days (or 'Golden Ages') of the organisation give further power to original values.

3.4   An organisation's culture is partly shaped by its environment, as it will adopt elements of the other cultural spheres (nation, region and industry sector) in which it operates. It will also embrace some of the cultural values of influential individuals and groups within the organisation: the cultures of particular professional/occupational groups, social classes and so on. Charles Handy noted that: 'Organisations are as different and varied as nations and societies of the world. They have differing cultures ... affected by events of the past and the climate of the present, by the technology of the type of work, by their aims and the type of people who work in them.'

3.5   Managers and leaders can have a strong influence on organisational culture, because they are in a position to model values and behaviours – and they have the power to influence the behaviours (and sometimes also the underlying attitudes) of subordinates. This is the basis of deliberate culture-change initiatives. At the same time, organisations with a strong culture tend to recruit managers who conform to that culture, so that the 'management culture' reflects – rather than shapes – the culture of the organisation.

3.6   The importance of organisation culture for management was highlighted by Tom Peters and Robert Waterman, in their influential study of successful corporations: *In Search of Excellence* (1982). One of the key features of excellent companies (which consistently produce commercially viable new products and respond effectively to change) was their use of organisation culture to guide business processes and to motivate employees.

3.7   Both Peters and Waterman and Deal and Kennedy argued that cultural strength is a powerful tool for shaping the behaviour and success of an organisation. Not all organisation cultures are 'strong' – but those that *are* contribute to improved business performance.

3.8   This school of thought defined 'strong' cultures as those in which key values were widely shared and intensely held, and in which employees allowed themselves to be guided by them. In other words, as summarised by Huczynski and Buchanan: 'Strength refers to the degree to which employees share a commitment to a range of goals and values espoused by management, and have a high level of motivation to achieve them.'

3.9   So how does 'strong' culture improve business performance? Peters and Waterman argued as follows.

* A handful of widely shared, strongly held guiding values can replace rules, guidelines and supervision: focusing employees' attention on strategic aims such as quality, innovation and customer service, and empowering them to take initiative and responsibility in pursuit of those aims. This reduces rigidity, increases flexibility, enables change (on the basis that if values change, behaviour will follow) and develops people.

* Strong culture increases employee job satisfaction, loyalty and commitment. People need both to feel part of something meaningful and to 'shine' as stars in their own right: strong culture can satisfy both needs, by emphasising the 'family' nature of the enterprise, by building myths to reinforce the 'heroic' nature of the enterprise and by using value-laden symbols as rewards and incentives.

Relationship values and behaviours

3.10   The culture of an organisation can have important effects on the relationships between buyers and suppliers. In the guidance for this module issued by CIPS four types of cultures are identified: bureaucratic, paternalistic, aggressive and progressive. It is interesting to look at the types of relationship behaviour that may typically arise in such cultures.

3.11 A **bureaucratic culture** is characterised by defined roles, hierarchical internal relationships and a strict adherence to laid down policies and procedures. This kind of culture is often referred to unfavourably, mainly because it is perceived as resistant to necessary change.

3.12 Because of this, relations with suppliers may be stable – perhaps too stable. There may be reluctance to engage with new sources of supply. Dealings with existing suppliers may follow rules laid down long ago and perhaps not sufficiently adapted to more recent developments.

3.13 A **paternalistic culture** refers to an organisation dominated by a single individual or small group of individuals. The typical scenario is that of a small or medium-sized family firm, where the founder or his descendants retain power mainly in their own hands. They often regard their employees as members of an extended family and take all the major decisions on their behalf.

3.14 This kind of culture can be frustrating for purchasing staff. Buyers working in such an organisation may find that they have little real power to conduct relations with suppliers, because final decisions on all important matters reside with the dominant father figure. Buyers working for customers of such an organisation may find it difficult to make contact with the real decision makers.

3.15 An **aggressive culture** is one where managers are inclined to challenge and dispute anything laid before them, either by their colleagues internally, or by external contacts such as suppliers. This style is not conducive to the closer relationships supported by modern supply chain thinking, and instead will lead to relationships at the adversarial end of the spectrum.

3.16 Buyers working in such a culture may well absorb the prevailing mentality (and indeed may have been recruited because they already have it). This may be advantageous in dealing with transactional supply relationships. However, buyers may dislike the general disposition to challenge and argue, and in that case may find their work unsatisfying. (There is the possibility, though, that an aggressive attitude towards external business contacts may coexist with a more friendly approach to internal colleagues.)

3.17 Buyers who deal as customers with this kind of organisation can expect very tough negotiating, even if the supplier is keen to win the business. This may be characteristic of highly competitive markets in which tight profit margins are the norm.

3.18 A **progressive culture** is one in which managers and their staff embrace change and hope to profit by new ideas. The concept of continuous improvement will be welcomed, leading to constant change, possibly incremental, possibly more dramatic. Staff will aim to take advantage of movements in market and economic conditions.

3.19 Buyers working for such firms enjoy flexibility in the relationship approaches they adopt with suppliers. This permits relationships to develop organically as conditions change. There is no requirement to stay in line with previous procedures merely for historical reasons, and indeed it may be considered unfavourably if frequent change is not observed.

Chapter summary

- Stakeholders are those groups, both internal and external, who have a stake in an organisation. Stakeholder analysis is a part of the general task of strategic analysis.

- Stakeholder mapping is a technique for categorising stakeholders in order to determine how each category should be managed.

- For a buyer, the most important external stakeholders are his suppliers, but he must also reckon with internal stakeholders, such as the user departments which are his 'customers'.

- The concept of internal customers and suppliers leads to consideration of transfer pricing between organisational units.

- There is potential conflict between technical specialists and professional buyers. Purchasing must develop close relations with technical specialists in order to hold constructive dialogue with them.

- Organisational culture is 'a pattern of beliefs and expectations shared by the organisation's members, and which produce norms which powerfully shape the behaviour of individuals and groups in the organisation'. It can also be defined as 'the way we do things around here'.

- Managers who use organisational culture effectively to guide business processes and to motivate employees will enjoy important benefits in terms of increased organisational effectiveness.

- CIPS identify four types of culture: bureaucratic culture, paternalistic culture, aggressive culture, progressive culture.

Self-test questions

1   List typical categories of external shareholders. (Table 5.1)

2   Draw a grid showing a model of stakeholder mapping. (Figure 5.2)

3   What problems are caused by a system of transfer pricing? (1.28)

4   Why may there be conflict between technical specialists and buyers? (2.4)

5   What is meant by standardisation, and what difficulties may be caused by a policy of standardisation? (2.9)

6   What is meant by a lead buyer approach? (2.14)

7   How does 'strong' culture improve business performance? (3.9)

8   Describe a paternalistic culture. (3.13)

9   Describe a progressive culture. (3.18)

CHAPTER 6

Supplier Appraisal

Learning objectives

2.1   Formulate objectives for relationships with suppliers.

- The external supplier's view of the selection process
- Manufacturing and service supply chains
- Upstream and downstream supply chain activities

2.2   Evaluate and apply techniques for supplier appraisal and selection.

- Supplier appraisal techniques
- Vendor rating
- Supplier auditing

2.3   Evaluate the effectiveness of the assessment process.

- Supplier appraisal deliverables
- Measuring the supplier appraisal process
- Effect of supplier appraisal upon relationship development
- Supplier appraisal in the context of the relationship cycle

4.7   Explain a range of techniques for managing multi-tiered supply relationships.

- Performance measures and their impact on the different parties within the supply chain, that is manufacturers, retailers, service providers
- The importance of measuring relationship development across the supply chain
- Difficulties involved in measuring performance across the supply chain
- The buyer and supplier perspectives on performance measurement

Chapter headings

1   Supplier appraisal techniques

2   Structuring the supply chain

3   The external supplier's perspective

4   Vendor rating

5   Other aspects of supplier appraisal

Introduction

In this chapter we look at methods of appraising suppliers, including the preliminary identification of potential suppliers. This leads on in the next chapter to actual selection of suppliers, ie award of contract.

1 *Supplier appraisal techniques*

A note on terminology

1.1 For many authors, there is no distinction between the terms 'vendor' and 'supplier'. The latter term seems to be preferred, but the former appears to be used on occasion for no other reason than artistic variation.

1.2 In this section we have followed the syllabus wording in talking about supplier appraisal. This accords with CIPS guidance in which a distinction is made between **supplier appraisal** (being the assessment of potential suppliers, prior to contract award) and **vendor rating** (which is the assessment of a supplier's performance in fulfilling a contract after its award). In other words, a supplier is someone we may be dealing with in future, whereas a vendor is someone we are already dealing with.

1.3 To complete the terminology, **supplier development** refers to activities carried out both before and after contract award, in which we aim to assist a supplier in developing and/or providing a product or service that we need. In general, this will mostly be carried out after the supplier has become a vendor, and so it might be more logical to refer to vendor development. However, to avoid confusion, we follow the CIPS guidance on this topic.

Factors to be appraised in supplier appraisal

1.4 To achieve planning objectives, it is essential for purchasing to appraise the supply markets. This is a form of purchasing research, which can be undertaken by specialist staff trained to investigate such matters. This is the usual organisational procedure in large purchasing departments. In smaller departments there may be no dedicated purchasing research staff, and instead individual buyers may be expected to conduct their own research.

1.5 The research should cover the following major areas in respect of each material or class of materials.

- **Demand analysis**. Standard procedures should be operated to ensure that particular attention is paid to high-value materials. The objective is to estimate likely usage in the period ahead.

- **Vendor analysis**. Buyers must evaluate the performance of current suppliers, as well as giving consideration to potential suppliers not currently being used. Once the decision on suppliers has been taken, attention will shift to the type of buying agreement to be implemented.

- **Market analysis**. Buyers must appraise general supply conditions in the market. What is the likely availability of each material, and are any shortages possible or probable? What is the prevailing price of each material, and what fluctuations (if any) are likely?

1.6 The research into supply markets conducted by purchasing departments is of an ongoing nature (though there is sometimes cause for a defined project of research to supplement this). Its objectives are:

- to provide information on which the organisation can plan to adapt to changes in the supply environment, whether to take advantage of new opportunities or to take defensive action in the light of perceived threats

- to secure competitive advantage by means of early information on innovations in supply markets.

1.7 To begin with, purchasing staff must define the scope of the research work. If they identify trends with a potential to impact on the organisation a sensible next step might be to conduct a limited research project, perhaps by means of consultations with suppliers. The aim of course is to obtain early warning of anything that could have a serious impact, for good or bad, on the organisation's supply chain activities.

1.8 Actual consultations with suppliers are not the only sources of information. For example, a buyer interested in the possibility of price changes in a certain material may be guided by any or all of:

- Historical trends
- Published price indices for particular industries
- Economic models
- Information from specialist forecasting agencies

The structure of supply markets

1.9 A useful starting point in the analysis of supply markets is to examine the main structural features that can be discerned. These are features that a buyer is unable to influence – the market just happens to be that way – but which may be an important influence on the buyer. Examples of these include:

- the number of buyers in the market
- the number of suppliers in the market
- methods of pricing in the market
- the degree of product differentiation in the market (are there many closely similar products or just a single product on which all buyers are dependent?)
- technological developments in the market.

1.10 In terms of demand, a market may range from a state of pure competition (where many buyers are active, and no one buyer is big enough to influence the price by his actions) to a state of monopsony. Strictly this would mean only a single buyer in the market, who would of course wield enormous influence over suppliers. In practice, the strict form of monopsony is rarely (perhaps never) seen, but close approximations exist. An example might be the railway industry in the UK: the number of buyers of rolling stock is very limited.

1.11 In terms of supply, a similar range of possibilities exists. At one extreme there is perfect competition: many suppliers exist, and no one supplier is big enough to dictate prices. The other extreme is monopoly. Public utilities such as the privatised water companies in the UK enjoy a position of virtual monopoly, though this is being challenged (eg by the introduction of competition in the gas supply industry).

1.12 The buyer must be aware of these characteristics in the supply markets, because they influence the strength of his negotiating position. For example, a buyer facing a monopoly supplier, in a market with little product differentiation and few substitute products, is in a weak negotiating position. If there are many suppliers, and many products of comparable quality, the situation is very different: the buyer's position is strong.

The need for supplier appraisal

1.13 The need for supplier appraisal may arise in several circumstances. For example, a supplier may apply to be placed on a list of approved suppliers. Alternatively, a buyer may need to source a part or component that has not been purchased before, or is not available from existing suppliers. Or it may be a case of a major one-off project that does not fall within the scope of existing suppliers.

1.14 In any of these cases, the buyer's aim is to ensure that the potential supplier can perform the contract to the required standard. This means that the process of assessment is an element of quality assurance. It will be particularly relevant in cases where no third-party validation of supplier quality – such as ISO 9000 accreditation – is available.

1.15 This is a bewilderingly complex subject, and the most difficult task is to place some kind of practical limit on the number and variety of factors that could form part of the assessment process. Reference to standard purchasing textbooks produces many different lists of the relevant factors, some of which are quoted in Table 6.1.

Table 6.1 *Factors involved in supplier appraisal*

Purchasing and Supply Chain Management by Lysons and Farrington	*Purchasing Principles and Management*, by Baily, Farmer, Jessop and Jones	*Purchasing and Supply Management*, by Dobler and Burt
Personal attitudes	Task variables, such as quality, service and price	Results of preliminary survey
Adequacy and care of production equipment	Financial stability	Financial stability
Means of controlling quality	Good management	Good management
Housekeeping	Results of site visits	Results of site visits
Competence of technical staff	Ability to support electronic data interchange	Quality of service
Competence of management	Just in time capabilities	Just in time capabilities

1.16 In this section we will adopt the following framework for discussion.

- Planning the appraisal
- Identifying potential suppliers
- Assessing financial stability
- Planning and conducting site visits
- Assessing task variables: quality, service, price, extent of automation, and just in time capabilities

Planning the appraisal

1.17 At the planning stage, purchasers will have to consider the following issues.

- The objectives of the appraisal (depending on the purchase situation, the importance of the purchase, the time/budget set aside for the process etc)
- The number of suppliers to be appraised
- The scale, rigour and formality of the process to be used (depending on the information already available, the importance of the purchase etc)
- The time set aside for the process (eg based on the location and feasibility of supplier site visits, the urgency of the purchase situation)
- The resources needed for the process (including personnel eg in a multi-disciplinary appraisal team, information and documentation)
- The likely perspective and response of the supplier(s) to the appraisal process
- Cost-benefit analysis: is the process worth carrying out?

Identifying potential suppliers

1.18 A wide variety of information sources is available to assist the buyer in identifying potential suppliers. In fact, the main danger is of spending too much time researching the sources on occasions when it is not appropriate. In particular, the extent of research obviously depends at least partly on the monetary value of the business likely to be done.

1.19 **Past experience** is a good starting point. Most of the tasks in a purchasing department are to a greater or lesser extent repetitive. A well organised purchasing function will ensure that a good supplier database is maintained, usually nowadays on computer. This will enable buyers to locate suitable suppliers quickly from those known to the organisation.

1.20 **Salesmen from suppliers** are another common source of information. Many buying organisations tap this source systematically by displaying both their finished products and major components in public, in effect inviting visiting salesmen to deploy their knowledge to the advantage of both organisations.

1.21 **Contacts with other buyers**, both inside and outside the organisation, can help in keeping up to date with new developments.

1.22 **Published catalogues** are received by all purchasing departments as part of suppliers' marketing efforts. They contain a mass of information, particularly for standard production parts, but this may be difficult to access unless there is a comprehensive system of indexing and filing. Some large purchasing functions employ staff just for this task of 'librarianship'.

1.23 **Trade directories** are also stocked by most purchasing departments, and contain lists of suppliers organised in terms of the products they supply. In some cases such directories are available in electronic form which simplifies access to the information and enables more frequent updating by the publishers.

1.24 **Trade journals** provide information in the form of editorial, news items and advertising.

1.25 **Trade shows and exhibitions** enable suppliers to display their wares and distribute product information and news of developments.

1.26 **Direct mail** from suppliers is an increasingly important source of information, but again is likely to lose most of its value unless it is carefully indexed and filed.

1.27 **Formal requests for information**, often through the medium of questionnaires, can be used to elicit information from suppliers who might be of interest to the buying organisation.

Assessing financial stability

1.28 The assessment of a supplier's financial position is often a very straightforward exercise, and should therefore be undertaken at an early stage. If there are doubts about financial stability, the supplier can then be eliminated from consideration without the need for more elaborate appraisal.

1.29 The importance of financial stability should be fairly clear. Dobler and Burt cite three typical nightmare scenarios that can arise if dealing with a financially weak supplier.

- You need to insist on maintaining quality, but the supplier is forced to cut costs.

- You have a financial claim against the supplier, but he does not have sufficient working capital to meet it.

- You need to insist on speedy delivery to meet a promised delivery date, but the supplier cannot afford to pay overtime.

1.30 The most accessible source of information on a supplier is their published financial accounts. This is not a textbook on financial accounting, but you should know enough to realise the importance of factors such as financial gearing (ie the extent to which the supplier relies on loan capital), working capital levels (ie the extent to which the supplier has assets in the form of cash and debtor balances, rather than tied up in long-term and inaccessible assets), and of course profitability.

1.31 Buyers should not resent a high level of profitability in their suppliers ('Your prices must be too high...'). On the contrary, unless there is evidence of definite exploitation of buyers, this should be regarded as an encouraging sign of reliable quality and sound management.

1.32 Of course, the supplier's financial accounts present only **historical** data, but supplemented by financial forecasting techniques (where appropriate) and comparison with the accounts of similar companies they are a most useful source of information to the buyer.

1.33 One other source of financial information is worth mentioning. In appropriate cases it will make sense to request information from credit agencies to enhance your knowledge of a supplier's financial standing.

Planning and conducting site visits

1.34 This is an important stage in the evaluation process (sometimes referred to as a **supplier audit** or **capability survey**), but it is important not to underestimate the amount of resources that it consumes. It will not be necessary in cases of small purchases where recurring business is not expected. And even in the case of potentially large contracts, it should be left until a late stage in order to eliminate as many suppliers as possible by less laborious means.

1.35 Despite this note of warning, it remains true that in appropriate cases site visits are a most important source of information on such matters as:

* production equipment and operations

* operation of key materials management activities

* existence of adequate production capacity

* expertise and motivation of personnel

* technological know-how of supervisory personnel

* management capabilities.

1.36 To get the best from the site visit, advance planning is vital. In many cases, the exercise is based on completion of a comprehensive questionnaire, part of which relates to advance planning while the remainder is completed during or after the visit. Usually, the supplier will be asked for information on the organisation's history and current standing, its key management personnel, its products and markets, its attitude to quality issues etc.

1.37 During the visit it is important to speak to appropriate personnel, at the buyer's discretion, while the plant tour is in progress. Their contribution can often throw valuable additional light on statements made by management. In particular, it is worth bearing in mind that procedures managers genuinely believe to be in force are not always performed as they should be, or even performed at all. In addition, the general level of skill, knowledge and enthusiasm of operating personnel can be an important indicator for the buyer.

Assessing task variables

1.38 An important differential between one supplier and another is the quality of management. This is particularly true when the proposed purchase is of a custom-made, large-value item. In these cases the buyer needs reassurance that the managerial resource is adapted to cope with planning, problem-solving and implementation. This goes much further than an assessment of production capability, though of course that too is an essential ingredient.

1.39 Allied to this is the quality of service that the buyer can expect. Service is a broad term, and encompasses such variables as on-time delivery, prompt response to queries or problems, prompt communication, suitable credit facilities and after-sales service.

1.40 Buyers will also be interested in the extent to which a supplier adopts the best modern practices. Are they able to cope with electronic data interchange? Do they have adequate just in time capability? Do they adopt a total quality management approach? Do they use statistical process control?

Carter's criteria for supplier selection

1.41   A supplier assessment framework developed by Ray Carter provides a convenient mnemonic for the key issues that buyers should be concerned with. Carter started from the notion that the traditional 'five rights' of purchasing (right price, right quality, right quantity, right place, right time) may not provide a sufficiently broad framework for assessing suppliers. It is not that these have been superseded. Rather, buyers should adopt wider-ranging criteria in the selection of suppliers.

1.42   Carter's 7Cs provided one possible list of such criteria. Other authorities have since added to his list, so below we highlight 10Cs.

- Competency of all staff all of the time: this includes managers, sales staff, technical and production staff etc
- Capacity of supplier (must have sufficient, flexible production capacity; must have sufficient financial capacity)
- Commitment to quality, evidenced by quality systems and perhaps by external accreditation such as ISO 9000
- Control of processes (again, ISO 9000 may be relevant)
- Cash (must be financially sound; we look at this in more detail later in the chapter)
- Cost (total acquisition cost, including extras, must be competitive)
- Consistency of output, delivery and service
- Culture (must be compatible with buyer organisation)
- Clean (ie environmentally sound)
- Compliance (or corporate social responsibility)

1.43   These criteria are particularly relevant in an age of 'mass customisation'. This refers to an environment where organisations seek fast, efficient, low-cost production of products tailored to the needs of individual customers. Such an ideal will hardly be attainable without the closest relationships between the organisation on one hand and highly flexible suppliers on the other.

2   *Structuring the supply chain*

Tiering of suppliers

2.1   An important strategic issue facing supply organisations is the structure of their supply chains.   One such issue is easily illustrated. Suppose that a manufacturer wishes to maximise his own part in the value adding process by taking in only a minimum contribution from outside suppliers. For example, the manufacturer buys in parts from a number of suppliers, and assembles them through a number of stages before the finished product is complete. The structure of the supply chain in such a case is as illustrated in Figure 6.1.

Figure 6.1 *All manufacturing performed by top-level purchaser*

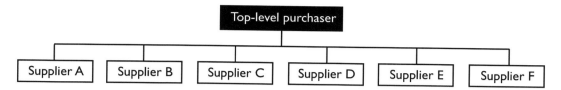

2.2   By contrast, suppose that the manufacturer sees strategic advantage in outsourcing all activities other than the final stages of production. In that case his direct relationship may be (in simplified terms) with a single supplier or (more realistically) with a single tier of suppliers.

2.3   Each supplier in this first tier would have an extensive role to fulfil in the manufacture of the final product. He would discharge this responsibility by making use of 'second tier' suppliers. The structure of the supply chain now looks like Figure 6.2.

Figure 6.2 *Top-level purchaser outsources most manufacturing*

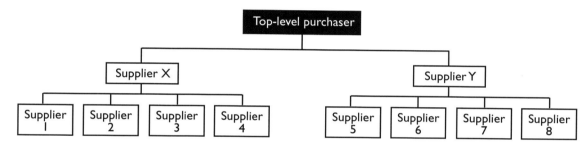

2.4   An organisation might adopt a deliberate policy of tiering its suppliers, so as to reduce the number of first-tier suppliers (suppliers with which it deals directly), and so 'reduce its vendor base'.

2.5   An organisation deals directly only with first-tier suppliers. Second-tier suppliers are suppliers to first-tier suppliers, and deal with the first-tier supplier, not the 'original equipment manufacturer' (OEM).

2.6   For example, an original equipment manufacturer might have 180 different suppliers with which it deals directly. In order to rationalise its commercial relationships, the OEM might pursue a policy of reducing the number of its first-tier suppliers to, say, 20 within a given time frame. To the extent that the OEM still needs products or services from some of the 180 suppliers who are no longer in the first tier, it will be the task of one of the first-tier suppliers to organise the other suppliers, who will become second-tier suppliers.

2.7   In a manufacturing operation, such as automobile manufacture, the OEM is the producer of the end product. First-tier suppliers would tend to be specialist assemblers, each making a particular sub-assembly. Second-tier suppliers would be component manufacturers, who would supply their products to a first-tier supplier.

2.8   The relationship between an OEM and its first-tier suppliers will be critically important, because each first-tier supplier will be organising the second-tier suppliers for the benefit of the OEM. The OEM will have a limited number of first-tier supplier relationships, and can focus on developing these as a long-term partnership. The first-tier suppliers will be expected to work with the OEM in making improvements and adding value throughout the supply chain, and in developing innovations in products and practices. Improvements in the supply chain will depend heavily on the contributions of the first-tier suppliers.

2.9   The reasons for tiering of suppliers might be any of the following.

- The OEM wants to develop long-term relationships with key suppliers, but only has the time and resources to develop a limited number of such relationships.

- Standardisation of parts and variety reduction has reduced the number of parts required, so that the OEM needs fewer suppliers than in the past.

- There has been consolidation of suppliers within the supply market.

Benefits of tiering

2.10   The benefits of tiering may be any or all of the following.

- The OEM has fewer commercial relationships to manage, and can direct its attention to improving these key relationships.

- The OEM can have strategic focus, without having to worry so much about the transactional and operational details of procurement.

- The OEM can share an objective to improve the supply chain with its first-tier suppliers: a shared effort is likely to bring more and better improvements.

- When responsibility is devolved to first-tier suppliers, operational decisions might be taken with a greater understanding of the operational detail, combined with a knowledge of the objectives and requirements of the OEM.

- First-tier suppliers might be able to co-ordinate supply activities more efficiently.

Characteristics of a first-tier supplier

2.11   The characteristics of a typical first-tier supplier are as follows.

- It is a direct supplier to the OEM.

- It is usually a supplier of a high-cost or complex sub-assembly.

- It is heavily dependent on the OEM, which in turn is heavily dependent on the first-tier supplier. It might even purchase assets dedicated to use on jobs for the OEM.

- There is a close and long-term buyer-supplier relationship with the OEM, and the partnership should ideally operate as a partnership of equals. The OEM should not be a dominant partner.

- It will often be involved in discussing new product ideas with the OEM.

- It is responsible for dealing with a number of second-tier suppliers. This number could be quite large. In effect, the first-tier supplier is put in charge of a section of the OEM's vendor base.

- It understands and shares the 'mission' of the OEM.

- It disseminates the standards and working practices of the OEM to the second-tier suppliers with which it deals.

- It must be a competitive producer to justify selection by the OEM.

- The supplier must also have the management capabilities to manage the second-tier suppliers efficiently.

- The relationship with the OEM is a long-term partnership. For example, the supplier will negotiate ways of removing costs from the supply chain (partnership relationship) rather than negotiate the allocation of costs between the buyer and the supplier.

The effects of tiering: upstream management

2.12　What are the effects of these different structures on management of the supply chain, from the perspective of buyers in the purchasing company at the top of the chain?

2.13　An immediate effect is that such buyers find themselves with far fewer transactions to handle and far fewer suppliers to manage. This greatly simplifies many operational tasks of purchasing.

2.14　At the same time, the purchaser must recognise the extent to which responsibility for his firm's product has been handed over to outsiders. This makes it necessary to ensure that the outsiders are thoroughly up to scratch in all relevant areas. In other words, it suggests that the relationships with suppliers, though fewer in number, will be closer and deeper than under the alternative model.

2.15　In particular, it is likely that the final purchaser will want to drill down through tiers in the supply chain to ensure that appropriate quality is present all the way down. This means that influences on lower-tier suppliers will come not only from the firms immediately above them in the chain, but potentially also from the very top of the chain.

2.16　For first-tier suppliers the implications are also significant. In effect, these suppliers have to take on the main responsibility for investment in product and process development. This implies a need for such suppliers to feel secure of continuing business from the top-level purchaser. Once again, this points to a partnership model of buyer/supplier relationships.

2.17　The competitive environment raises additional issues, particularly in relation to this last point about investment by first-tier suppliers. The top-level purchaser must consider carefully his attitude to these suppliers servicing his competitors as well as his own operations. In some cases, he may feel that this is unacceptable and will make it a condition of awarding the business that first-tier suppliers do not deal with competitors.

2.18　However, this will not always be an option. An important consideration is the level of investment required of the first-tier supplier. If this is very large, the supplier will have to cast his net widely to find other customers and so recoup his outlay. Inevitably, this will mean dealing with firms in the same or similar industries, and this is bound to mean that some customers are competitors of each other.

Controlling the tiered supply base

2.19   The organisation at the head of the tiering arrangement – say, the motor vehicle assembler in the motor industry, such as Ford or Renault – has the power to influence much of what happens lower down among the tiers of suppliers. This is true even in the case of suppliers well down the chain, who have little or no contact with the assembler. The influence spreads down from the top through the tiers.

2.20   As an example of this, a tier-one supplier may be pressured to adopt certain other suppliers at tier two. This may conflict with the tier-one supplier's own preferences. If he is forced to choose a supplier other than his regular partner, the tier-one supplier will feel that his own supply relationships are being damaged. Similarly, there are cases where the top-level purchaser may insist on a particular supplier (of raw materials, say) to be used by all organisations in the supply chain.

2.21   The top-level purchaser will also have a strong influence on costs and prices along the supply chain. In extreme cases, they may be strong enough to insist on price levels that suit themselves, with the threat that suppliers who refuse to play ball will be replaced by others.

2.22   This influence on pricing is strengthened in cases where the top-level purchaser insists on open book costing. By gaining access to suppliers' costing records the OEM can point to cost reductions that are achievable. Suppliers may then be pressured to pass on these benefits to the OEM, rather than benefiting from them directly.

2.23   Finally, the top-level purchaser can influence the systems and processes further down the supply chain. As an example, the OEM may insist on the use of electronic data interchange and barcoding. Suppliers who are not compliant will lose the work. This puts serious pressures on suppliers who are part of more than one supply chain, ultimately supplying more than one OEM: they may have to have more than one suite of systems to meet the respective demands of their top-level purchasers.

3   *The external supplier's perspective*

Understanding supplier reaction

3.1   It is important for the buyer to consider the appraisal process from the supplier's perspective. This will help the buyer to maximise the benefit of the process.

3.2   Sometimes an appraisal arises because a supplier has asked to be added to an approved supplier list. In this case it is safe to assume that the supplier is highly motivated. But if the approach comes from the buyer the response from potential suppliers will not necessarily be favourable. This can be for various reasons: see Table 6.2.

After the appraisal

3.3   The buyer should naturally provide feedback to each supplier. This will obviously happen as a matter of course with the successful supplier, but even unsuccessful suppliers deserve to know how the buyer evaluated them. This will help to preserve good relations, an important point if there is a chance of doing business together in the future.

Table 6.2 *Why suppliers may not welcome an appraisal*

Reason for supplier's reluctance	Steps a buyer can take
A particular supplier may not find the buyer's business attractive.	Check out potential suppliers first, using tools such as the supply positioning model.
They may have bad experiences of previous appraisals, possibly with other buyers.	Conduct the appraisal process fairly and transparently so that suppliers can see that they are not just wasting their time.
They may be unsure of the supplier selection process, perhaps suspecting that some other supplier has an 'inside track' or that the buyer is not serious.	Provide full information about how the selection process will work, and keep suppliers informed about progress through the various stages.
The timing of the proposed appraisal may be inconvenient.	Ensure that suppliers have adequate time to prepare for the appraisal, and avoid suggesting dates that will obviously coincide with suppliers' busy periods. Be sympathetic if a supplier suggests a different timetable.
They may believe that the process will be expensive and time-consuming, and of course it may not lead to profitable business in the end.	Be sympathetic to suppliers' likely perception of the cost of the exercise. Ensure that the exercise is streamlined as far as possible, consistent with obtaining the information required.
They may be wary of sharing confidential information.	Be prepared to sign a confidentiality agreement.

3.4 With the benefit of feedback from the buyer, added to his own immediate assessment after completion of the appraisal, a supplier can form a clear impression of the appraisal process. If the buyer has handled it well, the supplier will feel that his effort has been worthwhile even if ultimately unsuccessful. On the other hand, the supplier's reaction may be unfavourable if he feels that the process was unfair.

3.5 Table 6.3 shows the kind of responses, favourable and unfavourable, that a supplier may experience at this stage.

3.6 As a buyer, you should be acting in a way calculated to elicit favourable responses even from disappointed suppliers. The likelihood is that you may identify them as a potential supplier at another time in the future.

4 *Vendor rating*

Quantitative and qualitative assessment of suppliers

4.1 Our discussion so far in this chapter has focused on qualitative aspects of supplier relations. These are vitally important from both strategic and operational viewpoints. However, it is also important for buyers to assess supplier performance in a systematic and quantitative way. This is usually referred to as vendor rating. The objective from the buyer's point of view is to obtain objective information on which to base future sourcing decisions. The buyer is also able to inform the supplier of his rating and of areas where improvements are possible.

Table 6.3 *A supplier's possible reactions to the appraisal process*

Favourable reactions	Unfavourable reactions
We may be able to do business with this organisation in future.	We did not form a favourable picture of this organisation as a possible future business partner.
We managed to get to know the people well.	The people they fielded did not come across well to us.
We felt the process was handled fairly and efficiently.	We felt they were taking advantage of us, just inviting us to make up the numbers.
We will be able to benefit in the future from the potential cost savings and efficiency improvements we identified as a result of the exercise.	The exercise was an expensive waste of time and money, through no fault of our own.
They listened carefully to what we had to say and applied reasonable and even-handed criteria in evaluating it.	They gave us no chance to present the full strength of our case.

4.2   The process involves measurement of price, quality and delivery aspects of each supplier's performance. In broad terms, the supplier's price history is investigated and compared with competitors. Quality is measured by reference to percentage of rejects or number of production line hold-ups caused by faulty supplies. Delivery is measured by reference to number of deliveries on time, number of deliveries one day late etc

4.3   Some of these factors are difficult to measure. For example, detailed records must be kept of each delivery from each supplier and it must be possible for each one to compare actual delivery date with promised delivery date. To do this systematically inevitably requires computerised methods.

4.4   Even with a systematic computerised process there are problems with this procedure. For one thing, it is expensive to collect and analyse the data, and is probably only worth doing in the case of high-value items. Another difficulty is that the process inevitably incorporates assumptions about what caused certain problems. This is usually not clear-cut, and suppliers might well be able to defend themselves by reference to factors beyond their control. For example, was a late delivery the fault of the supplier or did it happen because the buyer placed an emergency order with insufficient notice?

4.5   As a supplement to these measures, many buyers make it a policy to visit suppliers on a regular cycle. The idea is to look at the supplier's operations, particularly in relation to quality issues, and discuss any shortcomings that are identified with a view to achieving improvements by the time of the next visit. This process is sometimes referred to as a **supplier audit**.

Vendor rating in practice

4.6   Two methods of vendor rating are in common use. The first is based on the use of a checklist such as that shown in Figure 6.3 (adapted from Dobler and Burt). For each factor listed, personnel within the buying organisation assess the supplier's performance as good, satisfactory or unsatisfactory. A weighting is applied to each factor. The factors within each main performance area are then aggregated and the supplier's overall performance in that area is summarised as good, satisfactory or unsatisfactory.

Figure 6.3 *Supplier performance evaluation form*

SUPPLIER _____	DATE _____		
Summary evaluation, by department	**Good**	**Satisfactory**	**Unsatisfactory**
Purchasing	_____	_____	_____
Receiving	_____	_____	_____
Accounting	_____	_____	_____
Engineering	_____	_____	_____
Quality	_____	_____	_____

Performance factors

Purchasing

	Good	Satisfactory	Unsatisfactory
Delivers on schedule	_____	_____	_____
Delivers at quoted price	_____	_____	_____
Prices are competitive	_____	_____	_____
Prompt and accurate with routine documents	_____	_____	_____
Anticipates our needs	_____	_____	_____
Helps in emergencies	_____	_____	_____
Does not unfairly exploit a single source position	_____	_____	_____
Does not request special consideration	_____	_____	_____
Currently supplies price, catalogue, and technical information	_____	_____	_____
Furnishes specially requested information promptly	_____	_____	_____
Advises us of potential troubles	_____	_____	_____
Has good labour relations	_____	_____	_____
Delivers without constant follow-up	_____	_____	_____
Replaces rejections promptly	_____	_____	_____
Accepts our terms without exception	_____	_____	_____
Keeps promises	_____	_____	_____
Has sincere desire to serve	_____	_____	_____

Receiving

	Good	Satisfactory	Unsatisfactory
Delivers per routing instructions	_____	_____	_____
Has adequate delivery service	_____	_____	_____
Has good packaging	_____	_____	_____

Accounting

	Good	Satisfactory	Unsatisfactory
Invoices correctly	_____	_____	_____
Issues credit notes punctually	_____	_____	_____
Does not ask for special financial consideration	_____	_____	_____

Engineering

	Good	Satisfactory	Unsatisfactory
Past record on reliability of products	_____	_____	_____
Has technical ability for difficult work	_____	_____	_____
Readily accepts responsibilities for latent deficiencies	_____	_____	_____
Provides quick and effective action in emergencies	_____	_____	_____
Furnishes requested data promptly	_____	_____	_____

Quality

	Good	Satisfactory	Unsatisfactory
Quality of material	_____	_____	_____
Furnishes certification, affidavits, etc	_____	_____	_____
Replies with corrective action	_____	_____	_____

4.7 This is a somewhat subjective procedure which runs counter to the idea of basing vendor rating on quantitative measures. The second method has a more quantitative feel to it. The idea is to pick out three or four major critical factors such as those already mentioned (price, quality and delivery). For each of these a method of measurement is determined. For example, the measure of quality performance might be '100 per cent less percentage of rejects in total deliveries'. A supplier whose deliveries contained 3 per cent rejects would score 97 per cent under this measure.

4.8 Next, each of the major factors is given a weighting, the total of weightings adding up to 1 (or 100 per cent). By performing a weighted average calculation the buyer ends up with a single figure for the overall evaluation of the supplier.

4.9 To illustrate this suppose that a buyer applies a weighting of 0.4 to price, 0.4 to quality performance, and 0.2 to delivery. (These weightings might change for other materials; for example, for a different material the most urgent factor might be on-time delivery, and this would then have a higher weighting than the other two factors.) Suppose further that a particular supplier scored 94 per cent on the price measure, 97 per cent on the quality measure and 72 per cent on the delivery measure. The overall rating for that supplier would be calculated as follows.

Performance factor	Weighting	Score	Rating
Price	0.4	0.94	0.376
Quality	0.4	0.97	0.388
Delivery	0.2	0.72	0.144
Overall evaluation	1.0		0.908

4.10 Using this method of calculation the supplier has achieved a rating of 0.908 compared with a total possible of 1. This score can be compared with that achieved by other suppliers and gives a good measure of where each stands in the order of preference.

4.11 Needless to say, this method too (despite its appearance of scientific precision) is not free from subjectivity. The weightings attached to each performance factor attempt to describe the relative importance of each, but this is clearly an impossible thing to do scientifically. Indeed, it may happen that some particular factor, such as delivery in a just in time environment, is so important that no compromise is possible, no matter how well a supplier performs on other criteria.

4.12 Similarly, however performance is measured on each factor there is sure to be some amount of estimation involved. Nevertheless, if consistently applied to all suppliers the method should provide a reasonable order of preference between them, even if not an absolutely 'correct' evaluation of any particular supplier. And if applied consistently year after year it should provide a measure of whether a supplier's performance is improving or declining.

4.13 All of this assumes that the information compiled in a vendor rating scheme is going to be used. It is not an exercise to be carried out just for the sake of it; it is a tool for making sourcing decisions and improving performance of suppliers who are chosen.

5   Other aspects of supplier appraisal

Supplying services

5.1   Services have the following characteristics and features which distinguish them from physical, tangible products.

- **Intangibility**: a service cannot be tasted, touched, seen or smelled before it is purchased. For instance, you will not see the results of going to the dentist before you purchase the service. Because of this a customer will look for other evidence of the service quality, such as the price, the promotional material, the location and the staff who provide the service.

- **Inseparability**: services are produced and consumed at the same time. A service cannot be stored. Using our dentist example again, we can see that both the patient and the dentist have to be present for the service to be provided. Therefore, the influence, personality and performance of the staff providing the service is paramount to success.

- **Heterogeneity**: the quality of a service will be variable. Because of inseparability, the service will be influenced by many factors such as the patient's mood, the dentist's mood, the weather etc. So it is difficult for a customer to be sure of the outcome of any service he participates in. This is different from buying a tangible product mass-produced on a production line: in this case, it is likely that one unit from the production process is indistinguishable from another.

- **Perishability**: a service cannot be stored so supply of a service is difficult to control. For instance, a dentist cannot store the service of filling a tooth. He may find demand high on some days, while there are no patients on other days. The result of this is that the dentist must always have the capacity to meet high levels of demand, which will be costly during slower periods.

5.2   The result of these distinguishing characteristics is that the marketing and the purchasing of services can be quite complex. Two important features in this context are people and process.

5.3   **People** refers to the actual employees delivering the service. Customer satisfaction can often depend on the person providing the service, because the service is inseparable from the person delivering it. If the employee is inefficient or poorly motivated then interaction with the customer will be affected. It is for this reason that organisations which provide services must be aware of the importance of their 'people'. Attention should be given to recruitment and selection, staff training and motivation in order to minimise heterogeneity of the service.

5.4   **Process** refers to the methods used to provide the service. Procedures for dealing with customers and for supplying the service must be carefully planned and managed to minimise heterogeneity. Many organisations – for example BT and many government agencies such as DVLA – have moved to computerised switchboards to achieve this. Because staff are not involved the customer receives the same standard of service every time he calls the organisation. Additionally, processes must be in place to ensure that the service is provided efficiently during peak hours. For instance, a hairdresser might employ Saturday staff because this is the busiest day of the week. Because a service is perishable the hairdresser will lose custom if he cannot meet demand.

The importance of the services sector

5.5 A major force in increasing the strategic role of purchasing functions has been the development of manufacturing operations. This trend is obviously absent from service companies (though philosophies such as total quality management and continuous improvement are equally relevant to any environment).

5.6 The result is that in many service companies the purchasing function is relatively undeveloped. Indeed, it is sometimes found that many purchasing responsibilities are undertaken by non-purchasing personnel because a centralised purchasing function is either completely absent or ineffective.

5.7 This is an area which is both a concern and an opportunity for the purchasing profession. It is a concern because service companies account for a huge share of gross domestic product in the UK and purchasing disciplines should not be neglected. It is an opportunity because such companies are at present failing to realise benefits which a strong purchasing input could bring.

5.8 Generalisations are always dangerous, but it is probably fair to say that in many service companies purchasing activities are dispersed throughout the organisation, rather than being under centralised control; and to the extent that a centralised function exists at all, its role is mainly clerical and administrative. This situation is changing as increased competition forces service companies to examine value added throughout their supply chains, but the stage of development is less advanced than in manufacturing organisations.

5.9 One characteristic that has retarded the development of purchasing functions in service companies is the absence of a clear link between inputs, processing and outputs. In the case of a manufacturing company this link is very clear: materials are bought in for £X, these are worked on at a cost of £Y and eventually converted into finished products for sale at £Z.

5.10 In a service company this process is much less clear, especially since the value of bought in materials is usually low as a percentage of sales output. For example, whereas a manufacturer might expect, say, 60 per cent of his sales revenue to be absorbed by the cost of bought out materials, for a service company the proportion might be as low as 10 per cent. Most of the inputs of many service companies consist of staff salaries, where purchasing expertise has little to contribute.

5.11 What items are bought out in a typical service organisation? This will obviously depend heavily on the exact nature of the organisation, but the following are likely answers.

- Office equipment and supplies such as stationery
- Computer hardware and software
- Motor vehicles
- Advertising and design services
- Maintenance services (for computers, vehicles and buildings)
- In some cases, capital goods (such as a provider of logistics services who must invest heavily in premises, materials handling equipment, heavy goods vehicles etc)

5.12 Whereas in a manufacturing company a purchasing manager's main 'customer' is the production function, in a service company hardly any of the buyer's effort is directed at 'production'. This is well illustrated by the list above. For this reason among others line managers in such companies have tended to think of purchasing purely as a support function and this has been a factor in the low priority accorded to purchasing expertise.

Measuring the supplier appraisal process

5.13 It is important for buyers to reach some kind of objective valuation of the appraisal process. This is necessary so that the respective offerings of different suppliers can be compared. To achieve this, the buyer must make appropriate enquiries as to factors that can be reliably measured.

5.14 Some of the possible factors to be investigated are listed here.

- For a manufacturing supplier, details relating to statistical process control (eg the number of production items falling outside accepted tolerances)
- For a service supplier, details relating to cost savings achieved by other clients
- Again for a service supplier, details relating to service level agreements with other clients and the extent to which these have been met
- Details of financial performance and stability (to some extent included in published accounts, though the buyer may look for further detail)

5.15 Of course, this kind of information is inevitably historical. The buyer can use it as one indication of likely future performance, but should also ask questions that specifically address the future. For example, he should enquire about the supplier's plans for capital investment, staff training and development, possible restructuring or management changes etc.

5.16 Other factors may be less tangible, but can also help the buyer to form an opinion as to the likely suitability of a potential supplier. For example, the interpersonal communication undertaken during the appraisal process can help the buyer to form an opinion as to likely future relations with the supplier. There will also inevitably be discussion about the supplier's relations with other customers – this can help to indicate what the buyer can expect in a future relationship. And finally the buyer will pick up hints just from walking around the supplier's premises: the state of repair of the manufacturing facilities, for example, the tidiness of the administration departments and so on. While not strictly objective measurements, this kind of indication may be very helpful in practice

Supplier appraisal and relationship development

5.17 The conduct of the supplier appraisal process is likely to have an ongoing effect on the eventual relationship between buyer and supplier. Needless to say, the buyer must always be professional in his attitude, no matter how hard he is working to extract the best possible deal from the supplier. Any kind of 'table thumping' at this stage will inevitably have a bad effect on future relations, or may even lead to the relationship being aborted.

5.18 The kind of behaviour that can be damaging at this stage might include failure (on either side) to divulge information in response to reasonable requests, undue insistence on a particular point of view with unwillingness to listen to the other party's story, or a generally confrontational attitude.

5.19 By contrast, if the buyer's attitude is 'firm but fair', and always professional, it lays the foundations for a mutually beneficial collaboration in the future. The point of undertaking the appraisal process at all is the possibility of an ongoing relationship. The supplier will be encouraged to enter such a relationship if he feels that the buyer is someone he can do business with in a professional way. He will be deterred from an agreement if it appears that the buyer's attitude or behaviour is unprofessional.

Chapter summary

- Research into supply markets should cover demand analysis, vendor analysis and market analysis.

- A useful starting point for research into supply markets is to examine the structure of the supply market, including such factors as the number of buyers and suppliers in the market.

- Important steps in the process of supplier appraisal include: identifying potential suppliers, assessing financial stability, planning and conducting site visits, and assessing task variables.

- An important strategic issue for buyers is the structure of the supply chain, in terms of the number of tiers of suppliers. Reducing the number of first-tier suppliers simplifies management of the supply chain for the top-level purchaser.

- It is not safe to assume that a supplier will necessarily welcome an appraisal, particularly if they suspect that the appraisal process is unfair.

- Vendor rating is a quantitative method of assessing supplier performance. However, the apparent mathematical nature of the process should not conceal the large amount of subjectivity involved.

- Services are distinct from physical goods in terms of: intangibility; inseparability; heterogeneity; and perishability.

- In service organisations, it is common to find that much purchasing activity is carried out by user departments, rather than by professional buyers.

Self-test questions

1   What is the objective of research into supply markets? (1.6)

2   In what circumstances may a need for supplier appraisal arise? (1.13)

3   List sources of information in identifying potential suppliers. (1.19–1.27)

4   What kinds of information will a buyer be looking for during a site visit to a potential supplier? (1.35)

5   What reasons might there be for adopting a tiered structure of suppliers? (2.9)

6   List characteristics of a typical first-tier supplier. (2.11)

7   List reasons why a potential supplier might not welcome a buyer's plan for an appraisal exercise. (Table 6.2)

8   What favourable and unfavourable reactions might a supplier experience on looking back at an appraisal exercise? (Table 6.3)

9   What aspects of supplier performance may be assessed in a vendor rating exercise? (4.2)

10   Describe two methods of conducting a vendor rating exercise. (4.6, 4.7)

11   List the factors that distinguish services from tangible products. (5.1)

12   What types of supply does a service organisation source from outside? (5.11)

CHAPTER 7

Supplier Selection

Learning objectives

2.4   Evaluate the constraints on supplier selection within the public sector.

- Legislation affecting supplier selection
- Supplier selection routes available to the public sector
- The buyer's perspective on selection legislation
- The supplier's perspective on selection legislation

2.5   Analyse the role of reciprocal trading in purchasing relationships.

- Definition of reciprocal trading
- Examples of organisations' policies on reciprocal trading
- Managing reciprocal trading in the selection process
- The impact of reciprocal trading on relationships during and after the selection process

2.6   Analyse and explain how to mitigate the potential risks of a change of supply source.

- Risks of change
- Cost of change
- Mitigation of risk and cost
- Communication and stakeholder management

Chapter headings

1   Supplier selection in the public sector

2   Reciprocal trading

3   Risks of changing a supply source

4   Evaluating suppliers for strategic capability

Introduction

In this chapter we complete our coverage of Section 2 of your syllabus (on assessing and selecting suppliers). We look at a number of disparate topics loosely concerned with selection of suppliers.

1   Supplier selection in the public sector

Private sector vs public sector

1.1   A major classification of buying environment distinguishes between private sector and public sector organisations. Most of the purchasing literature concentrates on private sector firms with the other category being treated as an add-on.

1.2   Although there are some sound reasons for this, it would be wrong to see public sector operations as merely a trivial addition to the mainstream economic activity carried out by private sector providers. On the contrary, the spending power of public sector enterprises is enormous. The sheer range of public sector service provision is staggering: roads, law and order, education, health services, emergency services, and much more.

1.3   The main influence on strategic decisions in a **private sector** firm is the achievement of commercial objectives. In most cases, this can be simplified further: private sector firms are profit-maximisers, and managerial decisions are assessed on the basis of the extent to which they contribute to organisational profit.

1.4   Related to this is the very strong influence of competition. In nearly all cases, a private sector firm will be one of several, or many, firms offering goods or services of a particular type. Consumers are free to choose between the offerings of different firms, and their choices of course have a dramatic impact on the revenue and profits earned by the firms concerned. Securing competitive advantage is a large step towards realising the objective of profit maximisation.

1.5   The 'constituency' served by a private sector firm is limited in number – shareholders, customers, employees, all referred to collectively as 'stakeholders' in the modern phrase. This helps the firm to be focused in its strategy: it is usually clear which outcomes will benefit the stakeholders. Moreover, all members of the constituency are there by choice. They could have invested their money elsewhere, or in the case of employees they could have offered their labour and talents elsewhere.

1.6   In all these respects, and others, **public sector** organisations differ from their counterparts in the private sector. The differences are well analysed by Gary J Zenz (in an American context) in *Purchasing and the Management of Materials*. His analysis forms the basis of Table 7.1 below.

Table 7.1 *Differences between public and private sector purchasing*

Area of difference	Private sector	Public sector
Objectives	Usually, to increase profit	Usually, to achieve defined service levels
Responsibility	Buyers are responsible to directors, who in turn are responsible to shareholders	Buyers are responsible ultimately to the general public
Legal restrictions	Activities are regulated by company law, employment law, product liability law etc	Most of this applies equally to public sector, but additional regulations are present too (eg compulsory competitive tendering)
Competition	There is usually strong competition between many different firms	There is usually no competition
Publicity	Confidentiality applies in dealings between suppliers and buyers	Confidentiality is limited because of public interest in disclosure
Budgetary limits	Investment is constrained only by availability of attractive opportunities; funding can be found if prospects are good	Investment is constrained by externally imposed spending limits
Information exchange	Private sector buyers do not exchange information with other firms, because of confidentiality and competition	Public sector buyers are willing to exchange notes
Defined procedures	Private sector buyers can cut red tape when speed of action is necessary	Public sector buyers are often constrained to follow established procedures

1.7 The implication so far appears to be that purchasing in the private and public sectors are two completely different disciplines. However, this is far from the truth and the differences cited above should not mask many essential similarities between the work of the public sector buyer and his private sector counterpart.

1.8 One reason for this is that differences in objectives, organisational constraints and so on may not necessarily lead to differences in procedure. For example, public sector buyers may not be seeking to maximise profit, but their concern to achieve value for money is stimulated by other influences, equally strong; in particular, the public sector buyer must achieve a defined level of service within a defined budget.

1.9 Similarly, the private sector buyer faced with a profit objective will identify customer satisfaction as a key criterion in meeting the objective. But equally, the public sector buyer will work in an environment where providing a quality service so as to delight 'customers' is an essential part of the organisational ethos. Often this commitment is evidenced by a customers' charter such as has been produced by such organisations as the Inland Revenue. Buyers in both environments will be concerned to a large extent with ensuring quality of output by influencing the quality of inputs.

1.10 In addition to this consideration, even where differences did once exist they are much less apparent now than before. An important reason for this in the UK was the Conservative government's strong commitment to introducing private sector disciplines into public sector organisations during the 1980s and 1990s, a policy which by and large continues today.

1.11 In some cases, the effects of this have been radical. Most previously public organisations have been privatised (for example the landline telecommunications industry). It is true that privatised monopolies remain subject to surveillance, but in all essential respects they function like any private sector organisation, and have to face up alone to competition from new technology.

1.12 Even in cases such as the National Health Service, which has remained in public ownership, developments such as GP fundholding (now abandoned) have introduced elements of a free market. Fundholding was the arrangement in which general practitioners were able in effect to 'purchase' health provision for patients on their list from whichever 'suppliers' (ie hospitals) they preferred. While this approach has been dropped, the more commercial ethos it introduced into the GP system has had profound effects on its culture.

1.13 In some cases, the political changes have led to public sector bodies becoming even more 'commercial' than private sector firms. This is the case for example in relation to competitive tendering. For a private sector concern the decision to use competitive tendering or not is exactly that: a decision. In most public sector contexts, no decision arises: use of competitive tendering is compulsory.

Areas of difference between public and private sector organisations

1.14 This last point gives rise to an important question concerning supplier relations. Modern approaches to supplier relations strongly emphasise the value of long-term partnerships between a buyer and a limited number of suppliers. Competitive tendering retains an important place in the buyer's portfolio of techniques, but is not generally suitable in relation to materials for which long-term partnerships are sought. The public sector buyer, constrained to use competitive tendering in all cases, therefore finds that the benefits of long-term partnership are unattainable.

1.15 Differences between public sector and private sector buying also arise from the question of accountability. As we have noted already, the stakeholders in a public service are more diverse than those of a private firm. Buyers in the public sector may be required to account for their actions to a wide constituency, most of whose members are entirely unknown quantities as far as managers in the public service are concerned. One effect of this is an insistence on detailed procedures and record keeping: it may be difficult later to justify a course of action which breaches defined procedures or which is poorly documented.

1.16 Budgetary control is another area where differences surface. The demand for funds in a private sector firm is limited, in that only some projects are commercially attractive. Other projects are not regarded as viable because, for example, they do not meet criteria for return on capital. In the public sector, by contrast, the demand for funds is limitless: no taxpayer ever complains that too much of a service is provided.

1.17 Another aspect of budgetary control concerns cash limits. A public sector buyer may enjoy less flexibility than his private sector counterpart. For example, a buyer in the private sector may weigh up the advantages and disadvantages of a bulk discount from a supplier. The public sector buyer probably has no option: if the bulk purchase would take him outside his budget he must forgo the discount.

1.18 Another difference is in the sheer diversity of items that may be purchased by a public sector organisation, which of course is related to the diversity of services it provides. Consider a local government authority in the UK: it may be a purchaser of construction materials for use in housing or road maintenance, of dustbin lorries for refuse collection, of sporting equipment for a community leisure centre, and much more. While large manufacturing organisations may purchase many thousands of different stock items, the diversity in their stock ranges will hardly compare with this.

1.19 Finally, difficult issues arise in connection with specifications in public sector buying. No matter how detailed a specification may be, there will always be areas of ambiguity, areas where slightly different approaches may be valid within the terms of the specification. Interpreting these 'grey areas' is a delicate matter, but in the private sector suppliers have a strong incentive to interpret them in a way that leads to perfect satisfaction on the part of the buyer. If they do not do so, the buyer will simply cross them off his list of possible suppliers for the future.

1.20 The considerations are different when a supplier acts in accordance with a public sector tender. Failure to provide complete satisfaction may lead to discontent on the part of the buyer, but he is not free simply to cross the supplier off his approved list. This is only possible if the supplier has demonstrably failed, but this will rarely be the case when any ambiguity was present in the specification.

The effects of European procurement directives

1.21 The European procurement directives are having an effect on purchasing in the public sector. Once a buyer has specified the product or service he requires, and has decided to use the tendering method, he must ensure that he complies with European Union directives. These do not apply to private sector buying, but do cover purchases by public authorities unless their value is below a certain (low) threshold.

1.22 Subject to certain exceptions, the directives require public bodies to use open tendering procedures. They must advertise the invitation to tender according to defined rules designed to secure maximum publicity.

1.23 In general, buyers are obliged to award the contract on the basis of the lowest quoted price, or on the basis of the economically most advantageous tender. If they choose the latter alternative, they must make the fact known to candidates, and must explain by what criteria they mean to assess 'economic advantage'. The purchaser is allowed to exclude firms if they fail to meet defined criteria relating to general suitability, financial and economic standing and technical competence.

1.24 The results of the tendering procedure must be notified to the Office of Official Publications of the European Communities, and will then be made public.

I.25 This regime of compulsory open tendering has certain disadvantages. All vendors are aware that a large number of bids are likely to be made, and this may deter some suitable applicants. Moreover, since very little prequalification of vendors is allowed under the directives, it is likely also that some will take risks in attempting to undercut potential rivals. The result may be a contract awarded at a price that gives no incentive to high quality performance. Finally, there is of course a great administrative burden on the purchaser who is faced with a large number of tenders to evaluate.

Procedures and time limits

I.26 Contracting authorities now have the choice of four contract award procedures: open, restricted, negotiated (with or without contract notice) and competitive dialogue.

I.27 For the **open procedure** there is no requirement for pre-qualification of suppliers. Tenders must be issued within six days of request by a prospective bidder. The contracting authority must set the closing date for receipt of tenders no less than 52 days from the publication of the contract notice.

I.28 For the **restricted procedure**, pre-qualification of suppliers is permitted but the contracting authority must indicate in the contract notice a predetermined range of suppliers to whom tenders will be sent. This must be not less than 5 and no more than 20. The contract notice must allow a minimum of 37 days for prospective bidders to register an interest and submit the required information for pre-qualification. Those suppliers who are pre-qualified must be allowed a minimum of 40 days to submit their tenders in response to the invitation issued by the contracting authority.

I.29 The **negotiated procedure** takes two forms: with publication of a contract notice, and without publication. In the latter case other formalities are dispensed with as well. The procedure without publication may be used for a number of reasons including when:

- the open or restricted procedure was discontinued, but only if the contracting authority invites to negotiate the contract every supplier who submitted a tender (not being an excluded tender) under the other procedures;
- there were inappropriate or no tenders under the other procedures;
- for technical or artistic reasons, or because of exclusive rights;
- because of urgency the time limits in the other procedures cannot be met;
- additional and/or repetitive goods/services/works are required.

I.30 Under the negotiated procedure where a contract notice is required, prospective bidders must be given a minimum of 37 days to register their interest to negotiate. Where there is a sufficient number of persons who are suitable to be selected to negotiate, the number selected must not be less than three.

I.31 Where contract notices are drawn up and transmitted by electronic means in accordance with the format and modes of transmission stipulated, the Regulations allow for the time limits for the receipt of tenders in open procedures, and the time limit for the receipt of requests to participate in restricted and negotiated procedures and competitive dialogue, to be shortened by seven days.

I.32   The time limit for receipt of tenders may be reduced by a further five days where the contracting authority offers unrestricted and full direct access by electronic means to the contract documents and any supplementary documents from the date of publication of the notice, by specifying in the text of the notice the internet address at which this documentation is accessible.

I.33   Where contracting authorities seek to take advantage of the above opportunity to shorten the time limits for the receipt of tenders on the basis of the electronic availability of their contract documents, they must publish the specifications and the additional documents in their entirety on the internet.

I.34   In general, buyers are obliged to award the contract on the basis of the lowest quoted price, or on the basis of the economically most advantageous tender. If they choose the latter alternative, they must make the fact known to candidates, and must explain by what criteria, and their relative importance, they mean to assess 'economically advantageous'. The buyer is allowed, in certain circumstances, to exclude bidders if they fail to meet defined criteria relating to general suitability, financial and economic standing and technical competence. This is discussed in more detail later in this section.

Debriefing

I.35   The results of the tendering procedure must be notified to the Office of Official Publications of the European Communities, and these are then published. Unsuccessful bidders have the right to a **debrief**, if they so request. This must be undertaken within 48 days of the unsuccessful bidder's request.

New provisions

I.36   New provisions have been added to take account of modern procurement methods and developments in best practice. These include specific provisions on **framework agreements, central purchasing bodies** (eg consortia purchasing), **dynamic purchasing systems** (eg electronic frameworks, electronic auctions), and **electronic auctions**.

Framework agreements

I.37   The regulations define a framework agreement as follows.

A framework agreement is an agreement between one or more contracting authorities and one or more economic operators, the purpose of which is to establish the terms governing contracts to be awarded during a given period, in particular with regard to price and, where appropriate, the quantity envisaged.

I.38   Under the new provisions in the Regulations, when a contracting authority enters into a framework agreement in accordance with the Regulations, it may enter into contracts based on such a framework agreement during its term of validity by applying the terms set forth in the framework agreement or, if all terms have not been fixed in advance in the framework agreement, by reopening competition between the parties to the framework agreement in relation to those terms.

1.39 The reopening of competition should comply with certain rules, the aim of which is to guarantee the required flexibility and respect for the general principles, in particular the principle of equal treatment. For the same reasons, the term of the framework agreements should not exceed four years, except in cases duly justified by contracting authorities.

Central purchasing bodies

1.40 The Regulations define a central purchasing body as follows.

A central purchasing body is a contracting authority which acquires supplies and/or services intended for contracting authorities or awards public contracts or concludes framework agreements for works, supplies or services intended for contracting authorities.

1.41 Certain centralised purchasing techniques have been developed in most Member States. Under these arrangements various contracting authorities are responsible for making acquisitions for resale to other contracting authorities or for awarding public contracts/framework agreements for other contracting authorities to use. In view of the large volumes purchased, these techniques help to increase competition and streamline public purchasing.

1.42 Provisions are therefore included in the Regulations for a definition of central purchasing bodies dedicated to contracting authorities. A definition is also given of the conditions under which, in accordance with the principles of non-discrimination and equal treatment, contracting authorities purchasing works, supplies and/or services through a central purchasing body may be deemed to have complied with the Regulations.

Dynamic (electronic) purchasing systems

1.43 The Regulations define a dynamic purchasing system as follows.

A dynamic purchasing system is a completely electronic process for making commonly used purchases, the characteristics of which, as generally available on the market, meet the requirements of the contracting authority, which is limited in duration and open throughout its validity to any economic operator which satisfies the selection criteria and has submitted an indicative tender that complies with the specification.

1.44 In view of the rapid expansion of electronic purchasing systems, appropriate rules have now been introduced to enable contracting authorities to take full advantage of the possibilities afforded by these systems. Against this background, it is necessary to define a completely electronic dynamic purchasing system for commonly used purchases, and to lay down specific rules for setting up and operating such a system to ensure the fair treatment of any economic operator who wishes to take part therein.

1.45 Any economic operator who submits an indicative tender in accordance with the specification and meets the selection criteria should be allowed to join such a system. This purchasing technique allows the contracting authority, through the establishment of a list of tenderers already selected and the opportunity given to new tenderers to take part, to receive a particularly broad range of tenders as a result of the electronic facilities available, and hence to ensure the optimum use of public funds through broad competition. A dynamic purchasing system may not last for more than four years, except in duly justified exceptional cases.

Electronic auctions

1.46   The Regulations define an electronic auction as follows.

> *An electronic auction is a repetitive process involving an electronic device for the presentation of new prices, revised downwards, and/or new values concerning certain elements of tenders, which occurs after an initial full evaluation of the tenders, enabling them to be ranked using automatic evaluation methods.*

1.47   Since the use of electronic auctions is likely to increase, such auctions are given a definition in the Regulations (shown above) and are governed by specific rules to ensure that they operate in full accordance with the principles of equal treatment, non-discrimination and transparency. To that end, provision is made for such electronic auctions to deal only with contracts for works, supplies or services for which the specifications can be determined with precision.

1.48   With the same objective, it must be also be possible to establish the respective ranking of the tenderers at any stage of the electronic auction. Recourse to electronic auctions enables contracting authorities to ask tenderers to submit new prices, revised downwards, and when the contract is awarded to the most economically advantageous tender, also to improve elements of the tender other than price.

1.49   However, to guarantee compliance with the principle of transparency, only the elements suitable for automatic evaluation by electronic means, without intervention by the contracting authority, may be improved. To this end, such elements must be quantifiable so that they can be expressed in figures or percentages.

Competitive dialogue

1.50   A new procedure, the **competitive dialogue**, has been introduced to complement the existing open, restricted and negotiated procedures. It is intended to be used for large complex projects in circumstances where, currently, the use of the negotiated procedure might be considered. The Commission's view of the negotiated procedure (as a fallback in circumstances where other procedures are not workable) remains unchanged.

1.51   In the competitive dialogue (and with the negotiated procedure with contract notice), in view of the flexibility which may be required and the high level of costs associated with such methods of procurement, contracting authorities are entitled to make provision for the procedure to be conducted in successive stages to gradually reduce, on the basis of the previously indicated contract award criteria, the number of tenders which they will go on to discuss or negotiate. This reduction should, in so far as the number of appropriate solutions or candidates allows, ensure that there is a genuine competition.

Benefits and drawbacks of the directives

1.52   The benefits of the EU directives may be summarised as in Table 7.2.

Table 7.2 *Benefits of the EU directives for buyers and suppliers*

Benefits for buyers	Benefits for suppliers
Wider choice of potential suppliers	Open access to public sector markets for more suppliers (via open tendering)
Purchasing decisions based on value for money (via competition), which supports key objectives	Ensures market is non-discriminatory and genuinely competitive: objective award criteria
Improved efficiency of the contract award process (including support for electronic/on-line methods, framework agreements, central contracting authorities etc)	Improved efficiency of the contract award process (including support for electronic/on-line methods)
Environmental/sustainability and other non-price criteria can be fairly used, and suppliers can be pre-qualified (within specified parameters)	Greater transparency: timely, reasonable, equal access to information on non-price criteria
Requirement to debrief offers opportunities to establish reputation as fair, honest, ethical	Right to debrief offers opportunities for learning, development (in return for investment in unsuccessful bid)
	Potential for longer-term, larger contracts (eg through support for framework agreements, central purchasing bodies)

1.53   The drawbacks of the legislation may be summarised as in Table 7.3.

Table 7.3 *Drawbacks of the EU directives for buyers and suppliers*

Drawbacks for buyers	Drawbacks for suppliers
Wider competition may deter potentially suitable bidders	Increased competition
Procedures take time, and may reduce responsiveness to urgent requirements	Good performance of a contract will not automatically be rewarded with repeat business.
Costs of time, putting together tender documentation, administering tender process, debriefs etc.	Costs of time, administration etc.
Competition on price may devalue quality/sustainability criteria	Competition on price may devalue quality/sustainability offering
Scope for negotiation is limited: buyers may not be able to secure maximum value for money	
Limited pre-qualification may create supplier risk	

Constraints on relationship development within the public sector

1.54   Here are some of the constraints on relationship development in the public sector.

- Public sector buyers are constrained by the EU Procurement Directives to use open advertisement and competitive tendering, over certain value thresholds.

- Preferred/compulsory tendering prevents buyers from letting contracts to proven suppliers with whom they have had positive results in the past. Long-term relationships with suppliers are therefore difficult to maintain.

- There are constraints on the maximum duration of a contract, again making long-term relationships difficult to establish.

- The public sector may be exploited (or seen as exploitable) by businesses, because of its large spends, inability to enter into long-term relationships, and inability to incentivise suppliers with automatic renewal or extension of a successful contract.

- The cost and time necessary to tender (plus the EU-wide competition) may prevent some organisations (particularly SMEs) from participation, thus excluding some suppliers with whom mutually beneficial relationships could be formed.

- The emphasis on best value may constrain relationships based on other pre-qualification criteria (such as quality, innovation or sustainability).

- Unless a competitive dialogue procedure is used, there is little opportunity to develop relationships based on early supplier/contractor involvement.

2   *Reciprocal trading*

Intra-organisational trading

2.1   This refers to commercial relationships between entities which are part of the same organisation. One aspect of this is the relationship between the purchasing function and its internal 'customers', which we discussed in an earlier chapter. In this section we look at another aspect of intra-organisational relationships: the situation where one group company supplies goods or services to another group company.

2.2   This situation adds a layer of complexity to the relationships that might exist in an open market. The terms on which two group companies may deal with each other are complicated by matters of internal policy and politics. As a simple example, there may be tax considerations which dictate the transfer price to be adopted by the selling company. This means that buyer and seller do not have the usual flexibility in negotiating and agreeing a price.

2.3   Intra-organisational trading may be regarded as one variety of a more general phenomenon known as reciprocal trading. In the simplest case, reciprocal trade means the practice of buying from a supplier simply because that supplier happens to buy from you. The practice can also take more complex forms.

2.4   Gary J Zenz (in *Purchasing and the Management of Materials*) cites the case of a paper mill placing an order for chemicals with a chemical producer on condition that the chemicals company buys paper products from the mill. The more complex form in this case might be a requirement that the chemicals firm buys its paper products not directly from the mill, but from a customer of the mill.

2.5 Reciprocal agreements often arise in cases of international trade, especially when a less developed company is importing goods or services. This has happened on a large scale in Eastern Europe in recent years since the fall of Communism and the opening of the Eastern bloc. An Eastern European country may agree to buy from, say, a UK company, but the UK exporter in return is obliged to purchase from the Eastern European country. This reduces the outflow of funds from the importer's country and safeguards hard currency reserves.

2.6 Note that simple cases where one company is both a customer and a supplier of another company are not necessarily examples of reciprocity. It is only when our decision to buy from Supplier X is taken **for the purpose of inducing Supplier X to buy from us** that reciprocity exists.

2.7 The stimulus usually comes from sales staff, quite properly exploring every avenue for maximising sales. A salesman for the paper mill in the above example may observe that the chemicals company is a good potential customer, but is not currently buying from the mill. The salesman may be tempted to apply pressure on the buying staff of the chemicals producer: 'If we buy from you, the least you can do is reciprocate by buying from us'.

2.8 This places the buying staff in a very difficult position. They are under pressure to purchase from the mill and the threat of losing a valuable customer may weigh heavily with them. But the fact that they are not currently buying from this particular mill is presumably because they have a preferable source elsewhere. Transferring their business is bad news for their existing supplier, and may be a less than optimal buying decision for the chemicals company.

2.9 Things are not much easier for buying staff in the paper mill. Naturally they would like their organisation to maximise sales and profits by every legitimate means. But to do so at the price of tying their hands on an important sourcing decision is undesirable. It would matter less if the chemicals producer were already their preferred source of supply, though even then circumstances might change in the future. And if the chemicals producer is not their preferred source, the buying decision is being taken for the wrong reasons.

Problems with reciprocal buying

2.10 The very description of these difficulties makes it clear that reciprocal buying is undesirable. It brings into the buying decision factors which have nothing to do with the buyer's principal duty, which is to secure the best possible purchase value for his organisation. To fulfil that duty he must look objectively at the various possible suppliers and choose the most suitable. Pressure to fit in with a reciprocal buying agreement removes that objectivity.

2.11 It is not just the buyer who suffers, but the organisation as a whole. It may be that extra sales are achieved, but unsuitable purchasing decisions may be the result. If so, there could be a heavy price to pay in terms of product quality and customer satisfaction.

2.12 An even more serious problem may be a possible breach of the law. In the UK, there are legal regulations which prohibit most attempts to stifle competition. Reciprocal agreements may well fall foul of these regulations and should only ever be entered into, if they must be undertaken at all, after taking legal advice.

2.13 Malcolm Saunders summarises these difficulties by posing the following three questions that should be answered in analysing an opportunity for reciprocal trade.

- How necessary is it to have a reciprocal agreement with the customer in order to win the sales contract?

- What are the benefits to the company of winning the sales contract?

- What are the costs to the company of using this customer as a supplier, as opposed to exercising a free choice? This question of course goes to the heart of the buyer's responsibility. By buying from Supplier X will quality or cost suffer?

2.14 Intra-group purchasing gives rise to similar problems. Clearly it is in the interest of a group of companies that they should not buy externally if a company within the group can provide what is required. But undue pressure to buy from fellow subsidiaries can lead to the same kind of suboptimal decisions as reciprocal buying, and should be resisted by purchasing staff as far as group policy permits.

2.15 To see the potential difficulties of intra-organisational trading most clearly it is worth looking at the extreme case. What would happen if the supplying company was in material breach of contract, perhaps because it supplied seriously defective goods which had a damaging effect on the buyer's production process? If this situation arose in a normal commercial context the buyer would seek compensation, if necessary through legal action. But in an intra-group context this would be almost inconceivable. It is clear that by accepting the intra-group supply the buyer also accepts limitations in his normal rights of redress against the supplier.

3 Risks of changing a supply source

The risk of change

3.1 Changing an existing supplier in favour of a new supplier causes upheaval and cost. Even so, a buyer will sometimes decide that this is the best course of action, perhaps because of problems with the existing supplier's performance, or because a new supplier's offering is impossible to resist. In taking such a decision the buyer exposes his organisation to a number of risks, and he must therefore proceed with great caution.

3.2 The most obvious risk is that the new supplier will fail to perform. For example, it may be found that the new supplier is unable to deliver goods of the right quality, or is unable to meet delivery schedules, or cannot supply in the way that we require (eg he may be unable to meet our requirements for JIT delivery).

3.3 Another risk, very pertinent to this examination syllabus, is concerned with relationship issues. Over a course of dealing, the buyer's staff will have had possibly extensive dealings with the old supplier's staff. A pattern of behaviour will have become established on either side, and the two teams will have become used to working with each other. With the new supplier, all of this has to be begun from scratch, and there is a risk that satisfactory relationships will not be established.

3.4   The buyer must also recognise a learning curve effect. Even if the new supplier is capable of excellent performance, it may take some time before he achieves that level. There may be 'teething problems' while buyer and supplier learn to work together effectively. Although this should not be a long-term problem, it can cause disruption in the short term.

3.5   There is also a risk of incompatibility in the systems and processes of buyer and supplier. Like all the other risks so far discussed, this should be identified at the stage of supplier appraisal (ie before contract award), but if it does not become apparent until later it can again cause temporary disruption.

3.6   Finally, there is a risk that the total cost of ownership will be greater with the new supplier than with the old one. If a reason for preferring the new supplier is his 'headline' price, the buyer must ensure that this does not mask other costs further down the line. For example, if it turns out that the new supplier charges higher amounts for regular 'extras' than the previous supplier, the intended cost saving may prove an illusion.

3.7   Naturally, the buyer will attempt to identify all such risks before contract award. If a mistake is made, the consequences to the buyer's organisation (and to the personal status of the buyer) may be very serious. The buyer does not want to be in a position of having to return on bended knee to the previous supplier.

The cost of change

3.8   Apart from the risks of things going wrong, there are also significant costs of changing supplier. These begin well before the stage of contract award.

3.9   Assuming that the situation arises because of dissatisfaction with an existing supplier, the first cost will be that of identifying potential new suppliers. This can involve extensive research and management time.

3.10   The next step may well be to initiate a tendering exercise. (In a public sector context, this may well be mandatory.) The process is complex and time consuming, and the cost of staff time may be considerable. Certainly it is much more expensive than merely renewing a contract with an existing supplier.

3.11   Once the contract has been awarded to the new supplier, additional costs arise during the transition period. For example, the buyer's organisation will need to deal with any items ordered from the old supplier but not yet delivered, as well as finalising any outstanding claims (for rejects, defective items etc). There is also the cost of changing internal systems and processes to align with the new supplier. Much of the burden is borne by internal user departments, rather than by purchasing.

3.12   There are costs involved in familiarising the new supplier with systems and procedures. For example, consider a decision to select a new supplier to provide canteen services for an organisation with multiple sites around the country. The new staff will need to be shown around all of the new locations, and will have to be informed of local requirements for their services. This takes time and adds to the burdens of staff who no doubt already have a full workload.

Mitigating the risk and the cost

3.13 Naturally, the buyer must work hard to minimise the adverse consequences of a change in supplier. The emphasis should be on advance planning, which can help to avoid most of the risks. This should have begun when the previous supplier was selected — it is common for buyers to include a clause requiring the supplier to share the costs of transition to a new supplier in the event of contract termination.

3.14 Buyers will normally be aware that contracts are up for renewal well in advance. Systems for flagging this and alerting the buyer should be routine. Once the upcoming renewal date is highlighted, buyers can discuss options with other stakeholders — either deciding to renew with the existing supplier, or to seek a new supplier.

3.15 If the decision is not to undertake a straightforward renewal, the next step will be to identify the risks and costs of switching. To the greatest extent possible, the buyer will wish to impose these upon the new supplier. However, if part or all of the costs must be borne in-house, then this must be budgeted for appropriately.

3.16 Where costs are shared with the supplier, it is important to be clear (in the contract) as to who owns any assets involved in the contract. For example, if the supplier incurs initial tooling costs and charges us for a part of the cost, we need to know whether the tools eventually belong to us or to the supplier.

3.17 Where the new supplier bears the costs of switching, he is likely to make allowance for this in his quoted prices. The buyer must be aware of this, and must ensure that he is not, in effect, paying these costs repeatedly over the course of the contract. It is also prudent to budget a certain amount for unexpected contingencies. Even the most careful planning may fail to unearth every possible cost, and a contingency allowance is a sensible way of catering for this.

3.18 So much for costs. In relation to risks, too, it is possible to place some of the burden on the supplier. For example, in addition to the key performance indicators included in the main body of the contract, there could be separate KPIs relating to the specific risks of the transition period.

Communication and stakeholder management

3.19 A switch in supplier can be a major upheaval in the buyer organisation. It makes sense to communicate carefully with the various stakeholders involved. These will obviously include relevant personnel in the purchasing team, but will also include user departments whose activities are affected by the change.

3.20 Communication should take place at all stages, beginning with the decision on whether a switch is appropriate. User departments can have a major contribution here: they are the ones who suffer from any unsatisfactory performance by the current supplier.

3.21 Once the decision is taken to switch suppliers, relevant stakeholders should be updated as to the implications for themselves. At this stage the stakeholders include the outgoing supplier. Clearly, it is necessary to work closely with both old and new supplier to ensure a smooth transition. And user departments must be informed in detail of the operational changes that they should expect as a result of the change.

4 Evaluating suppliers for strategic capability

Strategic relationships

4.1 In Chapter 1 we looked at strategic relations with suppliers as one end of a relationship spectrum. In the present context – supplier selection – the choice of a strategic partner presents issues in addition to those we have already explored in this chapter.

4.2 To begin with, the very term 'supplier selection' may be misleading. When considering a strategic relationship we are very often thinking of a supplier that has already been servicing our needs for some time. We are not so much selecting a new supplier, as developing closer links with an existing one.

4.3 However, there will be cases where we are considering a strategic relationship and there is no existing supplier. We then need to think carefully about the selection process.

- First, we must decide whether we wish to buy in the item or service required. If we decide to produce in-house, the issue of supplier selection disappears.
- Assuming we decide to buy in, we must next consider the type of relationship we seek and the skills and competencies our future partner must bring to the table.
- The next step is to identify possible partners by appropriate means of research. This could involve scanning the market, identifying possible suppliers, and pre-testing each possibility by reference to publicly available information (such as their accounts).
- We then need to approach the possible partners, either by means of a tendering exercise, or by direct approach to senior management within the supplier organisations. (Tendering would normally be mandatory in the public sector.)
- Having entered into dialogue with a number of possible partners (or possibly with just one – there may be only one realistic prospect) we must then evaluate their capabilities and determine whether we have a match.

Analysing the competencies of a prospective partner

4.4 Entering into a strategic relationship is a big step. The issues we examine are necessarily more extensive than in the case of a more tactical relationship. We could consider any or all of the following points.

- The nature of the supplier's products and services. Are they exactly of the kind we are trying to source? Or, in the case of a possible strategic alliance, are they complementary to our own products and services?
- The position of the supplier and product(s) in the market management matrix (see Chapter 2). Is this a match with what we are looking for?
- The managerial resource within the business. Is there strong management with a clear sense of strategic direction, and will they be able to envision and then implement a strategic relationship with our organisation?
- The skills and competencies available within the organisation's workforce. Will this be sufficient to carry out the relationship we have in mind?
- How are they regarded by other organisations in the sector, by the press, by customers, by the general public?
- The nature of their production processes. Have they invested sufficiently in automated processes? Are their systems sufficiently robust to ensure that we will get what we seek from them?

The risks of strategic relationships

4.5　Earlier in this chapter we examined the risks involved in switching a supplier. In many respects the risks are even greater when we are embarking on a new strategic relationship, and this may even be so if we continue to deal with the same supplier. The very fact that we are deepening the relationship exposes us to greater dangers. Our dependence on the supplier becomes greater, and the consequences to us if the relationship fails are more serious.

4.6　This could happen, for example, if our partner runs into financial difficulties. Or, at the other extreme, it could happen if our partner becomes extremely successful, to a point where our business is no longer sufficiently important to him to justify a close relationship. There could be other reasons: perhaps our partner may see benefits in linking with a third party, incompatible with the relationship already in place with us; or they may be taken over by a new organisation who view our business in a different light.

4.7　All of these possibilities are in some sense 'internal': they relate to our organisation, or to our partner organisation, or to the links between them. There are other 'external' reasons why things may go wrong. For example, our competitors may make such an impression in the market that our own business suffers. Or economic and market changes may make our offerings less attractive to customers.

4.8　For all these reasons, the risk management techniques outlined earlier are equally applicable when a strategic relationship is contemplated.

Chapter summary

- In a private sector firm the prime objective is to maximise profits. In the public sector it is not possible to identify a single organisational objective. Table 7.1 lists many other differences between the two sectors.

- The regime of compulsory competitive tendering in the public sector militates against modern notions of long-term partnership relations. This regime is embodied in European procurement directives.

- The EU directives permit a choice among four different contract award procedures: open, restricted, negotiated, and competitive dialogue.

- Reciprocal trading means the practice of buying from an organisation simply because that organisation is also a customer. This can lead to serious difficulties for buyers, who may be under pressure to make sourcing decisions for the wrong reasons.

- There are risks in changing a supply source. The new supplier may fail to perform, or it may prove impossible to build satisfactory personal relationships, or the buyer's systems may prove to be incompatible with the supplier's.

- There are also costs involved in changing a supply source: researching the supply market, initiating a tendering exercise, transitional costs, and costs of familiarising the new supplier.

- To evaluate potential suppliers for strategic capability we need a structured selection process. This is especially the case in view of the potentially serious consequences of supply failure.

Self-test questions

1   List areas of difference between purchasing in the public and private sectors. (Table 7.1)

2   Why do such differences not necessarily lead to different purchasing practices? (1.7–1.13)

3   What is the main requirement of the EU procurement directives? (1.22)

4   Why, in the context of public sector tendering, might the negotiated procedure without publication be used? (1.29)

5   What is a dynamic purchasing system? (1.43)

6   What is the competitive dialogue procedure? (1.50)

7   What is reciprocal trading? (2.3, 2.6)

8   According to Malcolm Saunders, what three questions should be answered in analysing an opportunity for reciprocal trading? (2.13)

9   What are the main risks for the buyer when contemplating a change in supplier? (3.1ff)

10   How can a buyer mitigate the risks and costs of changing a supplier? (3.13ff)

11   What factors might a buyer consider before entering into a strategic relationship? (4.4)

CHAPTER 8

The Process of Outsourcing

Learning objectives

3.1 Develop and apply procedures for undertaking an outsourcing exercise and maintaining effective outsourced relationships.

- The definition of and difference between service contracts, subcontracting, outsourcing and in-sourcing.
- The outsourcing decision-making process
- The outsourcing process
- Legal implications of outsourcing

Chapter headings

1 Defining the terms

2 The outsourcing decision-making process

3 The outsourcing process

4 Legal implications of outsourcing

Introduction

In the search for lean operations, many organisations in recent years have attempted to outsource non-core activities. This has important effects on the nature of relationships with suppliers and is the subject of Section 3 of your exam syllabus. We study this topic in this and the following chapter.

1 Defining the terms

Service contracts, subcontracting, outsourcing and insourcing

1.1 Your syllabus requires you to be able to define and differentiate between the above terms: see Table 8.1.

1.2 Although there is nothing inherent in the term 'outsourcing' to refer to the purchase of services, it is normally used in the service context. The problems of buying services have become increasingly important for purchasing professionals as the general expenditure on services throughout the economy has risen.

Table 8.1 *Terminology relating to outsourcing*

Definition	Explanation
A **service contract** is a supply contract concerned with provision of a service rather than a tangible product.	This is the simplest case. The buyer wishes to purchase a service, eg a consultancy assignment, and enters into a contract with a selected supplier.
Subcontracting is the use of an outside organisation to do work that we cannot do ourselves because of a temporary shortage of resources.	Company A contracts Company B (the main contractor) to perform certain work. Company B could do all the work itself, but has too much work on at present. To meet Company A's deadline, B subcontracts some of the work to C.
Outsourcing is the delegation of work previously carried out in-house to an external service provider.	The outsourcer will draw up a contract, typically for the long term, specifying the work to be done, the service levels to be achieved etc. The outsourcer retains responsibility for satisfactory completion of the work, but delegates day-to-day operations to the outsource provider.
Insourcing is the opposite of outsourcing.	The organisation previously outsourced the work, but now decides to bring it in-house.

1.3   This presents buyers with problems additional to those that arise in purchasing manufactured goods.

- Manufactured goods are tangible: they can be inspected and tested before purchase. Services are intangible.

- Goods emerging from a manufacturing process almost certainly have a high degree of uniformity which simplifies their evaluation. Every separate instance of service provision is unique and may or may not be equivalent to previous instances.

- The exact purpose for which a manufactured good is used will usually be known and its suitability can therefore be assessed objectively. It is harder to assess the many factors comprised in provision of a service: for example, what weight should be placed on the friendliness or smart appearance of the supplier's staff, compared with their basic efficiency in doing the job?

- A manufactured good is usually purchased for immediate use in some well defined way, such as incorporation in a larger product or onward sale. A service may be purchased for a long period, during which requirements may change subtly from the original specification.

- When purchasing a manufactured good a buyer can usually identify a number of suppliers offering products with essentially similar features (including price). Services are different: the offering from one supplier will inevitably differ from those of other suppliers in a whole range of mostly intangible ways.

The nature of outsourcing

1.4   Outsourcing is the ultimate expression of a buyer's attitude to a supplier as an extension of in-house resources. Facilities or functions that were produced in-house are instead performed by external contractors working very closely with the buying organisation.

1.5   In many cases the same personnel carry out the outsourced tasks, only instead of being employed by the buyer they work for the contractor. There are instances where the original staff remain *in situ*, and even work on the same equipment; the only difference is in the status of the staff (they now work for the contractor, not for the buyer) and the ownership of the equipment (transferred from buyer to contractor).

1.6   Outsourcing has been used in respect of many different functions. Organisations have contracted with external suppliers to provide cleaning or catering services previously performed by internal staff; banks have outsourced their information systems development to specialist external consultancies; major international businesses have outsourced their accounting and tax planning functions to firms of chartered accountants.

1.7   Gary J Zenz has a useful analysis of the steps that managers should take to make a success of outsourcing.

- Managers should establish a strategy for the proper balancing of management, contracting and consulting.
- Managers should establish a strategy to deal with possible reductions in staff.
- Managers should closely integrate the external suppliers.
- Managers should provide appropriate communication channels.

1.8   Zenz also identifies the questionable assumptions that sometimes underlie the decision to outsource.

- The assumption that strategy primarily involves competitive position in the market place. (The decision to outsource is often taken so as to concentrate on core areas where a competitive advantage is present. But this assumes that no other factors are relevant to shaping strategy.)
- The assumption that brand share is defensible without manufacturing share. (In other words, it is questionable whether producers can continue to reap full value from brands if they no longer take the full responsibility in manufacturing.)
- The assumption that design and manufacturing are separable. (The questionable assumption here concerns the feasibility of simply designing a product and handing it over to someone else to manufacture. In truth, production staff should have an input to the design process.)
- Market knowledge is separable from manufacturing.

1.9   'The problem with outsourcing is that while a series of incremental outsourcing decisions, taken individually, make economic sense, collectively they represent the surrender of the business's competitive advantage.' (Zenz)

2   *The outsourcing decision making process*

Strategic objectives of the organisation

2.1   Organisations have been understandably reluctant to outsource activities that they regard as core, ie activities that embody their key competencies and that confer competitive advantage. Any other activities have been regarded as possible candidates for outsourcing. Clearly the decision to outsource an activity can only be taken after a strategic assessment of what activities are core and non-core.

2.2 Once the candidates for outsourcing have been identified, the organisation must consider various criteria by which the decision can be evaluated. These will include both value for money and operational factors.

Value for money

2.3 Clearly a major reason for outsourcing is the possibility that it will be cheaper to buy the services than to provide them in-house. This is not necessarily an easy matter to establish, and assessing value for money in outsourced services is a delicate process.

2.4 The first step is to learn as much as the supplier is willing to disclose of his cost and profit structure. This will facilitate comparison with alternatives.

2.5 The overall cost of the service would obviously be compared with prices offered by alternative suppliers, and possibly with the costs of in-house operation if these are known. (They may not be if it is a new type of service that is being bought.)

2.6 More crucially, the effectiveness of the supplier must be evaluated by a comparison of actual outputs achieved with the original objectives specified. This of course implies that the buying organisation starts with a clear idea of what it needs and what it expects to get. The involvement of purchasing professionals in the early stages can be of great assistance.

2.7 It may not be completely obvious why a third party should be able to carry out the same service more cheaply than can be achieved in-house. However, it is possible that the supplier benefits from economies of scale in the particular activity we are outsourcing. Or they may benefit from greater productivity and efficiency arising from the volume of transactions they handle and the specialist experience they possess.

2.8 Apart from actual cost savings, the organisation can achieve a leaner balance sheet by divesting itself of assets that would otherwise be required in-house. This can have a favourable impact on the financial stability of the company, and in particular on its return on assets ratio.

Operational reasons for outsourcing

2.9 Costs are always an important issue, but there are other reasons why organisations may wish to outsource. For example, the outsourcer may be unable to keep up with the pace of technological change in a particular activity. Attempting to do so would divert management attention from the more important tasks of running the business effectively. This is a reason why many companies have outsourced their IT applications.

2.10 Another reason may be that we are simply not very good at the activity in question. Rather than attempting to improve our performance in an area that is not core to our business, it may be preferable to use the expert services of an organisation specialising in that activity.

3   *The outsourcing process*

Selecting areas to outsource

3.1   As we have already seen, organisations will only wish to outsource an activity if it is not core to their business. Among the non-core activities it is then important to identify likely candidates for outsourcing. Some typical areas have been discussed above, but considerations will differ from one organisation to another.

3.2   One tool that can be used in this context is the supply positioning model outlined in Chapter 2. Another relevant consideration is the extent of problems currently being experienced in the activities concerned. It is a mistake to outsource in the hope that an external supplier can fix problems that have defeated our own management. The better route is to ensure that things are working smoothly before handing over to the outsource provider.

Specification of the requirement

3.3   The above problems make it all the more important to observe traditional purchasing disciplines in order to achieve a satisfactory result. A few of the particular points that buyers should watch out for are spelled out below.

3.4   Firstly, the more work that can be done at the pre-contract stage the better. This means agreeing service levels, schedules, and the basis for charges in as much detail as possible before the final agreement is signed. Often, the difficulties which arise subsequently turn out to stem from different expectations held by buyer and supplier.

3.5   This point is particularly vital if the decision relates to outsourcing a function currently performed by in-house staff. The point is that once the decision to outsource is taken the buyer will typically close down its own internal service provision, disposing of equipment, making staff redundant, using office space for alternative purposes. Once this has been done, the supplier is in an extremely strong position and he must not have the opportunity at that stage to renegotiate on the basis that the original agreement embodied misunderstandings.

3.6   One possible precaution in this respect is to insist that the external contractor should 'audit' the service currently being carried out. His quotation must then be on the basis of providing at least an equal level of service in future. In the event of dispute as to what is included in this, it should be easy for the buyer to demonstrate that such and such a task was always carried out in the past and is therefore part of the contract.

3.7   Another basic point to look out for is the tendency for services to be bought without professional purchasing involvement. Often a user department will commission a consultancy assignment, or a finance officer will organise vehicle leasing. Too often, the role of purchasing is perceived too narrowly as being concerned with the purchase of manufacturing materials, and this perception should be opposed.

3.8 This concern leads on to an important point about the specification of the service. As suggested above, the drafting of the specification is a difficult but highly important task, in which it is essential to involve purchasing staff. However, it is equally important to involve user departments. For one thing, they are ideally placed to help determine the level of service required; for another, it is important for behavioural reasons to win the commitment of user departments. This is more likely to be achieved if they have participated in the project.

3.9 Supplier management is an important ingredient in successful service buying. Often the level of service agreed upon is expressed in terms which are difficult to measure (it is not like purchasing steel rods which definitely are, or definitely are not, of the diameter specified). It is vital that from the earliest stages the supplier is made aware of what the buyer regards as satisfactory performance, and what is unsatisfactory.

3.10 Certain legal and technical considerations must also be addressed. One example concerns staff employed by the contractor but working on the buyer's premises. Indemnity insurance may be appropriate. Another point is the issue of confidentiality. The contractor may by the nature of his work, or in the course of the negotiations, gain access to information which is commercially sensitive. It must be made clear very early that confidentiality is essential, and the contractor should usually be made to sign a confirmation that this will be observed.

Service level agreements

3.11 A crucial element in the success of external service provision is to reach clear agreement on the level of service to be provided. For example, suppose a company decides to hire external contractors to provide office cleaning services. Among the many points to discuss the following basic service level issues should be considered.

- How often is the service to be provided?
- During what hours will the service be carried out, and in particular will there be any disruption to office activities?
- How many staff (and, if relevant, what grades of staff) will be involved in providing the service?
- How far will the service extend (eg does it include cleaning of computer monitors, telephone equipment etc)?
- Does the service include special tasks caused by fault of the buyer's own staff (eg spillages)?
- What qualifications are needed by the staff members providing the service?
- What speed of response is expected from the supplier when the customer makes a request?
- What dispute procedures will be required?

3.12 Speed of response is a major consideration in many types of service provision. This must be carefully considered and agreed when service levels are discussed. It is easy for the purchasing organisation to complain that the service provider is not reacting quickly enough, but the supplier may retort that constant calls for 'urgent' attention suggest lack of forward planning by the purchaser. To avoid this kind of argument both sides must accept a responsibility for planning and communication, as well as agreeing the extent to which the supplier will be required to respond within a particular timescale.

3.13 The buyer needs to investigate the supplier's plans with some care. For example, he should enquire about the rates that the supplier intends to pay his staff. If these appear to be below average there is a potential impact on the quality of service likely to be delivered. This is particularly the case when the service is high on labour content.

3.14 Where services are currently being provided by in-house staff it is important to determine whether existing service levels are adequate. If they are not, it is not sufficient to require a similar level of service from the new supplier. Instead, defined improvements to the current level of service must be agreed in advance.

3.15 We have emphasised the importance of a professional purchasing input in this kind of decision. However, it is equally vital to ensure the full cooperation of user departments. They are uniquely well placed to determine the level of service that should be required. In addition, their support will be essential when the service goes live; they are unlikely to be supportive if they have not been consulted.

Quality assurance in services

3.16 By far the most important measure for assuring quality in service provision is the initial specification. Without detailed agreement on what is required it is most unlikely that the purchaser will be satisfied with what is eventually provided. However, even after the most thorough advance preparation it is not safe to assume that responsibility can simply be handed over entirely to the service provider. On the contrary, the purchasing organisation must closely monitor the delivery of the service.

3.17 Once again, the role of the user department is vital. They are best able to determine whether their needs are being met, and if not whether this arises from fault of the supplier or inadequate specification.

3.18 An important aid to assuring quality is the establishment of collaborative relationships. The supplier must be made to feel some 'ownership' in the service being provided, and to sense some loyalty between his own organisation and that of his customer.

3.19 Before entering into this kind of collaborative relationship it is up to the buyer to pursue traditional purchasing disciplines in his selection of the supplier. For example, he must be sure that the supplier is not of the type to fall into a common temptation in these situations: that of 'buying' the business by means of a low quote, with the intention of raising prices sharply once the buyer has become dependent.

3.20 The financial security of the supplier is also important. Remember that if a purchaser abandons internal provision of a service it is hard to re-establish it. To find at this stage that your supplier is in danger of insolvency is very bad news indeed.

3.21 A feature of this kind of agreement is that requirements change over time. Sometimes this results from external pressures; for example, new legislation on health and safety might mean that certain activities are more costly than expected. In other cases the needs of the user department simply evolve over time. In either case, buyers must be aware both of the cost implications and of the need to ensure that service provision is adjusted in the way required.

Service quality gaps

3.22 Note the concept of service quality gaps, ie the differences in perception that may arise between supplier and buyer. Four categories of 'gap' are identified.

- Consumer expectations, ie the gap between what consumers actually expect and what managers perceive that they expect

- Managers' perceptions of consumers' expectations, ie the gap between what consumers actually want and what managers lay down in service quality specifications

- Service quality specifications – the gap between what is delivered and what is specified

- Actual service delivery, ie the external communications gap between provider and customer.

Supplier selection

3.23 The next stage in the process is to select suppliers. An outsource contract is typically substantial in nature and for the long term, which means that purchasing disciplines are particularly important. Refer back to Chapter 7 for detailed discussion of the issues involved.

4 *Legal implications of outsourcing*

Introduction

4.1 An outsourcing organisation often has to make staff redundant, although sometimes they are transferred to the outsource provider. Both redundancy and transfer have legal implications.

4.2 The legislation in force at the time of writing (August 2006) is the Transfer of Undertakings (Protection of Employment) Regulations 2006. This is a complex area of the law, and you will only be expected to have a basic understanding of the key principles involved and how they impact on contracts for service provision. For this reason, we cover the basic principles set down in the 1981 Regulations, and then discuss the significant changes introduced by the new 2006 Regulations.

Transfer of undertakings

4.3 The Regulations apply to situations where an undertaking has a change of owner. This situation must mean that the staff are also transferred. The relevant issue here is that the staff will have their contracts of employment or service transferred to the new owner of the undertaking. The effect of this transfer under the Regulations is that the new owner of the undertaking must honour the existing terms and conditions of the workers' contracts. This will mean, in effect, that the workers will serve their new employer on the terms and conditions of employment that they enjoyed with their previous employer. In other words, the workers will have continuity of service.

4.4 Problems may arise in these situations where employees are made redundant and they are hired by the new owner of the undertaking under new terms of employment. We shall look at redundancy later.

4.5 It is essential to appreciate that the TUPE Regulations do not just apply to employees. They apply to workers generally – a much broader legal term. Potentially, casual workers could also be covered by the Regulations.

4.6 Transfer of undertakings can be fraught with problems. This is because they can potentially involve redundancy situations.

4.7 One of the first things to consider is whether the transfer falls into the category of a 'relevant transfer'. A 'relevant transfer' will involve situations where the ownership of the undertaking changes (eg where the undertaking is sold or is the subject of a merger transaction). If in doubt as to whether the Regulations apply to a given situation, the transferor (seller) should, to be on the safe side, assume that they do. The ambiguities are well illustrated by the case of **Süzen v Zehnacker Gebäudereinigung** (1997). In this case, a school cleaning contract was awarded to a new external contractor, having previously been held by a different external contractor. This was held to be the transfer of an activity only, not an undertaking, which meant that the employees were not protected.

4.8 The transferor (seller) has to initiate a consultation process with the affected workers. This consultation process should address the time of the transfer, reasons for the transfer and how it will be implemented. The process will involve the input of 'appropriate representatives' of the workers who, in the main, will be trade union officials, employee representatives or the workers themselves.

4.9 These consultations should take place ideally 28 days before the exchange of contracts, ie the acquisition of the undertaking or its disposal. There is, however, no statutory period for consultation.

4.10 Failure to consult affected employees or workers may mean that the seller could be liable to pay these individuals up to 13 weeks pay. The employee or worker does not have to demonstrate financial loss.

4.11 Special care should be taken to ensure that all employees or workers are consulted. This includes workers on maternity leave, sick leave and secondment. Failure to consult in such situations may invite liability under the Sex Discrimination Act 1975 and the Disability Discrimination Act 1995.

4.12 Dismissals connected with the transfer can be justified only on economic, technical or organisational (ETO) grounds. If a dismissal cannot be justified on these grounds then it may be potentially unfair, leading to a damaging and costly claim for unfair dismissal. At all times, however, the transferor must ensure that it has acted fairly in relation to the dismissal. Any such dismissal should be accompanied by a compromise agreement. If a dismissal on ETO grounds immediately precedes the transfer of undertaking, any liability remains with the transferor: this is the rule in **Secretary of State v Spence** (1986).

4.13 The transferor should draw up a schedule of all employees or workers affected by the transfer. This will give the transferee (new owner) valuable information concerning the various contractual rights of employees and workers. This will include any collective agreements which the employees or workers are party to. The transferor should write to each affected employee detailing the time of the transfer, the identity of the new employer and issues to do with continuity of employment.

4.14 Provision of information to the transferee will have to take into account issues raised by the Data Protection Act 1998 or the Human Rights Act 1998. It is essential to obtain the consent of the individuals affected by any exchange of information between the transferor and transferee.

4.15 Employees or workers have the right to object to the transfer in writing.

The 2006 regulations

4.16 The scope of the Transfer of Undertakings (Protection of Employment) Regulations 2006 is wider than that of its predecessor. Both outsourcing and insourcing will be covered by the new legislation. These situations are described as 'service provision changes' and examples include contracts that provide services such as office cleaning, catering and security. The Regulations provide for an exception where the service provision is on a one-off basis of short-term duration.

4.17 There is a new duty for the transferor employer to provide information to the transferee (preferably in writing) about the transferring employees before the relevant transfer takes place. This includes the following details.

- The identity and age of all the employees who will transfer; the information contained in their 'statements of employment particulars'
- Details of any disciplinary action or grievances in the previous two years
- Details of actual or potential legal actions brought by the employees in the previous two years.

4.18 The requirement is for the above information to be provided 'at least two weeks before the completion of the transfer'. The transferee can make a complaint to an Employment Tribunal if the transferor fails to provide this information and the Tribunal may award compensation for any loss which the transferee has incurred as a result of the failure by the transferor. The level of compensation must be no less than £500 per employee unless it is unjust to award this default minimum payment.

4.19 The Regulations contain special provisions which make it easier for insolvent businesses to be transferred to new employers. For instance, the provisions provide that some of the transferor's pre-existing debts to employees do not pass to the transferee, such as statutory redundancy pay, arrears of pay, payment in lieu of notice and holiday pay.

4.20 The Regulations provide some freedom for the transferor or transferee to agree variations to contracts of employment before or after a transfer where the sole or principal reason for the variation is a reason unconnected with the transfer (eg the unexpected loss of a large order), or a reason connected with the transfer which is an 'economic, technical or organisational (ETO) reason entailing changes in the workforce'.

4.21 The Regulations also clarify the circumstances where it is unfair for employers to dismiss employees for reasons connected with the transfer. Neither the transferor nor the transferee may fairly dismiss an employee because of the transfer itself or for a reason connected with the transfer, unless that reason is an ETO reason enabling changes in the workforce. If there is no such reason then the dismissal will be automatically unfair. If there is an ETO reason and it is the main cause of the dismissal, the dismissal will be fair if an Employment Tribunal decides that the employer acted reasonably in the circumstances in treating the reason as sufficient to justify dismissal and the employer met the other requirements of the law on unfair dismissal.

Chapter summary

- Outsourcing is the delegation of work previously carried out in-house to an external service provider. You need to be able to distinguish this from a service contract, subcontracting and insourcing.

- The term 'outsourcing' is normally used in the service context, but there is nothing inherent in the term to refer to the purchase of intangible services – it is quite possible to outsource part of a manufacturing process.

- It is normal for organisations to outsource only those operations that are not core to their main activities.

- Reasons for wanting to outsource include better value for money, and operational reasons such as a need to keep up with technological change.

- Advance planning and a detailed specification are essential elements in successful outsourcing.

- An outsource contract should contain detailed service level agreements by which the supplier's performance may be measured.

- Both user departments and professional buyers have important roles to play in successful outsourcing.

- Outsourcing gives rise to complex legal issues, mostly embodied in the TUPE Regulations. The key principle is that staff transferred to the outsource provider will retain the contractual rights that they used to have by virtue of their contracts with the outsourcer.

Self-test questions

1   Define subcontracting and differentiate it from outsourcing. (Table 8.1)

2   List characteristics that distinguish services from tangible products. (1.3)

3   Describe the 'questionable assumptions' which Zenz believes may sometimes underlie the decision to outsource. (1.8)

4   Why may it be possible for a third party to carry out an activity more cheaply than it can be done in-house? (2.7)

5   Why should an external contractor be asked to audit the activity under consideration for outsourcing? (3.6)

6   Why should user departments be involved in the outsource decision? (3.8, 3.17)

7   List the basic service level issues that might be considered in outsourcing office cleaning services. (3.11)

8   Describe what is meant by service quality gaps. (3.22)

9   Outline the basic principle of the TUPE Regulations. (4.3)

10   What is meant by a 'relevant transfer' under TUPE? (4.7)

CHAPTER 9

Managing an Outsource Contract

Learning objectives

3.2   Explain how performance should be managed in outsourcing exercises.

- Managing the outsourcing contract
- Establishing and implementing performance measures
- Monitoring performance measures
- Understanding why some organisations are in-sourcing

3.3   Evaluate the impact of outsourcing on relationships between customers and providers.

- Outsourcing relationships and the relationship spectrum
- Outsourcing relationships and partnerships
- How to manage change in an outsourced relationship

Chapter headings

1   Which areas may be outsourced?

2   Performance measurement

3   The impact on supplier relations

Introduction

In the previous chapter we examined the process by which an organisation decides on and then awards an outsourcing contract. In this chapter we look in more detail at the operational consequences that ensue.

1   Which areas may be outsourced?

Matrix analysis

1.1   A CIPS examiner has suggested a helpful matrix for determining whether an activity should be outsourced. This is based on analysis of two factors.

- The extent to which the activity is core to the organisation's main functions
- The competence of contractors available to carry out the outsourced activity

1.2   This analysis leads to the following matrix (first developed by Ray Carter).

Figure 9.1 *Outsourcing matrix*

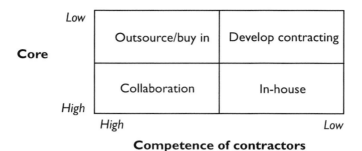

Competence of contractors

1.3 The conclusion from this is that an activity is a candidate for outsourcing if it is not core to the organisation's main functions, and if there are competent contractors able to carry out the activity. In this section of the chapter we look at a number of areas that are frequently outsourced.

Third-party logistics and distribution services

1.4 An important strand in modern management thinking is the need to concentrate on core activities in order to secure competitive advantage. The consequence of this philosophy is that more use is made of external suppliers for activities previously provided in-house.

1.5 Most manufacturers regard logistics as a support function rather than as a core activity. Even those who still maintain an 'own-account' operation are willing to make use of contractors to a greater or lesser extent.

1.6 The potential benefits that may be realised by manufacturers include the following.

- Contracting out frees up resources – above all, financial capital and management time – which can more profitably be devoted to core activities.

- Logistics specialists are well placed to recognise and respond to rising customer expectations. This would be a serious management burden if distribution remained in-house.

- Contracting out gives greater flexibility in times of difficulty. Firms with their own operation may suffer if employees go on strike, or if demand is very variable during the year. Access to outside specialists enables these risks to be spread.

- Buying firms gain access to specialist expertise which may enable them to develop improved distribution systems, offering better service than customers would otherwise have received.

1.7 All of these benefits presuppose that the external contracting is conducted on the basis of long-term relationships with a small number of suppliers. For example, any saving in management time would quickly be dissipated if negotiations with new suppliers, and the process of familiarisation, were ongoing; ideally, this should be a one-off exercise.

1.8 Despite the benefits outlined above, not all manufacturers are willing to outsource the logistics function. Several reasons may be suggested for this.

- Most fundamentally, a firm may be concerned that outside contractors will not give the required level of service. There has been some justification for such a view in the historical development of specialist logistics suppliers. Nowadays, however, the range of services offered has increased, standards are high, and advances in information technology have enabled buying firms to monitor the service provided very closely.

- A firm may fear that a large number of separate outside contractors – for storage, materials handling, haulage etc – would complicate matters. This too has been a justified worry in the past, but can now be overcome by making use of one of the various contractors that offer an integrated service covering all logistics areas.

- Finally, reluctance may stem from a general policy of wishing to retain control. Handing over major functional areas lock, stock and barrel to external suppliers runs counter to this natural instinct. Again, the solution lies within the varied offerings available from logistics providers. These range from management-only contracts (in which the buyer retains ownership of logistics assets, but contracts out their management), through various forms of joint venture, to full system takeover by the outside specialist.

Outsourcing information systems

1.9   An area where outsourcing has become particularly prevalent in recent years is that of information systems (IS). Many organisations have handed over their data processing functions, and in some cases their systems development functions as well, to external specialists.

1.10   The technical complexity of this area makes it an attractive candidate for outsourcing. The cost of maintaining IS expertise in house is high. But in some cases the move to outsourcing has been made for the wrong reasons. In particular, some organisations despaired of solving the so-called 'millennium bug' – the problem of computer systems that might have failed when the year 99 gave way to the year 00.

1.11   Outsourcing consultants are unanimous in condemning this approach. As with all outsourcing, the objective should be to draw on specialist expertise, not to abandon all responsibility for the outsourced activity. A consultant quoted in a 1998 issue of *Supply Management* summed it up as follows: 'The management that wants to outsource problems in order to get rid of them is a disaster waiting to happen. You've got to solve the problems first before you outsource'.

1.12   Even assuming that management are outsourcing for the right reasons, it remains difficult to measure the success of the project. The main problem is in defining the level of service. It is highly unlikely that one outsourcing supplier will offer exactly the same level of service as another, which means that the costs they quote are not strictly comparable. At the level of detail, what one supplier is offering to do will differ from the other's offering.

1.13   In practice this will lead to serious problems of evaluation, but once again it is clear that a proactive purchasing function has an important role to play. Essentially, the problem is one of specification: the buyer must know in advance, and in detail, exactly what he requires the supplier to provide. In the light of a detailed specification it will be much easier to monitor performance and to assess value for money.

Outsourcing facilities management

1.14   We have looked above at some specific services that may be outsourced, such as logistics services or IT services. A more radical approach to this general issue goes by the name of facilities management. Under this kind of agreement a specialist facilities management company is contracted to run services such as buildings maintenance, catering, heating and lighting, security and waste disposal.

1.15   At its extreme this approach is summed up in the words of a car manufacturer wishing to open an overseas manufacturing facility. 'Provide everything I need in support services: that's what I pay you for. All I want to do is make cars.' In a case like this the facilities management company will take on a very wide range of responsibilities, and the manufacturer must be certain that service provision will be up to the appropriate standard and at the right cost.

1.16   Experts in the field believe that the impulse towards outsourcing comes not from cost considerations (though of course value for money is important), but from a wish for greater efficiency. Buyers want to tap in to specialist expertise so as to increase the quality of service.

1.17   Another stimulus to this kind of agreement has undoubtedly been a desire to share risks. Buyers have sometimes welcomed the idea that if things go wrong it is an outside contractor that is to blame. While this may be regarded as a somewhat negative attitude – it would be better to concentrate on ensuring that things **don't** go wrong – it does highlight the fact that there are indeed serious risks in the services underpinning a company's operations.

1.18   Some of these risks were amusingly summarised in a 'nightmare' facilities management contract devised by a firm of solicitors specialising in the field. In their fictional example a company suffered the following series of disasters.

   •   Staff walked out after failing to receive their wages because of a technical problem with the payroll.

   •   Other staff left when the heating failed on an unexpectedly cold Autumn day.

   •   A subcontractor wiped out all the information on a customer database.

   •   Staff suffered food poisoning due to hygiene failures in the canteen.

1.19   The scale of these problems underlines the importance of quality assurance in all cases where services are outsourced.

2   *Performance measurement*

Stages in the outsource relationship

2.1   At all stages in the relationship, the buyer is concerned to ensure an appropriate level of performance from the supplier. It is helpful to consider how this concern is evidenced over the life of the relationship.

2.2   In the period leading up to award of contract, the buyer's objective is to agree terms that satisfactorily meet the objectives specified in the business case. He will focus on costs, service levels, and the minimisation of risk. Naturally, the supplier will be negotiating hard on all of these elements, and a satisfactory balance must be reached.

2.3 Once the contract has been awarded, the buyer will be concerned to ensure a smooth transition. Ideally, the supplier will immediately begin to perform to the levels of service specified in the contract, but it may be that 'teething problems' are experienced. If staff have transferred from the buying organisation to the supplier, the buyer will also be concerned about people issues: are the staff being treated according to the terms of the contract, which of course must reflect the provisions of TUPE?

2.4 With the transition phase over, it will be important to the buyer to see clear benefits arising. This is the justification of the entire exercise. Benefits may include reduced costs, improved service levels, and reduction in management effort within the buying organisation. To ensure that these objectives are being achieved, the buyer will need to focus on communication methods, such as reports and review meetings.

2.5 As the time approaches for renewal, the buyer should review the lessons learned at the time of initial contract award. If the relationship has not worked well, it may be necessary to consider a new supplier selection exercise. But if both sides have enjoyed benefits, a renewal of the contract may be appropriate. Even in this case, the buyer will want to incorporate changes arising from the experience gained over the life of the original contract. In particular, the buyer will want to discuss even further improvements in service levels and/or reductions in cost.

2.6 Clearly this cycle will repeat indefinitely. At all stages the buyer will be hoping to achieve continuous improvement in the supplier's performance, as measured by the service levels specified in the contract. At the same time, the supplier will legitimately be attempting to achieve economies of scale so as to make a fair profit for himself. If it appears that the benefits are not being shared with the buyer, this is a point to address at the time of contract renewal.

Costs involved in outsourcing

2.7 In the previous chapter we examined some of the benefits that a buyer will be looking to achieve by outsourcing. However, the buyer must also reckon on significant costs attached to the exercise. These are summarised in Table 9.1.

Table 9.1 *The costs involved in outsourcing*

Cost	Explanation
Preliminary costs	The costs of preparing and analysing the business case, the costs of identifying potential suppliers, the costs of the supplier selection process, the costs of agreeing terms and drawing up the contract
Contractual price	The actual sums payable to the supplier under the terms of the contract – hopefully, these will represent a reduction compared with current expenditure
Costs of getting it wrong	Costs arising if the supplier fails to perform
Costs of getting it right	Cost of all activities designed to ensure successful completion of the contract – changes to systems and processes, transitional difficulties, contract management costs, communication costs etc
Hidden costs	Costs of buying staff helping to implement the contract, costs of vagueness or ambiguity in the specification (leading to unexpected difficulties), costs of over-specifying etc.

Identifying suitable performance measures

2.8 To ensure that the supplier is performing to the required standard, it is important to identify suitable performance measures. Often these will be specified in the contract.

2.9 Needless to say, the measures chosen will depend very much on the details of the particular agreement. But in all cases they will include measures relating to cost and measures relating to service quality. Some measures will be 'hard', in the sense that they can be assessed objectively (eg the time taken to deal with a complaint or difficulty); others will be 'soft', in the sense that they are to some extent subjective. For example, the buyer will be concerned with the politeness of the supplier's staff, but this is not something that can easily be measured.

2.10 To define suitable performance measures, the buyer must focus on the key objectives of the outsource contract. Clearly, the measures chosen must be related to these so that they provide a good indication of how well the relationship is working. It is also important to keep the measurement process simple: a small number of easily understood indicators is preferable to a proliferation of complicated measures.

2.11 Communication is also important. The supplier must be aware of the measures regarded as important by the buyer. This is an important guideline for him in planning his work so as to satisfy the contractual requirements. He must accept that the measures are reasonable in the light of the contract. And communication is of course a two-way process: if the supplier is already performing similar services for other clients he may be able to suggest suitable performance measures from previous experience.

Why does it go wrong?

2.12 Numerous surveys, together with anecdotal evidence, suggest that outsourcing projects often fail to deliver the expected benefits. Some of the possible reasons for this are listed below.

- The organisation fails to distinguish correctly between core and non-core activities.

- The organisation fails to identify and select a suitable supplier, leading to poor performance of the outsourced activity, or in the worst cases to supplier failure.

- The outsourcing contract contains inadequate or inappropriate terms and conditions.

- The contract does not contain well defined key performance indicators or service levels, which means that it is difficult to establish where things are going wrong.

- The organisation gradually surrenders control of performance to the contractor.

Much of this can be avoided if the outsourcing exercise is carefully planned within a defined strategic framework.

2.13 These reasons, along with others, lead to the phenomenon of **insourcing**. As we defined in the previous chapter, this is the opposite of outsourcing, and involves an organisation taking work in-house, having previously outsourced it.

2.14 An obvious reason why organisations might do this is that the outsource provider might not be doing a very good job. There may be problems with service quality, or the supplier may not be delivering the expected cost savings. In this case it will be appropriate to terminate the contract.

2.15 Even here, though, one might expect the organisation to find an alternative provider. Presumably the work will be insourced only if the organisation believes that no external organisation is able to perform satisfactorily and at an economic price. However, there are other possibilities. For example, the organisation may have re-thought its conclusions on what activities are core and non-core. If it now believes that the activity is core, it may take it in-house for general strategic reasons.

3 *The impact on supplier relations*

Implications of outsourcing for commercial relationships

3.1 Outsourcing has some implications for commercial relationships.

- The organisation now has a dependence on an external supplier where none existed before.

- The organisation needs to consider what type of relationship it should be developing with the supplier.

- Many individuals within the organisation might be slow to recognise the implications of the change, and continue to treat the outsourced service as something that 'belongs' to the organisation. This can lead to difficulties in the relationship.

- The newly-established supplier organisation might fail to recognise the importance of delivering a high-value service, and could take an opportunistic approach, offering an unsatisfactory service or charging an excessive price.

- To be long-lasting, there should be a 'performance-driven' partnership, where the customer and supplier develop a partnership rather than have a cosy relationship, and the supplier recognises the need to seek excellence in performance

- There is no reason why the organisation should continue to use the new supplier for its outsourced services. There is a possibility of putting the outsourced service to competitive tendering from a number of potential suppliers.

The place of outsourcing relationships within the relationship spectrum

3.2 An outsource contract is typically substantial in nature and for the long term. This means that in terms of the relationship spectrum (refer back to Fig 1.2) such relationships are positioned towards the strategic end. However, it would be a mistake to expect as much from an outsource supplier as from a partnership or co-destiny relationship. This is because, by definition, the service being supplied is non-core and therefore the relationship is likely to be more distant.

Changes in relationships

3.3   The typical situation is that an internal department – for example, the IT department – previously carried out work which has now been outsourced to an external provider. User departments are likely to experience a different relationship with the external provider. This is the case even when the supplier has taken over the staff and assets that previously used to belong internally. The very fact that the personnel are now 'outsiders' inevitably affects the relationship.

3.4   The main difference will be an increase in formality. Naturally, user departments should always behave with complete professionalism in their dealings with the IT department, but there is likely to be a degree of informality if the IT staff are 'internal'. Once the IT function is carried out by an external supplier, the need for formality increases, even with no change in actual personnel.

3.5   This has an obvious effect on prioritising of tasks. If the IT staff are internal, senior managers can simply instruct them to drop Task A and move on immediately to Task B, if Task B happens to have become important. Once the activity is outsourced, this is no longer an option. Managers must go through agreed processes and this forces an increased degree of forward planning (which of course is always desirable in any case).

3.6   Another consequence is an increase in the requirement to report. As an external supplier, the department will have to account closely for the time it has spent (and charged for). This may lead user departments to scrutinise the IT department's work more closely. There may be a feeling that trust has declined. This may equally lead to a reduction in the amount of information exchanged informally – while formal reports may have to include defined items of information, there will be less informal 'grapevine' exchanges.

3.7   To avoid the adverse consequences of these changes it is important for client and supplier to communicate closely in a spirit of cooperation.

Chapter summary

- When considering areas that might be outsourced, two relevant points are the extent to which the activity is core to the organisation's main functions, and the competence of contractors available to carry out the outsourced activity.

- Common areas chosen for outsourcing include logistics and distribution services, information systems, and facilities management (among many others).

- It is possible to identify stages in the life of an outsource relationship and to check supplier performance in the light of the stage the relationship has reached.

- There are many costs involved in an outsourcing exercise. Our classification breaks these down into preliminary costs, contractual price, costs of getting it wrong, costs of getting it right, and hidden costs.

- Suitable performance measures must be chosen in relation to both cost and service quality.

- Some outsourcing exercises fail to achieve the outsourcer's objectives. This leads to the phenomenon of insourcing: taking the service back in-house.

- An outsourcing relationship is invariably situated well towards the collaborative end of the relationship spectrum.

- Outsourcing an activity can lead to a greater formality in relationships with user departments.

Self-test questions

1   What are the two axes on the matrix for determining which areas are suitable for outsourcing? (Figure 9.1)

2   What benefits may be realised by an organisation that outsources its logistics and distribution services? (1.6)

3   Why are some manufacturers reluctant to outsource logistics? (1.8)

4   Explain how the buyer will monitor the outsource agreement over the different stages in the relationship lifecycle. (2.2ff)

5   List as many costs as you can connected with an outsourcing exercise. (Table 9.1)

6   Why do outsourcing projects often fail to deliver the expected benefits? (2.12)

7   List the implications for commercial relationships when an activity is outsourced. (3.1)

8   Explain how an increase in formality may arise in dealings with user departments after an activity is outsourced. (3.3ff)

CHAPTER 10

Conflict, Communication, Power and Dependency

Learning objectives

4.1 Identify the causes of conflict in supply relationships and select appropriate methods for their resolution.

- The positive and negative roles of conflict
- Conflict factors
- Conflict factors related to the types of relationships in the relationship spectrum
- Stakeholder management and conflict

4.2 Evaluate the impact of both power and dependency on the management of supplier relationships.

- Power versus dependency
- Relationship issues resulting from power and dependency
- Managing power and dependency

4.3 Analyse the role of transparent communications between purchasers and suppliers in the effective management of supply relationships.

- Stakeholder communication
- Communication tools and techniques in the context of supplier management
- Transparency: open-book costing

Chapter headings

1 Conflict in supply relationships

2 Communication in supply relationships

3 Power and dependency in supply relationships

Introduction

In this chapter we assume that a supply relationship is now up and running. We look at the various ways in which suppliers and buyers interact within the relationship.

1 Conflict in supply relationships

The positive and negative roles of conflict

1.1 The nature and effects of conflict have been frequently studied, mostly in the context of single organisations. However, the academic analysis of intra-organisational conflict can easily be adapted to provide insights into conflict between buyers and suppliers in different organisations.

1.2 Several **ideologies of conflict** have been identified. These include the happy family view, the conflict view, and the evolutionary view.

1.3 The '**happy family**' view of organisations assumes that organisations are cooperative structures, in which there are no systemic conflicts of interest, and harmonious environments, in which conflicts are unnatural and exceptional. Conflict is blamed on bad management, lack of leadership, poor communication or inflexibility on the part of individuals or interest groups: strong culture, good two-way communication, cooperative values and motivational leadership should be able to eliminate conflict. (This is also called a **unitary** perspective.)

1.4 The **conflict view**, on the other hand, assumes that organisations are arenas for conflict on individual and group levels. Conflict is inevitable, as members compete for limited resources, status and rewards, and pursue different goals and professional values. Individual and organisational interests will not always coincide. Conflict is embedded in managerial choices about organisational goals, technology and structures, and in organisational politics. However, a mutual survival strategy, involving the control of conflict through compromise, can be made acceptable in varying degrees to all concerned. (This is also referred to as a **pluralist** perspective.)

1.5 The **evolutionary view** regards conflict as a means of maintaining the *status quo*, as a useful basis for evolutionary change. Conflict keeps the organisation sensitive to the need to change, while at the same time preserving social and organisational arrangements through the balance of competing interests.

Constructive and destructive conflict

1.6 Conflict can be highly desirable. It can energise relationships and clarify issues. John Hunt suggests that conflict is constructive, when its effect is to:

- Introduce different solutions to problems
- Define power relationships more clearly
- Encourage creativity and the testing of ideas
- Focus attention on individual contributions
- Bring emotions out into the open
- Provide opportunity for catharsis: the release of hostile feelings that might otherwise be repressed

1.7 Conflict can also be destructive, negative and damaging to social systems. Hunt suggests that conflict of this kind may act to:

- Distract attention from the task
- Polarise views and 'dislocate' the parties concerned
- Subvert objectives in favour of secondary goals
- Encourage defensive or 'spoiling' behaviour
- Result in disintegration of the relationship
- Stimulate emotional, win-lose conflicts, or hostility

1.8 Charles Handy redefined the term 'conflict' to offer a useful way of thinking about destructive and constructive conflict. He suggested that **differences** between people are natural and inevitable, particularly in organisations, where there is competition for scarce resources and unequal influence.

1.9 Differences may emerge as **argument**: a way of resolving differences by discussion, encouraging the integration of a number of viewpoints into a better solution. As long as the logic of argument is preserved and the arguing individuals have mutual trust and shared goals, argument can be beneficial and fruitful.

1.10 Differences may also emerge as **competition**. If competition is perceived to be open (with the potential for a win-win outcome) and the 'rules' are seen to be fair, competition can be extremely fruitful: setting standards (establishing best performance through comparison) and motivating individuals to better efforts.

1.11 If constructive conditions for argument and competition are not present, they can degenerate into what Handy defines as conflict: a harmful form of difference.

1.12 Robbins suggests that a contemporary approach to conflict:

- Recognises the inevitability (even necessity) of conflict
- Explicitly encourages opposition and challenge to ideas and the *status quo*
- Defines conflict management to include stimulation as well as resolution of conflict
- Considers the management of conflict as a major responsibility of all managers

Causes of conflict in buyer-supplier relationships

1.13 The underlying causes of conflict in supply relationships are often classified as follows.

- Interdependence: linked goals, shared resources, integrated systems and long-term relationship objectives – leading to frustration when one party fails to fulfil expectations, or when personnel or cultural change bring incompatibility
- Differences: in goals, values, expectations or perceptions, leading to the potential for misunderstandings and clashes
- Authority imbalances: different degrees of power or influence in a relationship, leading to competition, political behaviour, coercive use of power or exploitation
- Ambiguity: of objectives, expectations, roles or motives, leading to mistrust, misunderstandings, disappointments and clashes

- Conflicts of interest: eg the buyer trying to secure the lowest possible price (or the supplier trying to secure the highest possible price), at the expense of the other party's profits. A variety of other conflicts of interest is possible, however. One party may want an exclusive supply or distribution contract, while the other wants to broaden its supply or distribution base to minimise risk. A buyer may want its suppliers to off-shore production to low-cost-labour countries such as China, while suppliers may not want to shoulder the risk and cost of doing this. And so on.

1.14 Adversarial/transactional relationships are perhaps most likely to be subject to differences, ambiguity, conflicts of interest and power/resource competition. Collaborative/partnership relationships are likely to face increasing interdependence issues. Internal stakeholder relationships are just as likely to suffer from these causes of conflict as supplier relationships.

1.15 In more practical terms, situations which could give rise to conflict in a buyer-supplier relationship include the following.

- Unclear specifications or contract terms, leading to contract or payment disputes
- An adversarial approach on the part of a buyer or supplier, especially where the other party wants to enter into partnership relations
- Breaches of trust or confidentiality
- Disputed or delayed payment of supplier invoices, especially if this is repeated
- Breach of contract or failure of the supplier in any of the 'five rights' criteria
- Unreasonable demands made by buyers on suppliers (eg failure to give sufficient time or information for contracts to be effectively satisfied)
- Parties having different desired relationship outcomes or long-term objectives, or incompatible cultures.

Managing and resolving conflict

1.16 There are many approaches to the management of conflict and the suitability of any given approach must be judged according to its relevance to a particular situation. There is no 'right way'. In some situations, the best outcome may be achieved by compromise; in others, imposition of a win-lose solution may be required; in others, the process of seeking a win-win solution, whatever the eventual outcome, may be helpful.

1.17 Robbins provides a classification of possible strategies for resolving conflict: Table 10.1.

Table 10.1 *Robbins's strategies for resolving conflict*

Problem-solving	The parties are brought together to find a solution to the particular issue
Superordinate goals	The parties are encouraged to see the bigger picture and identify shared goals that override their differences
Expansion of resources	Resources are freed and mobilised to meet both parties' needs, eliminating the need for competition
Avoidance	One or both parties withdraws from the conflict or denies/conceals the incompatibility
Smoothing	One or both parties plays down the differences and 'papers over the cracks'
Compromise	Bargaining, negotiating and conciliating, so that each party makes some concessions in order to obtain some gains
Authoritative command	An arbitrator with authority over both parties makes a decisive judgement
Altering the human variable	Effort is made to change the attitudes, beliefs and perceptions underlying the conflict
Altering the structural variable	Effort is made to re-organise work relationships in order to minimise the potential for conflict

The win-win approach to conflict resolution

1.18 Another useful model for conflict resolution is the win-win model. Cornelius and Faire (*Everyone Can Win*) suggest that there are three basic ways in which a conflict or disagreement can be worked out.

- **Win-lose:** one party gets what he wants at the expense of the other party. However well justified such a solution is, there is often lingering resentment on the part of the 'losing' party, which may begin to damage working relationships.
- **Lose-lose:** neither party gets what he really wants. Compromise comes into this category. However logical such a solution is, there is often resentment and dissatisfaction on both sides: even positive compromises only result in half-satisfied needs.
- **Win-win:** both parties get as close as possible to what they really want. Whether or not the outcome is possible, the approach generates more options, more creative problem-solving, more open communication, enhanced cooperation and preserved working relationships.

1.19 Cornelius and Faire outline a win-win approach as follows.

- **Step 1: find out why each party needs what they say they want.** Getting to the other party's fears and needs in the situation facilitates meaningful problem-solving. It also encourages communication, supports other people's values, and separates the problem from the personalities involved.
- **Step 2: find out where the differences dovetail.** Diverging needs may seem like the cause of conflict – but they also offer potential for problem-solving, since the different needs may not be mutually exclusive, but dovetail at some point.

- **Step 3: design new options**, where everyone gets more of what they need. Techniques include: brainstorming; chunking (breaking a big problem down into manageable chunks and seeking solutions to those); and devising usable 'currencies' (suggestions and concessions which are easy or low-cost for both parties, and can be traded). The aim is mutual gain.

- **Step 4: cooperate.** Treat the other person as a partner, not an opponent.

1.20 The example given is of two men fighting over an orange. The win-win approach would ask each man why he needs the orange. One may want to make orange juice, while the other wants the skin of the orange to make candied peel: the conflict disappears. If they both want the juice, other options will be explored: sharing the juice; getting more oranges; diluting the juice; buying one man some bottled orange juice and so on. Even if compromise is settled on, the outcome will be a win-win, because both parties will have been fully assertive and willingly cooperative, enhancing the relationship between them (which adds to the 'win' outcome).

Managing and resolving conflict in contractual relationships

1.21 There are a number of formal mechanisms for managing and resolving conflicts in contractual relationships, depending on the nature of the relationship (eg the desire to preserve positive working relations), and the nature and 'stage' of the conflict.

- *Consultation* is a form of 'issues' management, in which potential causes of conflict are discussed, and suppliers have an opportunity to give their input, before the problem arises (or as soon as possible, once it has arisen).

- *Negotiation*, whether formal or informal, is a useful approach to conflict resolution at any level, in which parties discuss their issues in a structured way, and seek to reach constructive compromise through bargaining or mutual concessions.

- *Conciliation* is a process where conflicts or grievances are aired in a discussion, facilitated by an impartial conciliator, whose role is to manage the process and make constructive suggestions (and *not* to make a judgement for one side or the other). There is negotiation towards a mutually acceptable position – and, if possible, a 'win-win' outcome.

- *Mediation* may follow conciliation, if a voluntary settlement has not been reached. It involves the appointment of an independent person (or panel) who will consider the case of both sides and make a formal proposal or recommendation (not binding on either party) as a basis for settlement of the dispute.

- *Arbitration* involves the appointment of a mutually acceptable independent person (or panel) who will consider the arguments of both sides, in closed proceedings, and deliver a decision or judgement which is binding on both parties.

- *Litigation* is legal action to have a commercial or contract dispute resolved by the courts.

1.22 In buyer-supplier relationships, supply contracts will often include clauses setting out the methods that will be used to settle disputes, and how they will be 'escalated' (taken further or to a higher level) if necessary.

1.23 Litigation suffers from a number of disadvantages. Legal fees are costly. The matter may not come to court for a long time – and then may not be resolved quickly, because of the nature of the system. And the details of the conflict will be aired in public, possibly revealing confidential or reputation-damaging information.

1.24 It is therefore increasingly common for buyers and suppliers to treat court proceedings as a last resort, and to stipulate that disputes must first be referred to arbitration. This offers significant advantages. The proceedings are held in private, avoiding negative publicity and public disclosure of sensitive information. The process is less confrontational than litigation, which may be important if the parties wish to maintain positive ongoing trading relations. It is intended as a single process (avoiding the appeals that tend to draw out litigation), and is often speedier and less expensive. The arbitrator may be selected for specialist knowledge, as well as legal expertise.

1.25 It is worth noting that arbitration is also the most commonly used form of dispute resolution for international disputes, which are rendered much more complex by parties being under different legal regimes and jurisdictions. There are well established frameworks for international dispute arbitration, using the International Chamber of Commerce (ICC) court of arbitration, or the United Nations Commission on International Trade Law (UNCITRAL) arbitration code. Arbitration brings a measure of neutrality, so that no party is unfairly disadvantaged by the location of the proceedings, the language used, the procedures applied and so on.

1.26 Even so, both litigation and arbitration tend to result in 'win-lose' solutions, which are potentially damaging to ongoing relationships; both are costly and time-consuming; and both ultimately take the power of decision away from the parties concerned. Alternative dispute resolution (ADR) methods, such as mediation, have become increasingly popular, as attempts to reach less adversarial, more empowering solutions, where a mutually acceptable settlement is designed by the parties, with a view to continuing the relationship.

Conflict handling styles

1.27 The Thomas-Kilmann instrument (TKI) is a popular tool in conflict assessment. Thomas suggested that individuals' conflict-handling styles could be mapped on two dimensions, according to the intentions of the parties involved: their assertiveness (the extent to which they try to satisfy their own concerns) and their co-operativeness (the extent to which they try to satisfy the other party's concerns). The five extreme points on this map are shown in Figure 10.1.

Figure 10.1 *Model of conflict-handling styles*

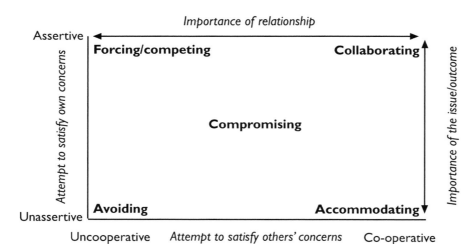

1.28   The various styles can be described as follows.

- In avoiding, you withdraw from the conflict or attempt to sweep it under the carpet. This allows you to avoid dealing with conflict, and avoids immediate tensions: it may be appropriate if the issue is genuinely trivial, or you need a 'cooling off' period, or someone else is better placed to deal with the conflict. However, underlying problems don't get resolved: long-term frustrations and resentments may emerge in other ways.

- In forcing/competing, you impose your solution on the problem. This allows you to get your way, and may be appropriate for issues that need winning: breaking down the inflexibility of others or implementing unpopular measures quickly in a crisis, say. However, the other party is likely to feel defeated and demeaned, and this can damage ongoing collaboration and trust.

- In accommodating, you concede the issue without a fight, to preserve harmony. This avoids upsetting people, and may be appropriate where maintaining the relationship is more important than the issue (or you realise you are wrong!). However, you are giving permission for the other person to take advantage of the situation, and your authority may be undermined.

- In compromising, you use bargaining or negotiation, so that each party trades some concessions for some gains. This reaches an agreement that both parties can live with, and enables you to get on with work: it may be necessary where power is evenly balanced and there is genuine conflict of interest. However, the solution is often more expedient than effective, and may leave both parties unsatisfied.

- In collaborating, you work together to try and find an outcome which meets the clearly stated needs of all parties as far as possible: a problem-solving or 'win-win' approach. This assumes that both positions are important, even if they are not necessarily equally valid. It takes time, but at the end of the process, both parties should be committed to the solution and satisfied that they have been treated fairly. This facilitates learning, generates more creative options and encourages trust.

1.29 Collaboration is regarded as the preferred way to resolve conflict when there is at least a moderate amount of interdependence among the parties (so that a win-lose situation would damage both); a perceived equality of power exists between the two parties (so that both can afford to be as open as collaboration requires); there are mutual advantages to collaboration that can be seen by both parties; and the collaborative process is supported by the organisation.

Conflict factors and the relationship spectrum

1.30 We have identified above some of the factors that lead to conflict. How are these affected by the position we occupy on the relationship spectrum?

1.31 At the adversarial end of the relationship spectrum, conflict may lead to seriously bad feelings on either or both sides of the relationship, and may indeed cause the termination of the relationship. This is because buyer and supplier are not placing a high value on the relationship, and a rift over a particular deal may be a bigger negative factor than any positive desire they have to continue working together.

1.32 At the other end of the spectrum – partnership relations – the situation is different. In this situation, the parties regard their relationship as more important than any particular deal between them. When a rift emerges, they are keen to resolve it by means of constructive debate around the issues. This may involve tough negotiations about the details of sharing costs and benefits, but always within the framework of a relationship that both parties wish to endure.

1.33 Buyers must beware of allowing conflict to cause adverse outcomes. As always, a positive, professional and firm approach is preferable to rudeness and hostility. The latter can only aggravate problems and in the worst case may even lead to termination.

Stakeholder management and conflict

1.34 Clearly the most important stakeholders in the context of supply relationships are the buyer and the supplier. Either one of these may have contributed to the conflict: it is not safe to assume that all problems are the fault of our suppliers. A first step in resolving conflict must involve careful and impartial analysis of the issues to identify what is causing the problem. This offers the best chance of **retrieving and retaining** a supply relationship in preference to terminating it.

1.35 It may then be appropriate to involve other stakeholders. For example, other departments in the buying organisation (finance, user departments etc) may wish to contribute their opinions on the causes of the problems and on the importance of maintaining the relationship.

1.36 One factor to consider in detail is the current position within the relationship spectrum, and in particular whether the dispute suggests that a move along the spectrum may be appropriate. Again, user departments may have an important say in this. For example, it may be that user departments believe that better results could be achieved by making use of such modern techniques as online auctions. If the supplier is currently regarded as a partner, he will understandably be upset by this. Buyers must evaluate the user department notion that a more distant relationship would be preferable.

1.37   At all times during this process, we must have a clear picture of our overriding objectives. What exactly are we trying to achieve by bringing this conflict into the open? At one extreme, some stakeholders may be seeking a means of terminating the relationship. At the other extreme, other stakeholders may believe the relationship is much more important than the problem giving rise to conflict. The buyer must either find a reconciliation of these positions, or choose between them, so as to determine his objectives and hence his approach to the problem.

1.38   Conflict should not be allowed to persist indefinitely. In the end, we must aim for some kind of resolution. This need not mean that we continue on the same terms with the supplier as previously; on the contrary, a range of resolutions is possible, including both termination at one extreme and moving to a closer relationship at the other.

2   Communication in supply relationships

Stakeholder communication

2.1   The more crucial the stakeholder, the more important it is to involve him in detailed communication about strategies, policies, plans and procedures. In the context of supply relationships, the most extreme example is suppliers with whom we have (or wish to have) a close strategic relationship, perhaps a partnership relationship.

2.2   In such cases, buyers and suppliers will display a high level of trust. They will be willing to share information which could be damaging if revealed. This might include detailed specifications, accounting information (such as profit margins), target customers, targeted cost reductions etc.

2.3   The stakeholders here are not only external suppliers. Internally, too, buyers must feel able to share information with other departments, rather than adopting a policy of 'knowledge is power' and refusing to share.

2.4   This is not necessarily easy to achieve. All kinds of obstacles may present themselves to the buyer seeking transparency. For example, he may have to overcome a history of mistrust and disappointment. Or he may have to break through inappropriate behaviour from the other party (perhaps arising from an adversarial approach to relationships). Or he may have to cope with changes in the relationship arising from changes in personnel.

2.5   The point of putting in the effort to achieve all this is to avoid the many adverse consequences that may ensue otherwise. These could include loss of customers, loss of revenue, higher costs, reduced market share and poor relations along the supply chain.

Communication tools and techniques

2.6   The late 1990s saw an explosion of development in many areas of communication.

   •   The infrastructure of telecommunications, allowing more data to be carried more quickly from one place to another. Such developments include the use of fibre-optic cable, the satellite transmission of data etc.

   •   The equipment and tools used to send and receive messages: fax machines, digital mobile phones, email and so on.

ISDN

2.7   ISDN is a digital telecommunications network which allows computer users to send data via telecom links without using a modem. It allows data to be transmitted much faster than conventional networks, so it supports high-speed access to the internet for more sophisticated use (eg video streaming). More than one service can be sent over the link simultaneously, allowing users to receive phone calls while online (eg for technical support, or to hold a 'virtual meeting' while viewing online data). Graphic data can also be transmitted, saving time and cost in tasks such as sending specifications and drawings to suppliers or buyers.

Fax

2.8   Fax technology allows hard-copy written or graphic data to be sent via a telecommunications link and reproduced on a remote fax machine. The latest machines can also be used as printers, photocopiers and scanners (to scan hard-copy data into a PC).

2.9   Fax allows for very fast transmission at the cost of a telephone call. Complex hard-copy data (diagrams, drawings, photographs) are identically reproduced at the target destination, giving all the advantages of written/visual communication, without delay. Machines can send and receive outside office hours and therefore across international time zones. These advantages can now be accessed even more effectively through email.

Email

2.10   Email (electronic mail) is rapidly replacing conventional mail – and even faxes and phone calls – as a fast, cost-effective and flexible medium.

- It is almost instantaneous, regardless of distance, allowing interactive real-time dialogue (eg through instant messaging).

- It has global reach, across international time zones, giving customers and suppliers '24/7' contact.

- It is economical (typically one twentieth the cost of a fax).

- It allows both one-to-one and one-to-many communication (eg sending information to all staff – or to all customers or suppliers, preferably on a permission basis, as part of relationship management programmes).

- The ability to print out a hard copy for reference/confirmation/evidence and to attach complex documents (such as spreadsheets, graphics or photographs) offers the advantages of conventional written formats

- Email transmissions can be standardised and monitored, when required, to minimise risks of misuse and to apply corporate identity.

2.11   You should, however, be aware that email also has its drawbacks, including the temptation to overcommunicate because of its ease and convenience. Email is an impersonal, instant-transmission medium; messages with inappropriate 'tone of voice' or content can be sent before the writer has a chance to reconsider. Email systems function as an informal grapevine; messages circulate freely, and are frequently inaccurate – and potentially defamatory or offensive.

Voicemail

2.12 Voicemail (or 'v-mail') systems enable a telephone caller to leave a message recorded in a 'mailbox' which can be accessed via the recipient's phone. This enables the organisation to leave messages for employees in the field or temporarily offsite, to be collected when they 'call in'. It also allows callers to leave messages when their target recipient is not available, or outside office hours. A 'personal' greeting can be given by individual extension users (not just a central switchboard).

Automated call handling and interactive voice-response systems

2.13 Automated call handling (ACH) is a system by which a recorded or computerised voice asks callers to select from a menu of options by pressing buttons on their telephone handsets, without intervention by a human operator. It is often used to route calls through a switchboard, but can also be used to complete transactions (for example, paying bills by credit card, accessing information or booking tickets).

2.14 Interactive voice response (IVR) is a similar system, whereby users make selections by responding verbally to closed questions with key words ('yes', 'no', numbers, days of the week, etc) which can be recognised by the receiving software. This is now used extensively in the booking of taxis, for example.

2.15 The advantages of such systems are that they allow customers (or other contacts) to place orders, pay bills and access information (eg price lists, timetables) at any time and with only a telephone. ACH switchboards allow calls to be swiftly routed to the right department or extension for the nature of the query or transaction. However, such systems can be frustrating for the user (particularly if there are lengthy menu sequences to go through), and may be less congenial than talking to a 'real' human being.

Computer-telephony integration (CTI)

2.16 CTI systems link the telephone system to a computerised database of customer, product or market information. The organisation (or call centre) thus has real-time access to information requested by callers, and to relevant electronic forms and systems through which to process transactions while the customer is on the phone.

2.17 CTI also enables service staff to 'recognise' callers' telephone numbers and call up details of their account or previous contacts, both to streamline service (by cutting down on the information to be elicited for each new transaction) and to create apparently personalised communication (as part of a customer relationship marketing approach, say).

Video-telephones and video-conferencing

2.18 Video-telephones are still regarded as 'futuristic' by most people, but mobile versions are already on the market. Video-conferencing has traditionally involved users going into specialist conferencing studios for link-up to other locations. ISDN technology, however, has paved the way for 'dial-up' systems, since there is no need for dedicated links. More accessible options include webcasts: users attach digital video cameras and microphones to computer terminals, which feed audio-visual data to each participant via the internet.

2.19 A high proportion of the impact of interpersonal communication is non-verbal. Once initial wariness (or lack of awareness) has been overcome, and systems and products have developed further and come down in cost, 'virtual' face-to-face communication will allow organisations to harness the advantages of meetings and discussions for 'personal' service, relationship-building, negotiation and counselling without having to incur costs of travel, interview/meeting space and so on, and without taking remote or dispersed location into account.

Internet, intranet and extranet

2.20 The internet is a worldwide network of telecommunications-linked computers.

2.21 An intranet is a set of networked and/or internet-linked computers which is used to communicate within an organisation. Only employees are able to access relevant web pages and internal email facilities (as well as having access to the wider internet). Intranets may provide employees with access to a wide range of internal information: performance databases and reporting systems; induction and employment information (online policy and procedure manuals, job vacancies and training opportunities); noticeboards (for posting messages, announcements and bulletins); internal email facilities; mailings of employee newsletters and work updates; and so on.

2.22 Intranets offer significant advantages for integrating internal communications. They support multidirectional communication and data-sharing; link remote sites and workers in 'virtual' teams; give employees wider access to corporate information for personal identification, ideas-swapping and culture-creation; encourage more frequent (because convenient) use of reference sources and updating of information; and save on the costs of producing and distributing the equivalent printed documents and messages.

2.23 Extranets give selected outside users authorised access (by password) to particular areas or levels of the organisation's information network. Examples include the registered-user-only pages of corporate websites (encouraging customers to sign up for permission-based and personalised marketing contacts), and the member-only pages of professional bodies' websites. Extranets are particularly useful tools for relationship marketing and inter-organisational alliances. Business partners, for example, can share data and information systems for more efficient transaction processing or to provide added value to customers.

2.24 An extranet may be used to publish news updates and technical briefings which may be of use to clients or supply chain partners; provide shared services (sharing data and systems to enable partners to cross-sell each others' products and services, say, to offer customers 'one-stop' shopping); exchange transaction data (orders, payments, delivery tracking and so on); share training and development resources; provide online presentations and promotions to business partners (while excluding competitors); and publicise trade or consumer promotions, conference attendance, loyalty schemes and other marketing tools.

Transparency: open book costing

2.25 Open book management originated as the idea that a company should reveal financial information about its business to its employees. The purpose of this is to:

- develop the interest of employees in the performance of the company

- educate employees to understand that their own well-being (eg annual bonus) is linked to the financial performance of the company and

- educate employees to see a connection between the work they do and the financial performance of the company.

2.26 Open book management will, it is argued, encourage employees to associate themselves more closely with the company, and adopt a more collaborative and positive approach in their work.

2.27 A similar concept can be applied to the relationship between a company and its supplier. However, a distinction is made between:

- open book costing and

- cost transparency.

Open book costing

2.28 With open book costing, suppliers provide information about costs to the purchaser. Having cost information from the supplier will, it is argued, reassure the purchaser about getting value for money, and that the supplier will not be making excessive profits.

2.29 Open book costing is used in the automotive industry, and is also used in some service industries, such as facilities management, catering and logistics. It is also necessary with contracting work where the agreed price is based on some form of cost-related formula.

2.30 It has been suggested that open book costing is appropriate as part of a supplier development programme, so that:

- the customer can get to know more about the supplier's operations and processes, and

- the customer can identify areas where the supplier might be able to make improvements to reduce costs or add value in some other way.

2.31 In principle, open book costing can be a way for the customer to help the supplier, and creates a win-win situation. In practice, however, open book costing is unlikely to appeal to suppliers, because the customer is dictating the requirements. The flow of costing information is all one-way, from the supplier to the customer. The supplier might be reluctant to divulge confidential information that the customer might pass on to another supplier, thereby reducing its competitive advantage. Faced with a demand from the customer for cost information and a reluctance to provide confidential information, the temptation for a supplier might be to provide inaccurate cost data.

2.32 Even if open book costing does result in added value, the supplier cannot be certain of enjoying any of the benefits. The customer might take all the benefit of cost reductions, for example, either to keep itself or to pass on to its own customers.

Cost transparency

2.33 The main drawback to open book costing is that the customer is in the driving seat and the flow of cost information is all one-way. Cost transparency is something different. With cost transparency, the customer and the supplier share cost information, for activities where they have a common interest. The flow of information is two-way.

2.34 The objective of cost transparency is to reduce costs, because an understanding of the costs of the customer or supplier will help the other party to appreciate where the opportunities for savings might lie.

2.35 If the two organisations exchange financial information openly, they will also develop a better understanding of their concerns and objectives. For example, a company might want to buy a particular product to certain specifications, but for a price no higher than a stated maximum amount. Financial information from the company might help to explain to the supplier the reasons for the customer's maximum price requirement. Equally, a supplier might provide financial information to a customer to demonstrate that it is not making unreasonable profits on the items that it is supplying. An exchange of financial information could:

- promote greater mutual understanding, and
- encourage closer collaboration for mutual benefit.

2.36 Cost transparency is not currently widely-adopted, but might gain greater acceptance if strategic supplier-customer relationships continue to develop. However, there is still a strong tendency for managers to want to protect confidential information, such as profitability margins and technical details.

3   *Power and dependency in supply relationships*

Power versus dependency

3.1 Cox and others (in *Supply Chains, Markets and Power: Managing Buyer and Supplier Power Regimes*) have analysed the possible power and dependency relations that may exist between buyer and supplier: see Figure 10.2.

3.2 What the diagram indicates is that where B is important to A, but A is not important to B (top left sector), then B is the dominant partner in the relationship. The bottom right sector indicates the opposite situation: A is important to B, but B is not important to A, so A is dominant. In the top right sector, each partner is important to the other and their relationship is one of interdependence. In the bottom left sector, neither partner is important to the other: they are independent of each other.

Figure 10.2 *Relationships between buyer and supplier*

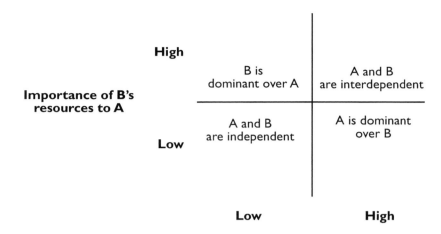

3.3 In certain special cases, this kind of market situation is sufficiently important to have earned a name. We look below at the three special cases of monopoly, oligopoly and monopsony.

3.4 A **monopoly** is a market in which just one supplier exists. It is doubtful whether any pure monopoly exists, because almost always there are alternative possible suppliers. However, there are markets in real life which approximate closely to monopolies in that it would hardly be realistic to contemplate any supplier but one. For example, in the UK, most households will have their water supplied by the local water company, and it is not feasible to look beyond this.

3.5 In a monopoly situation the single supplier clearly has great power over buyers. This opens up the possibility of abuse, but governments are alert to the danger and in most cases markets that are monopolies or near monopolies are closely regulated.

3.6 An **oligopoly** is a market dominated by just a few large suppliers. For example, in the UK the telecommunications industry is dominated by just a handful of very large companies such as British Telecom. Once again, this places suppliers in a very strong position relative to buyers.

3.7 A **monopsony** is a market in which just one buyer exists. As with monopolies, it is hard to think of a pure monopsony. However, a close approximation in the UK was the market for rolling stock in the days before British Rail was split up into fragments. In a mirror image of the monopoly situation, monopsony confers great power on the single buyer.

Relationship issues resulting from power and dependency

3.8 Some of the relationships described above carry dangers for one or other of the parties concerned. Broadly speaking, each party wishes to avoid the situation where the other party is dominant. In terms of Figure 10.1, Company A wishes to avoid the top left quarter, whereas Company B wishes to avoid the bottom right quarter.

3.9 However, while the dangers of over-dependency are obvious enough (what happens if our partner finds better business elsewhere?), there are also dangers in an over-dominant position. Many buyers are reluctant to take too much of a supplier's turnover, even though the supplier might be keen to get more business. This is partly because of CSR obligations – the buyer must to some extent have the interests of his suppliers at heart. Partly, too, the buyer positively wishes the supplier to have a good range of customers. That makes him a better supplier, more attuned to the possibilities within the market, and more able to share his knowledge with the buyer.

3.10 Having said all this, it remains true that ultimately a buyer will choose his suppliers on the basis of hard commercial criteria. If he feels a need to change supplier, he will do so even if it is painful to the supplier because of the amount of business involved. To protect themselves from this kind of damage, suppliers will usually wish to diversify their customer base.

Managing power and dependency

3.11 As a first step in managing such problems, buyers should use appropriate tools to identify the dangers. The supply positioning model, supplier preferencing and the market management matrix can all be helpful in this context.

3.12 Some of the dangers arise for suppliers. For example, a buyer may seek to insist that a supplier should use particular processes and standards. This may suit the buyer, and if his position is dominant the supplier may be forced to accede, at least in the short term. However, in the longer term, the supplier should adopt a strategy of lower dependency on that particular buyer, perhaps by actively seeking to widen his customer base.

3.13 Buyers should be aware that a particular supplier is dependent on them. This is an issue that should form part of regular communication between buyer and seller. If the buyer senses that a particular supplier is over-dependent, he should normally advise the supplier to diversify, and may be able to recommend possible customers. This recognises the fact that over-dependency is not good news for either party to the relationship.

3.14 Buyers are also exposed to risk. For example, a dominant supplier may threaten to cease supply unless the buyer accepts a price increase, or a change in specification. If this arises in the context of a close strategic relationship the buyer will have every right to be aggrieved: such opportunistic behaviour runs counter to the principles of such an agreement and is likely to drive the buyer towards seeking another supplier. Even in the context of a more transactional relationship buyers will wish to reduce their dependency on a particular supplier.

Chapter summary

- Conflict in supply relationships can be constructive or destructive. A buyer must be alert for opportunities to manage conflict constructively.

- Robbins provides a useful checklist of strategies for resolving conflict.

- An aim of managing conflict is to arrive at a win-win solution.

- The effects of conflict can depend partly on the position of the supply relationship along the relationship spectrum.

- Modern communication tools and techniques (such as ISDN, fax, email, voicemail, automated call handling etc) can provide significant assistance in managing conflict.

- Open book costing is a system under which suppliers provide information about costs to the purchaser. Cost transparency goes one step further: buyer and supplier both provide information about costs.

- A relationship involves dominance and dependency when one partner is much more important to the other than *vice versa*. Where parties are equally important to each other (or equally unimportant) we have an interdependent (or independent) relationship.

- Certain extreme cases of dominance are referred to as monopoly (only one supplier in the market), oligopoly (just a few major suppliers in the market) and monopsony (only one buyer in the market).

- There are dangers in an over-dominant relationship as much as in an over-dependent relationship.

- Buyers can use tools such as the supply positioning model, the supplier preferencing model and the market management matrix to identify the dangers of this kind of relationship.

Self-test questions

1   What is meant by an evolutionary view of conflict? (1.5)

2   What may be the effects of destructive conflict? (1.7)

3   List as many as you can of Robbins's strategies for resolving conflict. (Table 10.1)

4   Outline the steps in the win-win approach to conflict resolution advocated by Cornelius and Faire. (1.19)

5   Distinguish between the adversarial and the collaborative ends of the relationship spectrum in terms of their effects in the management of conflict. (1.31, 1.32)

6   Explain what is meant by ISDN. (2.7)

7   What are the drawbacks of email as a communications method? (2.11)

8   What is an intranet? How may an intranet improve internal communications? (2.21, 2.22)

9   Distinguish between open book costing and cost transparency. (2.33)

10   Sketch the matrix of power and dependency relations outlined by Cox and others. (Figure 10.2)

11   What is an oligopoly? (3.6)

12   Why may it be dangerous for a buyer to have an over-dominant relationship with a supplier? (3.9)

CHAPTER 11

E-purchasing

Learning objectives

4.4   Appraise the use of e-purchasing in supply relationships.

- E-purchasing and the relationship spectrum
- E-purchasing and supply situations
- Appropriateness of e-tools and their effect on relationships
- Suppliers' perspective of e-purchasing
- Stakeholders' perspective of e-purchasing

Chapter headings

1   E-purchasing and the relationship spectrum

2   E-purchasing tools

3   E-purchasing and supply situations

4   The supplier's perspective on e-purchasing

5   Online auctions

Introduction

In recent years the impact of technology on the work of buyers has been dramatic. In this chapter we look at aspects of electronic purchasing (e-purchasing).

1   E-purchasing and the relationship spectrum

Definitions

1.1   The use of electronic methods by buyers has notably increased in recent years. Traditional purchasing disciplines remain as important as ever, but the trend towards electronic processing has an important impact on commercial relationships.

1.2   We begin by defining some terms, using the CIPS definitions provided in their paper on e-sourcing.

Table 11.1 *Defining the terms*

Term	CIPS definition
E-purchasing	The electronic acquisition of goods and services, including all processes from the identification of a need to purchase to the payment for these purchases, including post-contract/payment activities such as contract management, supplier management and supplier development
E-sourcing	Using the internet to make decisions and form strategies regarding how and where services or products are obtained
E-procurement	Using the internet to operate the transactional aspects of requisitioning, authorising, ordering, receipting and payment processes for the required services or products

1.3   What do these definitions tell us?

- E-purchasing is the most general term. The term 'purchasing' covers just about everything that might form part of a buyer's job. When those activities are conducted electronically, the result is 'e-purchasing'.

- E-sourcing is one part of e-purchasing. According to CIPS, 'it covers those parts of the buying process which are at the discretion of specialist buyers'.

- E-procurement is the other part of e-purchasing. According to CIPS, it 'may be seen as the focus of local business administrators, with one of the key goals being to devolve the buying process to local users, covering the requisition against contract, authorisation, order, receipt and payment'.

1.4   E-sourcing and e-procurement together make up the entire purchasing cycle, which the CIPS paper illustrates as follows.

Figure 11.1 *The e-purchasing cycle*

E-Purchasing Cycle

1.5 As with many such models, one is left wondering exactly how the diagram works. You should always look critically at such concepts and ask exactly what the model is telling you.

- For example, you might ask what is the significance of the circular layout? Is it meant to imply that the purchasing of a particular item is an iterative process? Surely not – once we've ordered, received and paid for the item we surely do not start at the beginning by identifying the need for an item we have already purchased. Perhaps a vertical layout would make more sense?

- And what does it mean to have the terms 'business case, legal, security, CSR' in the centre of the diagram? Does it imply, for example, that the process of developing the business case goes on in among the other activities? Again, surely not – if we need to develop the business case, surely we do this at the beginning of the process.

1.6 In a later paper, CIPS divided the circular model into six segments, with titles as shown in Table 11.2.

Table 11.2 *Segments in the e-purchasing cycle*

E-sourcing	E-procurement
Segment 1: understanding, defining and planning	Segment 4: ensure delivery
Segment 2: approach the market	Segment 5: effective utilisation
Segment 3: secure the right deal	Segment 6: payment, review and disposal

1.7 We will look again at this analysis in the context of e-purchasing tools (see next section of this chapter).

The impact of e-purchasing on commercial relationships

1.8 A serious danger that buyers must be aware of and must manage is the risk of alienating existing suppliers. A supplier who has invested time and money in servicing a customer is likely to be unhappy if he hears that his efforts are to be undermined by a buyer intent on offering the business by means of online auction. Indeed, in some cases existing suppliers have refused to participate when a buyer decides to take this route.

1.9 The use of reverse auctions has caused concern when linked to supply chain thinking. Suppliers may bid prices which are not sustainable, just to get the business. Reverse auctions are more cost-driven than the waste-driven ideas of supply chain management, and so could be viewed as encouraging an adversarial relationship approach when a more strategic one may be called for.

1.10 In general, the impact of e-procurement and other ICT tools on buyer-supplier relationships can be summarised as follows.

- Enhanced communication tools (such as intranets, extranets and the internet) enhance the exchange of information within the supply chain, and hence potentially the development of transparency and trust. They also overcome barriers of distance and time-zones in international supply.

- ICT-based information systems can produce a wide variety of *analyses and reports* to support management decision-making relevant to relationship management: demand and capacity forecasting, supplier appraisals, customer/stakeholder feedback (eg using online surveys) and so on.

- The use of centralised, shared *databases* helps to ensure the coherence and consistency of information used by, or given to, all parties for joint planning and decision making and collaborative activities.

- Database management also supports supplier/customer relationship management programmes. These have various applications for identifying 'key' relationships, and ensuring that users can draw on the full range of contact history, transaction history and other information necessary to conduct each encounter efficiently and with a view to building the relationship.

- E-procurement tools can free up buyers' time – previously taken up by routine and repetitive clerical tasks – for creative, strategic and relational aspects of their roles.

- Virtual meetings technology, video-conferencing and web-casting save travel time and cost in getting people together for conflict resolution, negotiation and collaboration.

- Tools such as the internet and websites support wider choice of suppliers, through improved appraisal/selection information, and better access to opportunities for SME and overseas suppliers.

- E-tools may help buyers monitor and manage supplier performance and compliance (eg with environmental/ethical standards), especially where regular site visits are not feasible. This may be particularly important in international outsourcing (or 'offshoring') projects.

- Adversarial or arm's length relationships are supported by e-tools such as reverse auctions, electronic spot buying and so on.

- Procurement and supply *processes* can be streamlined by e-procurement tools, and still further by integration of supplier/client systems (eg using EDI). This may make possible significant mutual benefits such as cost reduction, the elimination of waste, and support for swifter and more agile supply.

- ICT-supported improvements in information, decision and service quality and cost efficiency may help to enhance internal relationships, by raising the contribution, status and credibility of the procurement function.

- However, e-procurement tools may be variously viewed by internal stakeholders, which may create conflict within internal relationships. Purchasing staff may view them as empowering, users as restrictive of choice, and management as a means of cost reduction, for example.

- E-procurement tools also may be variously viewed by external stakeholders, which may create conflict within external supply chain relationships. Suppliers are often resistant to reverse auctions, for example, as advantageous only to the buyer.

Using the internet

1.11 There are opportunities for using e-procurement to enhance the customer–supplier relationship and add value for all participants in the supply chain. The potential benefit comes from feeding real-time information about customer demand to suppliers over the internet.

1.12 Purchasers routinely use the internet for a variety of purposes.

- Using web browsers to search suppliers' catalogues. This permits immediate access to information on product features, availability, prices, delivery methods and prices etc.

- Electronic ordering. This takes the process one step further: once the buyer is satisfied, he can place his purchase order online.

- A further step still is payment by electronic funds transfer or by purchasing cards (see below)

- Buying departments can track shipments and receive delivery information by directly accessing the websites of transportation companies.

1.13 Apart from accessing information from suppliers, buyers can also use the internet to publicise information about themselves: their mission statement, their environmental policy, details of how the purchasing system operates etc.

1.14 The beauty of this approach is the reduction in transaction costs. Instead of sending out a copy of, say, an environmental policy to every supplier on the list, it is sufficient to post the document onto a website and the job is done in a single hit. The use of online auctions is another example where traditional processes can be extremely streamlined by electronic means. Overall, this means that information technology can make a vital contribution to the ideal of lean supply.

Legal considerations in e-procurement

1.15 Transactions between buyers and sellers are increasingly conducted by electronic means. Discussion and negotiation about terms and conditions of sale, previously undertaken by post, are now often contained in an exchange of emails. Many sellers offer their goods for sale on a website; buyers cannot negotiate terms, they can only click OK or decline to click.

1.16 These developments may affect the contractual position of the buyer and seller. You need to be aware of two important European directives concerning e-signatures and e-commerce.

1.17 The Electronic Signatures Directive of 1999 has led to the Electronic Communications Act 2000 (ECA). The main principle here is that a digital 'signature' is valid. You may wonder why this is important. After all, for most contracts, no particular form of document is required, and in principle the contract need not even be in written form. However, in practice, it is important to have a written contract with a valid signature in case of later dispute over what exactly has been agreed. The ECA confirms that a digital signature can be used in such a case.

1.18 The E-Commerce Directive lays down rules about the content of a company's emails and website. It is now essential for companies to include certain basic details on their emails: name, geographic address, trade register in which the company is registered, supervisory or regulatory authority that regulates the company (if any), VAT registration number (where relevant).

1.19   The directive also affects the position of buyers ordering through a website. The buyer must be given certain information before the order is concluded.

- Technical steps to conclude the contract
- Whether the contract will be filed with the supplier and how it can be accessed
- Technical means for identifying and correcting input errors before the order is placed

1.20   The seller must also issue a receipt for orders placed via a website.

1.21   If a supplier fails to comply with these provisions, a buyer can claim damages. And if a service provider has not made its terms and conditions available, or acknowledged receipt of the order, or made available a means of correcting errors, the contract may be cancelled at any time.

1.22   Buyers who are using electronic communication to negotiate and conclude orders should think carefully about their standard terms and conditions. It is sensible to consider amending these to cope with the additional risks and uncertainties of electronic trading. It is also a good discipline to attach a copy of your standard terms and conditions of purchase whenever you email a supplier about a potential purchase.

E-procurement and real-time information

1.23   There are opportunities for using e-procurement or the internet to enhance the customer-supplier relationship and add value for all participants in the supply chain. The potential benefit comes from feeding real-time information about customer demand to suppliers over the internet.

1.24   Here are some examples of recent initiatives.

- Dell Computers have direct contact with their customers, who buy their computers direct from Dell representatives rather than through a middleman. Dell's supply chain involves 'virtual integration' with its suppliers, communicating information and co-ordinating activities via an extranet, as if they were all part of the same company. Dell is developing a Choiceboard service, whereby customers will be able to specify the computer they require. The order information submitted by a customer can be fed straight through to Dell's suppliers.
- Wal-Mart, the US retail store chain, makes immediately available to its suppliers, through the internet, sales data from its electronic point of sale check-out desks in its stores and from its web sales. The sales data will allow Wal-Mart's suppliers to make their own forecasts of likely future demand and plan their production schedules on the basis of these forecasts rather than waiting for an actual order from Wal-Mart before taking any action. This speeds up the supply chain.
- Tesco, the UK supermarket chain, is introducing a similar system. Its suppliers will receive real-time information about Tesco customer demand, and suppliers will be invited to send in quantities of goods that they believe will meet future demand, without having to wait for a formal order from Tesco.

1.25 Through this type of arrangement, companies such as Wal-Mart, Tesco and Dell should be able to substitute information to suppliers in place of inventory. Reducing inventory should reduce costs, and is consistent with a just-in-time (JIT) management philosophy. The internet will make 'virtual partnership' between customers and suppliers easier to arrange. The following comments on the potential of the internet are worth noting.

- 'Under e-commerce, delivery will become the one area in which a business can truly distinguish itself.' (Drucker, 1999)

- 'I'm only half joking when I say that the only thing better than the internet would be mental telepathy.' (Michael Dell, Chairman of Dell Computers, 2001).

Developments in IT and their effects on purchasing

1.26 Good quality, usable information which is available in real time can be used as a tool for faster and more accurate decision-making. In addition to e-procurement, there are many other ways in which the rapid developments in information and communications technology (ICT) have helped purchasers:

- to call off stock electronically from partners via desk-top procurement systems, or to allow partners to control stock and deliveries (vendor stockholding), eg with low-value purchases such as stationery or lubricants, helping to reduce transaction and stockholding costs;

- to use the internet and specialist directories such as *Kelly's* to give more tailored international information (a thorough supplier appraisal must still be carried out);

- to join forces with other organisations using linked or compatible programmes to provide real-time information for use in supply chain management;

- to locate stock accurately (enhanced by global positioning systems, GPS);

- to measure the effectiveness of routes and warehousing;

- to link with other organisations and share information as part of an enterprise resource planning (ERP) platform or a linked extranet system, on matters such as demand forecasting and capacity scheduling;

- to enhance new-product development by the use of CAD/CAM systems where organisations in partnership can work together, using the principles of early supplier involvement (ESI), to monitor and progress products through the design phase and forward to prototype development in a tightened timeframe while still ensuring that the product meets purchasing, operational and management criteria and, ultimately, customer requirements;

- to benefit supplier associations from the development in knowledge management, which allows for the sharing of ideas and information throughout the association.

1.27 Note, however, that the development of linked systems is often an onerous and time-consuming process that requires a great deal of commitment and trust by all parties. In addition, ICT developments are in danger of removing the human elements from relationships, and may take us back to 'transactional' relationships, even where a closer relationship is desirable.

2   E-purchasing tools

Listing the tools

2.1   We have already mentioned that CIPS divide the e-purchasing cycle into six segments. In their analysis of the segments they also list specific tools that may be useful at each stage. This analysis is summarised in Table 11.3. Each of the suggested tools is explained in turn in the paragraphs that follow.

Table 11.3 *A list of e-purchasing tools*

Segment of the e-purchasing cycle	Tools available
Segment 1: understanding, defining and planning	Data warehousing Trend analysis tools Spend analysis tools Supplier performance data Collaborative development forums Soft copy specification to transmit
Segment 2: approach the market	Market intelligence tools Secure tender portal handling Confidential/dedicated email facility Electronic reverse auction
Segment 3: secure the right deal	Negotiation planning data Create e-contract and update contract management system
Segment 4: ensure delivery	Delegated authority to select/requisition E-requisition Extranet/intranet communication Catalogue and/or punchout communication Expediting by exception Barcode plus RFID, GPS
Segment 5: effective utilisation	Receipt and inspection: barcode/handheld devices, bluetooth Automatic update of systems Capture supplier performance data Update customer systems Generate automatic payment
Segment 6: payment, review and disposal	Eliminate traditional invoicing process: self billing, automated invoice matching, electronic invoice generation Funds transfer: BACS, CHAPS Update data warehouse Capture supplier performance data

Explaining the tools

2.2   **Data warehousing.** A data warehouse has been defined as 'an application with a computer database that collects, integrates and stores an organisation's data with the aim of producing accurate and timely management of information and supporting data analysis'. Another possible definition is 'a copy of transaction data specifically structured for querying and reporting'. Either way, the buyer is able to use the database to extract information which will help him in planning a purchase.

2.3 **Trend analysis tools.** This refers to software (eg forecasting systems) used to identify trends in the buyer's requirements for particular items.

2.4 **Spend analysis tools.** This refers to software used to break down total expenditure into categories useful to the buyer: eg spend per item purchased, spend per supplier, spend per internal business unit.

2.5 **Supplier performance data.** This is software used to analyse how well suppliers perform in terms of delivery, quality etc. Buyers will use this to determine whether particular suppliers are suitable sources for particular items.

2.6 **Collaborative development forums.** This refers to a secure website permitting only restricted access, where appropriate personnel from buying and supplying organisations can exchange ideas and plans relating to new developments.

2.7 **Soft copy specification to transmit.** This is self-explanatory: instead of using manual methods to provide suppliers with specifications, the process is instead carried out electronically.

2.8 All of the above tools are used in Segment 1 of the cycle: understanding, defining and planning. We now move on to Segment 2: approach the market.

2.9 **Market intelligence tools.** This refers both to specialised software designed to provide information on suppliers and supply markets, and also to general internet search engines, such as Google. Specialised software is usually developed by dedicated providers and may be accessed by buyers in return for a subscription.

2.10 **Secure tender portal handling.** A web portal is a website providing personalised capabilities to visitors. In the case of a tender portal, the capabilities in question are those related to the conduct of a tendering exercise: transmitting specifications and invitations to tender, receiving and recording responses from suppliers etc. Naturally, access is limited to appropriate personnel by means of passwords.

2.11 **Confidential/dedicated email facility.** This is self-explanatory.

2.12 **Electronic reverse auction.** This refers to software by which buyers can conduct an auction in which potential suppliers bid ever lower prices to win a contract. (The gradual **lowering** of bids is what gives the name of reverse auctions.) Another aspect of this is **electronic marketplaces**: these are sites where buyers can advertise their requirements and sellers their capacity and capabilities.

2.13 All of the above tools are used in Segment 2 of the cycle: approach the market. We now move on to Segment 3: secure the right deal.

2.14 **Negotiation planning data.** Buyers can use data provided by potential suppliers to investigate the attractiveness of their offerings. It is usual to use spreadsheets models to analyse the effects of changes in the parameters or variables ('what if? analysis').

2.15 **Create e-contract.** Contracts can now be concluded by electronic means: see earlier in this chapter. The software will automatically update the contract management database.

2.16 The above tools are used in Segment 3 of the cycle: secure the right deal. We now move on to Segment 4: ensure delivery.

2.17 **Delegated authority to select/requisition**. With appropriate electronic systems in place buyers can feel more confident in allowing user departments to place purchase orders. The software can prompt action that might otherwise be forgotten by the users (eg requesting agreed discounts). The user may be acting in relation to an *ad hoc* requirement, or departments may be ordering requirements generated by an MRP or MRP II system.

2.18 **E-requisition**. This simplifies the process whereby the purchasing department captures requisitions from users, and provides information about both the requisitioner and the requirement.

2.19 **Extranet/intranet communication**. An intranet is an internal network linking computers within the buyer's organisation. This enables staff to access information about many aspects of the organisation, including that related to purchasing. An extranet goes one step further: external organisations, subject to password protection, are allowed to access similar information. This can permit suppliers, for example, to display catalogues tailored for the buying organisation, while staff within the buying organisation can access the catalogues so as to make orders.

2.20 **Catalogue and/or punchout communication**. The use of electronic catalogues has just been mentioned. **Punchout** is an e-procurement software application that makes it possible for a buyer to access a supplier's website from within the buyer's own procurement application. The buyer leaves ('punches out' from) his own organisation's system and goes to the supplier's web-based catalogue to locate and order products.

2.21 **Expediting by exception**. Electronic systems enable simple and rapid tracking of transactions, as well as flagging items that have not happened when they should have. These 'exceptions' can then be chased as appropriate, while buyers are free to ignore the large majority of items that are progressing smoothly.

2.22 **Barcode plus RFID, GPS**. The kind of tracking system just described is often made possible by the use of barcodes along with radio frequency identification (RFID) and global positioning systems (GPS).

2.23 All of the above tools are used in Segment 4 of the cycle: ensure delivery. We now move on to Segment 5: effective utilisation.

2.24 **Receipt and inspection/automatic update of systems**. Once goods are received they are scanned in using electronic equipment such as barcode readers. This will automatically update the status of the item within the computer records. For example, an item previously recorded in the system as 'on order from supplier' may change to 'received from supplier'.

2.25 **Capture supplier performance data**. The same process of automatic data capture can equally be used to monitor suppliers' performance in terms of delivery, and possibly also in terms of quality. For example, if goods are captured on the system as 'inspected and rejected', that gives important information about the level of rejects from that particular supplier.

2.26 **Update customer systems**. This appears to refer to internal customers within the buying organisation. It means that a user department is automatically informed when a requirement has been satisfied by receipt of the goods. Equally, the stores department can be informed.

2.27 **Generate automatic payment triggers from acceptance**. This means that the system automatically authorises payment procedures to begin in cases where the goods have been received and checked to be in satisfactory condition.

2.28 **Eliminate traditional invoicing process**. The traditional system is based on paper invoices being received, copies being circulated to relevant departments, and a manual system of authorisation and payment. With e-purchasing this tedious process may be avoided. For example, a system of self-billing may be in operation: the buyer pays on the basis of goods received, with no need for the supplier to generate an invoice at all. Or there may be a system of automatic invoice matching: when an electronic (or even paper) invoice is received it is matched on the system with a purchase order and goods received data, and immediately passed for payment.

2.29 **Funds transfer**. Electronic funds transfer by BACS (Bankers' Automated Clearing System) or CHAPS (Clearing House Automated Payment System) provides added security as compared with the use of cheques, and also reduces manual operations.

2.30 **Update data warehouse and capture supplier performance data**. These items have been referred to earlier.

Linking the tools to the relationship spectrum

2.31 Needless to say, not all of the electronic tools listed above will be appropriate in all circumstances. To some extent, the use or non-use of a particular tool will be suggested or even dictated by the type of buyer-supplier relationship. This leads to the possibility of linking particular tools to particular types of relationship.

2.32 It would be a waste of time to do this in too much detail (much better to simply use a little commonsense in light of the particular situation), but some pointers are given in Table 11.4. Note that many of the tools are relevant in all types of relationship, because it is almost always desirable to simplify, streamline and automate processes. Thus many buying organisations will routinely pay suppliers by BACS regardless of the type of relationship they have. And equally it will always simplify processing if incoming goods are scanned by barcoding technology, no matter what supplier they have arrived from.

Table 11.4 *Linking e-purchasing tools to the relationship spectrum*

Type of relationship	Notes on e-purchasing tools
Adversarial and arm's length relationships	Online auctions are more suitable for this end of the spectrum. Electronic payment processes may be more trouble to set up than the short-term nature of the relationship can justify.
Transactional and closer tactical relationships	An important principle here is for the buyer to set up ordering processes and then hand them over to users. This suggests use of online catalogues. Automated payment processes may be justified if the volume of transactions is moderately high.
Single sourced relationships	Online auction may well be justified if there is a good level of competition in the supply market. Electronic tendering and use of online catalogues also suggest themselves.
Outsource relationships	This will usually be suitable for an electronic tendering process.
Closer relationships	At this end of the spectrum – strategic alliances, partnerships, co-destiny relationships – online auctions are quite inappropriate and likely to damage relations with suppliers. It is to these relationships in particular that collaborative development forums apply. Sharing of information, eg by extranet communication, is vital.

3 E-purchasing and supply situations

Interpreting the syllabus

3.1 There is a somewhat gnomic caption at this point of your syllabus: 'e-purchasing and supply situations'. It would take advanced powers of divination to work out what this is referring to, but fortunately it appears from CIPS guidance that the caption refers to ways in which tools of e-purchasing can help the buyer in five particular situations that he may encounter.

- There is a monopoly supplier.
- There is a cartel of suppliers.
- An adversarial relationship exists but the buyer would prefer a different relationship.
- A supplier regards the buyer as a nuisance (in the special meaning that term bears in the context of supplier preferencing).
- A supplier treats the buyer as exploitable, while claiming to regard him as core.

The five unfavourable situations

3.2 It would be difficult to find an example of a true **monopoly** market. In other words, in almost every case it will turn out that other suppliers exist who can supply the desired item, or something indistinguishably close to it. Electronic tools (such as internet search engines) can help the buyer to identify alternative suppliers, or alternative products sufficiently close to meet his requirements.

3.3 Moreover, the buyer may be a more attractive customer from the monopolist's perspective if he can automate his own systems by increased use of electronic processes. This too can help the buyer in his dealings with the monopolist.

3.4 Although a true monopoly market will rarely or never be found, a slightly less extreme situation is much more common. This is the situation where the market is controlled by a small number of dominant suppliers: an **oligopoly**.

3.5 There is a temptation for the few suppliers in an oligopolistic market to join forces and create a **cartel**. The cartel would agree on output levels of each member and on the prices to be charged to customers. It effectively creates a monopoly from an oligopoly, because the few suppliers act together as a single entity. The best known cartel is OPEC (the Organisation of Petroleum Exporting Countries), which controls most of the oil production in the world.

3.6 Anti-competition law in the UK forbids firms from forming cartels, but informally buyers can often spot evidence of collusion in oligopoly markets. For example, if an oligopolist raises his prices, his rivals may do likewise. In a perfect market a firm that does this risks pricing itself out of the market, but in an oligopoly the few firms 'competing' may decide simply to follow the leader.

3.7 Once again, electronic tools have a role to play in assisting the buyer. For example, the buyer may use a search engine to identify alternative suppliers. And the use of online auctions can be tailored in such a way as to make collusion difficult (for example, by inviting different suppliers to tender for different items – though this may not be an option in the public sector).

3.8 The third situation is where **an adversarial relationship exists**, but the buyer would prefer a different relationship. The advice from CIPS in this situation is to use an e-auction: this 'will make suppliers compete if they feel that the business is interesting to them'. It might also be said that electronic tools such as extranet communication can themselves form part of a closer relationship.

3.9 The fourth situation is where the supplier **regards the buyer as a nuisance**. This is not always undesirable: if the items supplied are of low importance there may be no great incentive for the buyer to seek a closer relationship. However, if this does not suit the buyer's objectives, he may use search engines to identify an alternative supplier. Electronic tools may also help to change the supplier's perspective. If part of his reason for regarding the buyer as a nuisance is the transactional difficulties, then greater automation by the buyer can improve matters.

3.10 Finally, a supplier may indicate interest in a buyer's objective of achieving a partnership relationship, while in truth he regards the buyer as 'exploitable' (refer back to the supplier preferencing model). In this situation the buyer has various options. He may negotiate with the supplier, explaining in what ways he believes the relationship is falling short of target. Or he may abandon his objective and re-classify the relationship. Or he may use a search engine to identify an alternative supplier.

4 *The supplier's perspective on e-purchasing*

Benefits for suppliers

4.1   Our discussion of e-purchasing has highlighted many potential advantages for buyers. However, we must also consider the subject from the perspective of suppliers. What advantages and disadvantages may suppliers perceive in the use of e-purchasing techniques?

4.2   The most immediate advantage for suppliers is the general benefit provided by increased automation. In all areas of business, this has led to increased efficiency and accuracy of processing transactions, as well as reduced costs.

4.3   Many examples of this could be cited. There is no longer a need for producing and mailing paper invoices. Payment is received more quickly and with less processing. Electronic communications, eg automatic updates on delivery schedules, remove the need for expensive man hours spent on phone calls. The list could go on.

4.4   Suppliers also enjoy the many benefits that technology has created in terms of generating sales. Every supplier organisation now uses a website to attract potential customers. This not only opens up a much wider potential market, but also reduces the need for expensive selling staff. In addition, when orders are accepted by electronic means, the effort and cost of processing them is much reduced.

4.5   Suppliers can benefit from being invited to tender in an online auction. If the auction is transparent, they get to see the prices quoted by their competitors, which is useful information not normally available. They can use such information when bidding for business in future.

4.6   Finally, the greater ability of buyers to identify potential suppliers has a 'mirror image' benefit for suppliers: any particular supplier has a greater chance than before of being invited to tender.

Disadvantages for suppliers

4.7   As usual, the situation is not entirely clear cut. Balancing the above benefits are a number of disadvantages.

4.8   Firstly, the benefits of reduced transaction costs come at a price. In particular, supplier organisations must spend significant sums of money on information and communication technology. Most suppliers would admit instantly that this is justified, and indeed essential to survival, but it is wise to recognise the costs involved.

4.9   Not all of these costs are entirely under the control of the supplier. For example, the supplier can choose to spend as much or as little as he likes on website development. But he may not be able to choose how much he spends on ensuring system compatibility with a buyer. In a case like this, if he wishes to acquire or retain the business, the cost of systems development may be unavoidable.

4.10 Another issue concerns online auctions (discussed in greater detail below). On the one hand, this technique should open up the potential for doing business with a wider class of buyers. But many suppliers complain that buyers are over-using the technique. In particular, a supplier who already has the business may argue that the buyer is wrong to seek a better deal by means of an online auction. Often their argument will be based on a claim that the nature of a supply is more strategic than a reverse auction implies.

4.11 It is natural for an incumbent supplier to feel this way, because it may lead to loss of business. In particular, they may feel that it encourages an undue concentration on price. If a supplier believes that his offering is differentiated by quality, delivery, service etc, he may feel disadvantaged by a focus on price. However, a supplier not currently having the buyer's business can only regard the online auction as a welcome opportunity to tender.

5 Online auctions

The nature of online auctions

5.1 As indicated above, one particular aspect of e-purchasing has attracted much comment in the literature, especially in regard to its effect on supplier relationships. This is the increasingly common practice of using online reverse auctions. We have already touched on this topic, but it seems set to become a hot topic in the exams and we therefore devote a separate section to it here.

5.2 In an online reverse auction, a buyer posts the specifications of the item(s) or lots he wishes to buy, and the price he is willing to pay. Suppliers then bid competitively to offer the best price for the items over a specified bidding period. All bids are available for everyone to see (minus the names of the suppliers). The 'winners' are declared according to agreed 'auction rules' (eg in regard to whether the lowest bid must be accepted). Both buyer and supplier are then bound by the sale.

Potential benefits of online auctions

5.3 Many benefits of online auctions are claimed for buyers (particularly by software firms attempting to market their online auction systems). The possible advantages include the following.

- Reduction in acquisition lead time and efficient administration: eliminating the time-consuming offline processes of supplier selection, quotation requests/comparisons and so on.

- Savings over and above those obtained from negotiation, as a result of competition.

- A 'wake up' call to existing suppliers on the need to reconsider their cost base and pricing in order to remain competitive.

- Access to a wider range of potential suppliers and sources of market information, including a global supply base.

- Less time 'wasted' on interpersonal interaction eg meeting supplier representatives.

5.4   Supporters of online auctions also point to benefits for suppliers.

- Opportunities to enter previously closed markets or accounts (especially for smaller suppliers)
- Reduced timescales/costs of negotiation
- Good source of competitor/market pricing data
- Clear indication (ideally) of what is required to win business

Potential drawbacks of online auctions

5.5   Despite the potential benefits, online auctions have also come in for criticism. Here are some of the potential drawbacks.

- Online auctions are based on a zero-sum, adversarial or 'win-lose' approach: profit for either party is at the other's expense
- Suppliers are vulnerable to coercion (being forced to participate on threats of lost business) and manipulation (eg 'fake' bids by a buyer to force down prices; intention to use existing supplier, forcing prices lower by 'apparent' competition).
- Suppliers may feel exploited, leading to loss of trust and goodwill in the buyer-supplier relationship
- Possible long-term adverse effects on the economic performance of the supplier: forced (by real/apparent competition) to price reductions which are unsustainable
- Possible long-term adverse effects on the economic performance of the buyer: supplier failure (and/or loss of goodwill) may reduce the future supply base and incur further costs (eg quality problems). If prices continue to fall, suppliers may merge to achieve economies of scale, tipping the balance of power to the supply base.
- Promised massive savings not materialising, due to factors such as: supplier switching costs, cost of managing/developing new suppliers, quality problems, legal disputes, retaliatory pricing by alienated suppliers (especially when buyers have urgent requirements) – and overstated savings claims by 'market makers' (auction service providers) in the first place.
- Suppliers get the message that price is the most important factor in winning business: risk of downgrade in quality, investment in quality improvement to compete on cost
- Inability to take adequate account of non-price criteria (eg quality and customer service) and stakeholder input into criteria

In what circumstances are e-auctions suitable?

5.6   Reverse auctions are potentially suitable (or most successful) in the following circumstances.

- When purchasing certain commodities such as bulk materials, stock commercial goods, or non-technical services that can be easily specified, and where switching costs are negligible.
- When purchasing some services (eg freight services or hotel accommodation) where there is surplus supply.

5.7 'Lowest-price reverse auction processes should be used only where there is little concern about production specifications or the suppliers selected. They are not appropriate for complex products or projects requiring collaboration or considerable negotiation.' (*Lysons & Farrington*).

5.8 If a buyer is thinking of using online auctions, he should at least take certain preliminary precautions.

- Ensure that service levels can be achieved by winning bidders.
- Ensure that supply sources are secure.
- Ensure that suppliers are educated in the use of e-auctions, and that the benefits of e-auctions are promoted to them.
- Ensure that there is a good business case for e-auctions, recognising that they are not suitable for all circumstances.
- Gather detailed information for justification and planning of the auction.
- Consider the challenges and risks likely to be faced, and make plans to manage them.
- Consider in detail the financial and non-financial resources required to implement e-auctions, and the type of products best suited to them.

Executive decision-making traps

5.9 An influential article by M L Emiliani argues that senior managers typically adopt online auctions because of pressure for cost reduction (eg due to global competition); pressure for fast investment returns; and the belief that technology-based tools give quick results. Given the amount of reported negative outcomes and experiences of e-auctions, their decision-making process must be flawed.

5.10 Emiliani classifies the reasons for this ('decision-making traps') as follows.

- **Anchoring**: giving disproportionate weight to the first information received (eg usually market makers' claims of savings/benefits) – discounting concerns expressed by lower level employees
- **Status quo**: preference for solutions that preserve the current state (eg power-based bargaining, purchasing decisions based on price – rather than, for example, developing supplier collaboration to manage costs)
- **Sunk cost**: decisions that support past decisions (eg continuing the use of e-auctions, even though initial end-of-auction savings are not maintained in practice) because of the financial/personal investment already made – and reluctance to admit errors
- **Confirming evidence**: seeking information (eg initial/apparent price reductions) that supports the viewpoint, while rejecting contrary evidence (eg subsequent cost escalation etc). Low-price bids confirm suspicions that suppliers have over-charged in the past.
- **Framing**: making a decision based on how a question or problem is framed (eg marketing claims that e-auctions secure cost savings that directly enhance bottom line profit and increase EPS in a predictable way over time – making the decision look easy!)

- **Estimating/forecasting**: estimating or forecasting uncertain events, using faulty/biased information due to other traps (eg using overstated savings data as a basis for estimating own results; using inaccurate demand forecasts as a basis for supplier pricing)

- **Overconfidence**: believing that the estimate or forecast is accurate (when they aren't, if specifications/quantities change, lead times are long, quality/delivery problems occur etc)

- **Adjusting savings estimates downwards 'to be on the safe side'**: framing/anchoring decision-makers to believe that most of the savings claimed can be realised – when they can't.

- **Recallability**: predictions about the future based on memory of past events (eg remembering initial end-of-auction euphoria; forgetting subsequent disappointing results, costs/difficulties of supplier switching etc)

Chapter summary

- E-purchasing is a general term, embracing both e-sourcing and e-procurement.

- There is a danger of alienating existing suppliers when a buyer moves to a policy of e-purchasing.

- Buyers routinely use the internet for purposes such as searching catalogues, electronic ordering, electronic funds transfer, and tracking shipments.

- Recent legislative changes have made it clear that a digital 'signature' is valid in forming a contract.

- Modern developments in IT have had a major impact on the work of buyers, eg in the use of desktop procurement systems, internet sourcing etc.

- CIPS analyse the e-purchasing cycle into six segments and identify a large number of electronic tools that may be suitable at each segment.

- To some extent, the selection of electronic tools is governed by the position of the supply relationship along the relationship spectrum.

- There are various unfavourable supply situations that a buyer may encounter, in which use of electronic tools can bring benefits. These situations include a monopoly supplier, a cartel of suppliers, an adversarial relationship where the buyer would prefer something different, a supplier regarding the buyer as a nuisance, and a supplier treating the buyer as exploitable.

- There are many benefits for suppliers in the use of e-purchasing: increased efficiency and accuracy of processing transactions, reduced costs etc.

- However, there are also disadvantages for suppliers: the costs of automation, the concern about online auctions etc.

- Many advantages are claimed for the use of online auctions: cost savings, increased efficiency, access to a wider supplier base etc. However, online auctions also carry disadvantages (adversarial approach, damage to supplier relations etc) and should be used only after careful consideration.

Self-test questions

1   Define e-purchasing, e-sourcing and e-procurement. (Table 11.1)

2   List the six segments in the CIPS e-purchasing model. (1.6)

3   For what purposes do buyers use the internet? (1.12)

4   What details are companies legally required to include on their email communications? (1.18)

5   List some of the impacts of modern IT developments on the work of buyers. (1.26)

6   List as many electronic tools as you can, categorised according to the segment of the e-purchasing cycle to which they are relevant. (Table 11.3)

7   What is meant by a collaborative development forum? (2.6)

8   What is an electronic marketplace? (2.12)

9   What is meant by punchout communication? (2.20)

10   How can electronic tools help a buyer facing a monopoly supplier? (3.2, 3.3)

11   How can electronic tools help a buyer facing a cartel of suppliers? (3.5–3.7)

12   How can suppliers benefit from being invited to an electronic auction? (4.5, 4.6)

13   List potential drawbacks of online auctions. (5.5)

14   What preliminary precautions should a buyer adopt before using an online auction? (5.8)

CHAPTER 12

International Supply Contracts

Learning objectives

4.5   Appraise the relationship aspects of international supply contracts.

- Factors affecting international supply contracts
- Managing risk in international relationships
- Factors affecting performance measurement and ongoing monitoring
- International supplier development

4.10 Analyse the relationship challenges of multinational suppliers in the context of a global supply chain.

- Barriers to successful ongoing relationship management
- Multinational organisations as customers in local and national supply chains
- Multinational organisations as suppliers in local and national supply chains
- The positive impact of multinational organisations in developing economies

Chapter headings

1   Factors affecting international supply contracts

2   Managing risk in international relationships

3   Performance measurement and monitoring

4   Multinational companies

Introduction

Developments in technology and transport have led to increased use of overseas sourcing. Dealing with overseas suppliers gives rise to particular problems that do not surface in the domestic context. These issues are the subject of this chapter.

1   Factors affecting international supply contracts

The motivation for sourcing overseas

1.1   In this section we look at an important factor involved in the choice of suppliers, not primarily related to maintaining quality but with an impact on supplier relations. This is the question of choosing suppliers locally, nationally and internationally.

1.2   Certain obvious advantages of sourcing locally present themselves immediately. Communications are easier. Delivery costs should be lower. Delivery lead times should be faster and more reliable. Just in time techniques are more likely to be feasible. Rush orders are easier to cope with. No language problems arise. Given all this, why should firms even consider sourcing from national or international suppliers? Some of the possible reasons are discussed below.

1.3   The most obvious reason is availability of the required materials. There may simply be no local supplier who can meet the requirements. Even if there is, it may well be that a larger national or international supplier benefits from economies of scale that the local firm cannot match, leading to a price and/or quality advantage for the bigger firm.

1.4   Another factor applies in public sector contexts. As we have seen, there are European Union rules that regulate the activities of public sector buyers. Contracts with a value above a certain threshold must be advertised: it is not an option for a buyer to source locally without inquiring widely for potential suppliers.

1.5   International sourcing introduces special additional factors. Historically, sourcing from abroad has been attractive primarily because of the opportunity for cost savings. Certain overseas countries have been strongly competitive because of cheap wage rates and easy access to abundant supplies of local raw materials. Countries nearer home have been at a price disadvantage as a result.

1.6   Another reason has been the quality revolution which was pioneered in the Far East, and especially in Japan. Often, Western purchasers have found that reliability, quality and even cost considerations favoured suppliers from such countries, despite apparent disadvantages arising from physical distance.

1.7   Finally, an important feature of some markets has been the rise in countertrade. Under a countertrade agreement, a company exporting to a foreign country may be 'requested' (ie required) to purchase materials from organisations in that country. Typically, these agreements have taken place with countries that suffer from lack of hard currency, including many countries in Eastern Europe. The main problem is that in some cases the goods offered in return for securing export sales suffer from quality defects that discourage potential trading partners.

1.8   The discussion so far has hinted at particular problems in dealing with suppliers abroad. These difficulties are elaborated below.

1.9   Perhaps the most awkward issue to deal with is that of quality. As already mentioned, one reason for the increase in international sourcing has been the desire of Western firms to benefit from the quality advances pioneered in the Far East. However, not all overseas countries operate to the same quality levels as have become accepted in developed economies. The problem is exacerbated by the difficulty of making specifications unambiguous when a foreign language is involved. Absence of agreed international standards may also be a problem in some cases.

1.10   Price too is a more difficult issue than when dealing in home markets. The specific difficulties of dealing with foreign currencies come to the fore. This issue is discussed later in this chapter.

1.11 Delivery is likely to be slower and more uncertain. Political instability can wreck even the most tightly controlled schedules, but even without this complication sheer distance must be reckoned with. To compensate for longer lead times importers may order in large quantities, but this has important disadvantages in terms of stockholding costs.

1.12 Finally, the complications of international shipping procedures and documentation place additional burdens on purchasing staff. This is also the case in relation to payment methods.

Problems encountered when buying abroad

Culture and communications

1.13 One of the more obvious problems in dealing with overseas suppliers is that they are not British! This remark is not intended in any racist or xenophobic sense. It is merely intended to make the obvious point that the residents of a particular country, such as the United Kingdom, share a common culture and a common language, both of which influence their business dealings with each other. When dealing with overseas suppliers it is necessary to adjust to a different culture and language.

1.14 The difficulties here are both technical and behavioural. Technical difficulties concern the simple issue of understanding what is being offered and accepted, and what has eventually been agreed. Behavioural difficulties are related to how people interact with each other and form pleasant and rewarding business relations.

1.15 To deal first with the technical difficulty of communication, it is clearly vital that agreements once concluded are expressed in language that both parties understand. But before that stage is reached oral discussions will take place during which offers and commitments will be expressed that have a great influence on the course of negotiations. Buyers must make every effort to ensure that such discussions are unambiguous.

1.16 It is an essential element in a binding contract that the parties reach agreement. That element is absent if there is misunderstanding: one party believes he understands what the other has said, but in fact has not done so. Even leaving aside the legal niceties, it is clear that successful business relations are endangered if the two parties have different ideas as to what has been agreed.

1.17 Native speakers of English are in a fortunate position in that their first language is widely recognised as the standard language of international trade. However, that should not lead buyers to think that they can ignore communication difficulties. Even if negotiations are conducted in English, it is important to ensure that the supplier understands technical terms and idioms in the same way as the buyer.

1.18 An effort to acquire some understanding of the relevant foreign language can be a great help in this respect. It is also a major step in improving business relations. It is a positive sign that the buyer has made efforts to adapt to the supplier's position and will usually be welcomed even if the level of proficiency is not great.

1.19 This leads on naturally to the less technical and more behavioural problems of dealing with overseas suppliers. As in all negotiations, it is important to make a positive impression on one's business partners. This is more difficult in the case of overseas partners because of cultural differences.

1.20 Many of these differences have been described in the purchasing literature. For example, it is common to refer to Japanese patterns of business behaviour which can cause confusion to British and American buyers.

1.21 One instance of this is the much greater link between social and business relations in Japan; social communication forms a larger part of the negotiation process than is common in Britain or America. Buyers doing business in Japan should not assume that extensive entertaining by their hosts is an unimportant prelude to the main talks.

1.22 Another instance sometimes cited is the Japanese practice of avoiding a direct 'no', so as not to cause embarrassment to their guests. This can sometimes leave a British or American buyer believing that something is still up for debate, when the truth is that the supplier regards it as unacceptable.

1.23 Instances such as this could be multiplied by reference to other countries where business practices differ from those of Britain and America. However, the best practical measure is to benefit from the experience of others. Buyers doing business with overseas suppliers should brief themselves by discussing such points with colleagues who have previous experience.

Table 12.1 *Suggestions for negotiating with overseas suppliers*

1.	Speak slowly and ask questions to check understanding.
2.	Print business cards in both English and the foreign language.
3.	Study the culture in advance.
4.	Be prepared for negotiations to be drawn out over a longer period than usual.
5.	Become familiar with local regulations, tax laws etc.
6.	Prepare in advance on technical issues, financing arrangements, cost and price analyses etc.
7.	If possible, ensure that the person recording the discussions is drawn from your team
8.	Arrange discussions so that the other team can 'win' their share of the issues.

Documentation, Customs procedures, payment and legal issues

1.24 A variety of other problems arise in overseas buying. One of the major ones – currency management – is discussed in the next section of this chapter. Here we round up sundry other difficulties.

1.25 The documentation associated with international trade is extensive and often bewildering. The standard textbook *Elements of Import Practice* by Alan Branch devotes a chapter to this issue, in which no fewer than 24 separate documents are discussed. They include documents of title, shipping documents and many types of certificate relating to the goods (insurance, health, quality etc). Of course, not every one of these will apply to every transaction, but the buyer who sources from overseas must certainly reckon on a substantial increase in form-filling.

1.26 Goods imported will have to proceed through UK Customs. This leads to more paperwork, possible delays and a need to master fairly complex compliance procedures.

1.27 The supplier will also be concerned about the method of payment. The buyer would prefer payment to follow delivery and inspection; the supplier may prefer the reassurance of advance payment at least in respect of part of the total. Buyer and supplier must agree on whether open account trading is acceptable (as would be normal between businesses in the same country), or whether more elaborate payment mechanisms must be used. For example, it is common for suppliers to insist on a letter of credit issued by the buyer's bank to guarantee payment once the appropriate documents are received.

1.28 Finally, the legal systems in the buyer's and the supplier's countries will be different. The parties to an agreement must agree on two important matters.

- Which country's law should apply in the event of a dispute under the contract?
- In which country's courts should any dispute be conducted?

1.29 The relationship challenges of sourcing internationally can therefore be summarised as follows.

- Difficulty of identifying new sources of supply, monitoring supplier performance and so on (with reduced proximity for site visits etc)
- Transport risks: time/distance for delivery, difficulties of guaranteeing timely delivery, increased risk of supply disruption, damage/loss of cargo etc
- Exchange rate and currency risk
- Political and economic risk in the supplier's country/region: risk of instability, policy change etc
- Different legal frameworks (and issues of jurisdiction over trade disputes)
- Different language
- Different cultural and ethical values (which may create misunderstandings and disputes, or increase the risk of reputational damage to the buyer through unethical conduct by the supplier)
- Time zone and infrastructure differences (for communication and logistics)
- Complexity of documentation, customs procedures, tariffs/duties placing a burden on the buyer
- The use of third parties (eg agents, freight forwarders or staff contractors)
- Pressure to use e-procurement/e-commerce solutions (for which tools, skills and willingness may or may not be available).

2 *Managing risk in international relationships*

Introduction

2.1   The difficulties we have already discussed make it doubly important for buyers to manage risk when sourcing from overseas. In this section we discuss a number of techniques that can help with this.

- The use of incoterms
- Managing foreign currency risk
- The use of specialised payment methods
- The use of local expertise
- The impact of corporate social responsibility

The use of incoterms

2.2   When buying from abroad, a purchaser may find himself involved in up to four separate contracts: the actual purchase contract, a contract of carriage, a contract of insurance, and a contract of finance (perhaps involving a letter of credit). The buyer must be able to cope with all of these, despite the language differences that may exist.

2.3   The communication difficulties involved in international trade have long been recognised as a problem. In particular, the interpretation of certain commonly used technical terms is of key importance to both buyers and suppliers, and must be absolutely free from ambiguity. A step in this direction was taken in 1936 when the International Chamber of Trade (nowadays the International Chamber of Commerce) published the first edition of Incoterms.

2.4   This publication, which has been updated several times since then, sets out agreed explanations of many of the terms used in international trade to define obligations of seller and buyer. The incoterms were fully revised in line with developments in commercial practice, and republished in September 1999. The current revision is effective from 1 January 2000 and consists of 13 standard commercial terms. Many of these have been used for centuries in international trade and different interpretations had become possible, which are now standardised by incoterms.

2.5   Buyers and suppliers may contract with each other on whatever terms they think most suitable. They are not obliged to use incoterms. However, by doing so they remove many of the ambiguities that could otherwise be introduced into their agreement. If the agreement specifically refers to an incoterm, both parties understand immediately what their rights and obligations are in that respect. There is minimal danger of subsequent misunderstanding or dispute.

2.6   Parties may negotiate to determine which type of incoterm agreement is most suitable. In doing so the buyer should observe the need to develop a good business relationship on a long-term basis.

Examples of incoterms

2.7   Some of the more common expressions defined in incoterms are explained below. We use the example of goods produced in Lyons by a French supplier and shipped from Rotterdam to Southampton.

2.8   Goods sold on **ex works** terms (EXW) are the supplier's responsibility only as far as the factory gate. In other words, the supplier's obligation is merely to make the goods available at his factory or warehouse by the agreed date. 'Ex works Lyons' represents the least possible obligation for the supplier, and the largest possible involvement for the buyer. The price paid covers the goods only, as the buyer must arrange and pay for carriage and insurance. It would be usual for the British buyer to appoint an agent in France to handle this.

2.9   The supplier takes more responsibility under **FOB** (ie free on board) terms. His obligation is to place the goods in the ship at the agreed port of shipment. He must therefore pay for the cost of transporting the goods to that point, and for their insurance in transit. (Of course, he will pass on such costs in the price he charges the customer.) Once the goods have been placed on board ship, responsibility passes to the buyer. He pays for shipment and for insurance during the voyage.

2.10   The term 'FOB Rotterdam' would be used to describe this in our example. A similar term is 'FAS Rotterdam', which means free alongside ship. The difference is that the seller's obligations end slightly earlier, when the goods are placed alongside the ship at the named port of shipment.

2.11   Even greater obligations attach to the seller under **CIF** (ie cost, insurance and freight) terms. He must arrange and pay for transport and insurance to cover the goods right to the port of destination, including any unloading charges once they arrive. Again the price charged to the buyer would obviously reflect the additional obligations assumed by the seller. The term 'CIF Southampton' would be used to describe this in our example.

2.12   The above terms, together with the others described in Incoterms 2000, are briefly summarised in Table 12.2.

2.13   From the buyer's point of view a very important consideration is the true delivered cost, ie the actual amount he has to pay inclusive of all 'add-ons' such as freight, insurance, customs duties etc. Careful study of the applicable incoterms will enable him to calculate this in any particular case.

Managing foreign currency risk

2.14   A buyer sourcing from abroad must also take account of the difference between his home currency and that of the exporter. In the discussion that follows we use the example of a buyer in the UK purchasing goods from a Swiss supplier to the value of SFr 1m (ie one million Swiss francs).

Table 12.2 *A summary of Incoterms 2000*

Group		Terms of category	Duties of seller/buyer
E	Departure – all carriage paid by buyer	Ex works or EXW	The seller's only duty is to make the goods available at own premises. May assist with transit but not a requirement.
F	Main carriage paid by buyer	FCA, FAS, FOB	Seller will undertake all pre-carriage duties but main carriage arrangements are the responsibility of buyer.
C	Main carriage paid by seller	CFR, CIF, CPT, CIP	Seller arranges for carriage of goods, but once despatched has fulfilled obligations
D	Arrival – main carriage paid by seller	DAF, DES, DEQ, DDU, DDP	Seller's obligations extend to delivery of goods at the specified destination; e.g. seller is liable for damage in transit.

2.15   The Swiss supplier prices his goods in francs for the same obvious reason as a British company would price goods in sterling: francs are the main operating currency of the supplier, even if some of his goods are exported. He needs francs to pay his own local suppliers, his local and state taxes, his employees etc.

2.16   Meanwhile the British importer does not usually deal in francs. There is therefore a mismatch, and this is the problem that we discuss in this section. Somehow the funds available to the importer, expressed in sterling, must be transformed to funds of the type required by the exporter, expressed in francs.

2.17   The actual process of conversion is no problem in the present case, as anyone who has ever travelled abroad will know. Banks are quite happy to exchange francs for sterling. There may indeed be a difficulty in conversion if the currency concerned is not 'hard' (for example, if a British company deals with a Russian company, because the Russian rouble is not a hard currency). However, that is not the issue that we are addressing here.

2.18   The real issue is the fact that the relationship between one currency and another, even when dealing only with hard currencies, is not a stable one. Today one can purchase SFr 1.63 for £1 sterling. Yesterday the exchange rate was 1.61. Over extended periods, much greater fluctuations are likely. This is highly relevant to typical purchase agreements: a purchase agreed today may not need to be paid for until, say, three months hence. What will have happened to the exchange rate in the meantime?

2.19   One argument is to say 'Who cares anyway?'. Given that exchange rate movements are going to happen, should we not just resign ourselves to them and hope for the best when the time comes to pay up? In practice, this is not a sensible argument, at least when large amounts are involved. An adverse movement in exchange rates can wreck a buyer's carefully negotiated price and make budgets and product costings meaningless.

2.20 To illustrate this, suppose our British purchaser agrees his SFr 1m contract today with payment due in three months. What will be his situation if the exchange rate has moved from 1.63 to 1.50 in the meantime? At today's exchange rate, he might expect to pay £613,497 to acquire SFr 1m from his bankers (1,000,000 ÷ 1.63 = £613,497). In three months it will cost him £666,667 to acquire the same number of francs (1,000,000 ÷ 1.50 = £666,667). The supplier will be no better off – he receives SFr 1m either way. But for the buyer, the movement in the exchange rate has made the deal £53,170 more expensive, a 9 per cent increase in product cost.

2.21 In such a case we say that the franc strengthened against sterling (£1 did buy 1.63 francs, but later could buy only 1.50 francs); equivalently, we could say that sterling weakened against the franc.

2.22 Clearly the buyer is taking a big risk by accepting a contract expressed in francs. Should he then ask the supplier to invoice him in sterling instead? The problem with this is that the risk is in effect being transferred from buyer to seller. To see this, just think about how much the seller should charge on an invoice dated today and expressed in sterling.

2.23 To charge the buyer £613,497 would be fine if only the buyer would pay immediately. Then the supplier could rush off to his bank and ask for SFr 1m in return for his sterling. (We are ignoring the bank's transaction charges, and the difference between buying and selling prices for francs.)

2.24 But in fact the £613,497 will not be received today; it will be received in three months. Depending on the exchange rate prevailing at the time the supplier may receive more or less than SFr 1m when he converts the sterling. To protect himself against this risk he is very likely to charge more than £613,497 – say £650,000. That way, even if the exchange rate has moved to 1.54 in three months the sterling he receives will be worth at least SFr 1m.

2.25 This illustrates the problem that arises if the buyer asks for an invoice in sterling. It is true that he eliminates his exchange risk and can budget with certainty. But the supplier takes the risk instead and will load his price accordingly. A more practical difficulty is that the supplier may simply refuse.

2.26 To reduce these difficulties, various techniques are available to the buyer. We mention two such techniques (with brief description): leading and lagging, and forward exchange contracts.

2.27 **Leading and lagging** is very simple in principle. It involves changing the timing of payments so as to take advantage of changes in exchange rates.

- Leading means making a payment in advance of the due date.
- Lagging means making a payment later than the due date.

2.28 Lagging involves a delay that may not be acceptable to the supplier, and raises general issues of ethics and buyer-supplier relations. For these reasons it is not recommended.

2.29 Leading involves paying in advance. Obviously this would be acceptable to the supplier. Whether it is advisable for the buyer depends on two things.

- The opportunity cost of the cash paid out. By paying now rather than later the buyer forfeits the use of the money in the interval. There is an opportunity cost associated with this, namely the amount that the money could have earned for the buyer by being used in some other way.

- Which way the exchange rate moves. The point of making a lead payment would be to forestall an adverse movement in the rate of exchange. If in fact the movement turns out to be favourable, the buyer will have made a poor decision.

2.30 All of this should make it clear that making a lead payment is in essence a gamble. The buyer is speculating that an adverse movement is about to take place and he pays early to avoid it. He is also deliberately forgoing the use of the funds for a period when they could have been earning a return for him. This only really makes sense if either the exchange rate movement can be predicted with near certainty (unlikely), or the supplier can be persuaded to offer a substantial discount for accelerated payment.

2.31 The one positive thing that can be said about this method is that it removes uncertainty. The buyer knows exactly how much he is paying.

2.32 Using **forward exchange contracts** is a much more sophisticated method of removing uncertainty about future payments. In essence, the buyer agrees now with a bank to purchase the required amount of foreign currency at the appropriate date in the future. The price at which the currency is to be purchased is determined now, so that the buyer knows exactly how much it will cost him.

2.33 By offering rates that are guaranteed for a date in the future the bank is in effect speculating on its ability to predict the movement in exchange rates. How the bank does this, and how it protects itself from errors, are not the subject of this section. What is important for a buyer is that the mechanism enables him to guarantee now how much his currency requirements will cost him in the future.

The use of specialised payment methods

2.34 Payment for goods purchased from abroad may in some cases be no different from payment in a domestic transaction. For example, companies who have a long history of trading together will have developed a mutual trust enabling ordinary trade credit terms to be operated. The seller simply invoices the buyer and the buyer pays on the due date.

2.35 This situation however is far from being the norm in international trading. The distances involved, the risks of international transportation, the limited direct contact between the parties, and the different legal systems involved, all reduce the seller's confidence of being paid. To protect the seller's position, alternatives to open account trading have been developed.

2.36 The simplest alternative, though highly undesirable from the buyer's point of view, is payment in advance. The dangers of this are so obvious as to require no comment, and in practice this procedure would be highly unusual. More probably, buyer and seller would resort to one of the various methods that have been developed to provide reasonable security on both sides. These methods involve the use of banks as intermediaries. By far the most common method is the use of a letter of credit, and this is described below.

Letters of credit

2.37   Using letters of credit is essential in international trade, and importers need a reasonable understanding of how they work. However, the procedure is somewhat complex and to help your understanding it is worthwhile to bear in mind what the system attempts to achieve.

- For the seller, the aim is to ensure payment without recourse to litigation, especially since such litigation might involve a foreign jurisdiction. Preferably, the seller would like the source of funds to be located in his own country.

- For the buyer, the aim is mainly to ensure that payment is not made until he has received assurance that the goods have been transferred to himself.

2.38   These aims are achieved by the use of two banks as intermediaries: one in the seller's country (the advising bank), and one in the buyer's country (the issuing bank). In brief, the buyer instructs the issuing bank to open a credit with the advising bank in favour of the seller. The seller will be able to draw on this credit – ie obtain funds from the advising bank in his own country – once he has delivered to the advising bank any documents specified by the buyer, such as a clean bill of lading.

2.39   Having paid the seller, the advising bank passes on the documents to the issuing bank and is reimbursed for the sum advanced. The issuing bank in turn presents the documents to the buyer in return for payment. The end result is that the buyer has paid, and the seller has received, the contract price, while the intermediary banks have received fees for handling the transaction.

2.40   The seller will invariably insist that a confirmed irrevocable letter of credit is used.

- 'Confirmed' means that the advising bank has confirmed the arrangement with the seller in its own country, and the seller therefore has confidence in receiving funds from a local source once he has delivered the required documents.

- 'Irrevocable' means that the issuing bank receives an irrevocable authority from the buyer, and also undertakes irrevocably to act on that authority. This means that the issuing bank must honour the credit, even if the buyer attempts to revoke the agreement (as might happen, for example, if some dispute arose between buyer and seller).

2.41   The banks involved in this transaction act as agents of the buyer, and they run the risk that he, as principal, will refuse to ratify their actions. This he might do, for example, if the documents tendered to him do not comply with the requirements that he laid down. To protect themselves against this possibility, banks will normally refuse to accept documents from the seller unless they comply in every respect with the buyer's stipulations.

2.42   Use of letters of credit is by no means a fail-safe system. In particular, the number of parties involved can mean that delays arise. It can happen, for example, that goods arrive at the port of destination before the buyer has received the bill of lading from the issuing bank. The carrier will be reluctant in that case to hand over the goods. In practice, the buyer may persuade him to do so by indemnifying him against any loss he may suffer as a result.

2.43 Despite this kind of difficulty, the letter of credit is a central feature of modern international trade and you should ensure that you are familiar with the main principles. Note that most of the main banks issue useful booklets explaining the principles. For example, an exceptionally clear booklet entitled *Letters of Credit* is published by HSBC. It includes the very useful diagram reproduced in Figure 12.1 which summarises the procedures already described.

The use of local expertise

2.44 Many of the difficulties arising in overseas sourcing stem from lack of local knowledge. This can be overcome if the buying organisation can somehow access personnel from the overseas country. One possibility is to employ an agent based in the overseas country. Clearly the buyer must aim to select someone trustworthy and energetic. There will be a cost, often expressed in terms of commission based on the value of business done.

2.45 Another possibility is the employment of local staff. For example, a buyer conducting significant business with Chinese suppliers might open a buying office in, say, Shanghai and employ local staff to run it. They would be able to use their local knowledge and expertise to provide advantages unavailable to staff based in the domestic country.

The impact of corporate social responsibility

2.46 You should refer back to Chapter 4 for detailed discussion of CSR issues. In the context of overseas sourcing it is particularly important to consider the employment practices operated by the overseas supplier and any adverse effects on the environment caused by the supplier's operations.

2.47 Buyers increasingly accept that they have an obligation to ensure their suppliers conform to recognised CSR standards.

3 Performance measurement and monitoring

3.1 This is mentioned in your syllabus in the context of international sourcing, but we defer our discussion of it until we cover syllabus area 4.8 in the next chapter.

4 Multinational companies

Barriers to relationship management

4.1 A multinational company is one that operates from bases in several different countries. This should be contrasted with a global company, which is a company that sells to or buys from countries throughout the world, regardless of where its base is located.

4.2 The syllabus caption 'barriers to successful ongoing relationship management' suggests that there are particular problems in maintaining relationships with multinational companies. Unfortunately, it is not easy to see what these might be, and the CIPS guidance for this module provides no clues. Nor is there any discussion of such issues in any of the recommended texts for this module.

Figure 12.1 *Letters of credit flowchart*

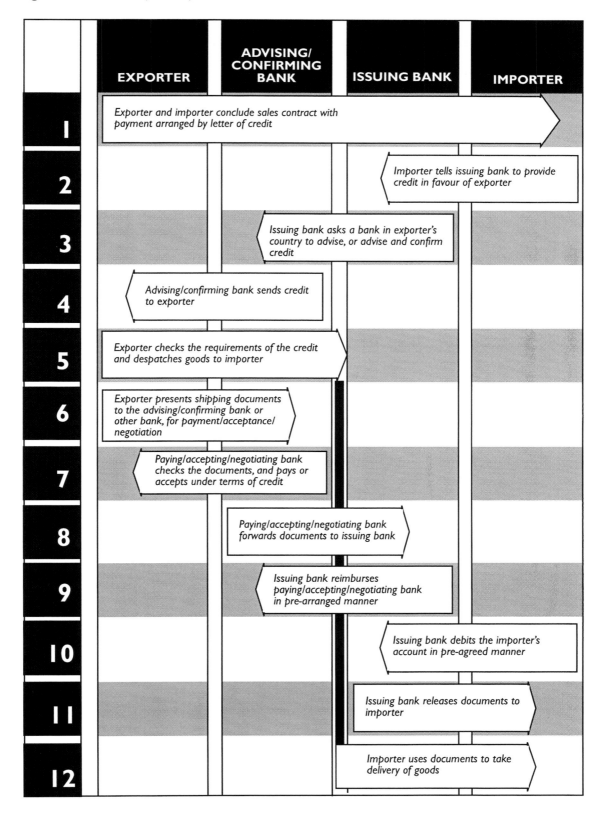

	EXPORTER	ADVISING/ CONFIRMING BANK	ISSUING BANK	IMPORTER
1	Exporter and importer conclude sales contract with payment arranged by letter of credit			
2				Importer tells issuing bank to provide credit in favour of exporter
3			Issuing bank asks a bank in exporter's country to advise, or advise and confirm credit	
4		Advising/confirming bank sends credit to exporter		
5	Exporter checks the requirements of the credit and despatches goods to importer			
6	Exporter presents shipping documents to the advising/confirming bank or other bank, for payment/acceptance/ negotiation			
7		Paying/accepting/negotiating bank checks the documents, and pays or accepts under terms of credit		
8		Paying/accepting/negotiating bank forwards documents to issuing bank		
9		Issuing bank reimburses paying/accepting/negotiating bank in pre-arranged manner		
10			Issuing bank debits the importer's account in pre-agreed manner	
11			Issuing bank releases documents to importer	
12			Importer uses documents to take delivery of goods	

4.3 In the absence of any guidance, we may speculate that difficulties arise from the dispersed nature of a multinational's operations. This in effect means that dealing with a multinational can be like dealing with many different organisations across the world. It may be unlikely that a single relationship model will be appropriate.

4.4 There may also be difficulties arising from the imbalance of power between a large multinational manufacturing organisation (MMO) and its suppliers. As a buyer, the MMO potentially has significant power because of:

- Its size – and therefore the size of its requirements, which may represent a significant volume, value and proportion of business to suppliers. It may also represent a significant proportion of a total market or market segment, creating virtual monopsony (single-buyer-dominated) conditions – as discussed in Chapter 10.

- Prestige and high-profile branding – representing reputational capital for its selected suppliers

- Wide choice of suppliers through global purchasing, enabling low dependence on suppliers and ease of supplier switching. This ease of switching may be further increased by the pressure on MMOs to standardise their offerings, and therefore supplies.

- Its ownership of global patents and intellectual property – representing a strong 'lock in' factor once suppliers have developed processes and components specific to the MMO's designs

- Political and fiscal support for its activities (where they generate export earnings, employment, improved standards of living in developing markets and so on).

4.5 Size and ease of switching are key factors in high buyer power (relative to suppliers) according to Michael Porter (in his Five Forces model). If you are familiar with French & Raven's classification of the sources of power, you may also recognise that MMOs have a high degree of legitimate power (resulting from contracts and government support, say); expert power (ownership of IP); referent power (strong brand and reputation); reward power (recognised control over resources that are scarce and/or valued by the supply chain); and coercive power (the aggressive use of leverage arising from dominance in the market).

4.6 MMOs typically use their dominance, and the dependency of suppliers on their business, in various ways.

- To force down supply costs (ie supplier margins) to enhance their own competitive advantage. Because of the relatively low supply risk arising from their dominance, global supply networks and ease of switching, MMOs are likely to operate from a tactical profit or tactical acquisition strategy (Chapter 2): this enables them to use aggressive leverage to drive down costs.

- To enforce standardisation of goods and services, regardless of where production is located. This may create strong 'asset specificity' or dependency where suppliers adapt processes to products/services that may not have a market elsewhere.

- To demand quality and ethical performance from suppliers. This may be seen as an advantage to suppliers (and to local economies), particularly if it is supported with investment in infrastructure development, training, standards development and monitoring and so on. However, it may also be seen as a further erosion of supplier profit margins.

4.7 It should be added that MMOs – like all organisations – have a choice about how they wield their power.

- As we noted in Chapter 10, socially responsible buyers may be reluctant to take too much of a supplier's turnover, for example, or to insist on relationship-specific adaptations, in order to avoid over-dependency – and to maintain a versatile and market-sensitive supply base.

- Socially responsible MMOs (and those sensitive to the risk of reputational damage) may wish to avoid some of the potential negative impacts of their dominance on suppliers (eg forcing costs so low as to drive them out of business or cut safety corners) and on local economies (eg low wages, environmental damage or high-risk dependency).

- Even in dominant relationships with suppliers, power may be exercised non-coercively, ethically and constructively in the form of: mutual obligations (expressed through negotiated contracts); fair competitive pressures to meet price and non-price criteria; commercial/operational support and incentives to integrate/adapt systems and pursue quality standards (supplier development); and the offer of ongoing business where performance and price criteria are met.

Multinationals as customers and as suppliers

4.8 The size of multinational companies gives them great power in their dealings as both customers and suppliers. For example, as customers their buying power enables them to exert extreme pressure on suppliers. Most suppliers will be keen to gain or retain business from such a large-scale customer, and as a result will feel compelled to shave their profit margins to the barest minimum in order to offer an attractive price. In many cases the multinational company will insist on examining the supplier's cost base to determine whether price reductions are possible.

4.9 Another pressure on the suppliers of a multinational is to ensure standardisation of their offering. For example, a hotel chain must ensure that the quality of its facilities and its services is equivalent in all areas of the world. Otherwise they risk losing the business of their multinational customers on the grounds of poor consistency.

4.10 These pressures are not necessarily a bad thing. By insisting on the highest possible standards from its suppliers a multinational may be raising the quality of provision of suppliers across the world, and particularly of those in developing countries. By the same token, multinationals can be an important influence for adoption of CSR policies in regions where otherwise standards might remain low.

4.11 As suppliers, multinationals may take advantage of their presence in many different markets across the world. For example, it may suit them to offer different products in different countries. Frequently this can mean that a new and more advanced version of a product is released first in the United States, while other countries are constrained to manage with older and less sophisticated versions.

4.12 The existence of multiple markets equally permits multinationals to practise differential pricing. If they calculate that the market in Western Europe will bear a higher price for their products than markets in the Far East, say, they can charge different prices in the two regions. In theory European customers might be able to circumvent this by buying those products in the Far East and importing them, but the practical difficulties and extra costs may well mean that this is not feasible.

Multinationals in developing economies

4.13 There is an ongoing debate about the impact of multinationals in developing economies. Critics of big business argue that the impact is damaging: they cite exploitation of local labour forces, pollution and other environmental damage. By contrast, many commentators argue that the impact of multinationals is benign: they create employment, stimulate the local economies, and provide access to technology which the host country could not by itself afford.

4.14 The arguments will no doubt rage on, but your syllabus refers only to 'the positive impact of multinational organisations in developing economies'. For this reason, we explain the point of view that multinationals bring benefits rather than damaging the host countries.

4.15 Strong support for this view is contained in a report by the McKinsey consultancy. In 2004, the McKinsey Global Institute calculated the impact of foreign direct investment on local industries – manufacturing and services alike – in Brazil, China, India and Mexico. The industries included automotive, banking, consumer electronics, food retailing, and IT and business process outsourcing.

4.16 In 13 of the 14 cases examined, McKinsey's found that the impact of the foreign multinationals was unambiguously favourable to the host country. Positive effects included improved productivity and output, thereby raising national income while lowering prices and improving the quality and selection of services and products for consumers. Foreign investment nearly always generated positive spillovers for the rest of the economy.

4.17 A major conclusion of the McKinsey research is that the biggest benefit of foreign direct investment is its ability to raise local standards of living. This is because, contrary to what is argued by critics of multinationals, the main reason for entering overseas markets is to extend markets for products and services. (The critics, by contrast, argue that multinationals invest in local economies primarily for lower-cost production of goods that are then exported.)

4.18 The improved standard of living stems above all from the fact that wages paid by multinationals are at least equivalent to, and in most cases higher than, the wages offered by their domestic competitors. The multinationals are still able to achieve cost savings, because they pay lower wages than they would in their domestic operations.

Chapter summary

- There are certain obvious advantages of sourcing locally: faster lead times, lower delivery costs etc.

- However, these may sometimes be outweighed by reasons for sourcing from abroad: competitive prices, more reliable quality, the rise of countertrade.

- The particular problems of dealing with overseas suppliers can be classified under the headings of: culture and communications; and operational problems, such as documentation, Customs procedures, payment and legal issues.

- There are several techniques used by buyers to minimise risk in international sourcing: use of incoterms, management of foreign currency, specialised payment methods, use of local expertise. Buyers must also exercise principles of corporate social responsibility.

- Incoterms are internationally recognised terms relating to overseas trade. They define where a supplier's and a buyer's duties begin and end.

- Movements in foreign exchange rates pose a threat to buyers. Supplies may cost more to purchase than envisaged (sometimes less). Two techniques for managing the risk are leading and lagging, and foreign exchange contracts.

- The risks of overseas payment are minimised by the specialised payment method known as letters of credit. These give the seller reassurance of collecting payment from a bank in his own country, while the buyer is reassured that payment will only pass once the goods are satisfactorily received.

- Multinational companies exercise great power as suppliers and as customers. Their effects on developing economies have been the subject of much debate, but your syllabus emphasises their benign effects over any possible damage to local economies.

Self-test questions

1   What are the obvious advantages of sourcing locally? (1.2)

2   What are the obvious disadvantages of sourcing from overseas? (1.9–1.12)

3   Give examples of cultural differences in dealings with overseas suppliers. (1.19–1.23)

4   How do incoterms reduce the risk for a buyer in sourcing from overseas? (2.5)

5   Describe the responsibilities of a supplier under FOB terms, and under CIF terms. (2.9–2.11)

6   In the context of foreign exchange management, what is meant by 'leading and lagging'? (2.27)

7   Describe how a payment is made using letters of credit. (2.38, 2.39)

8   How do multinationals use their presence in different markets to leverage their muscle as suppliers? (4.11, 4.12)

9   How do multinationals benefit less developed economies? (4.17)

CHAPTER 13

Supplier Development and Relationship Development

Learning objectives

4.6   Evaluate a range of techniques to develop stronger relationships between purchasers and suppliers.

- Supplier development
- Supplier development opportunities
- Supplier development versus supplier relationships
- The stakeholder and supplier development

Chapter headings

1   Supplier development

2   Relationship development

3   Costs and benefits of development activities

Introduction

In this chapter we look at ways in which buyers can cooperate with suppliers in order to improve the relationships between them. Unusually, we focus on how buyers can give assistance without seeking immediate reimbursement. The reward they aim for is a long-term goal of improved quality, service and price from their suppliers.

1   Supplier development

What is supplier development?

1.1   Supplier development is the process of assisting suppliers to provide us with something we need. We may provide the supplier with goods, machinery, advice and technical assistance, improved technology, or anything else that will enable him to deliver to us at improved quality or reduced price.

1.2   To do this effectively, we need to engage in dialogue with the suppliers concerned. The emphasis is on working as a team, taking advantage of the knowledge and skills of all team members. This sits well with modern notions of closer, less adversarial relationships with suppliers.

1.3 Supplier development may take many forms. Research by Monczka, Trent and Handfield (published in their text *Purchasing and Supply Chain Management* 1998) identified the following main possibilities. In an earlier publication (*Purchasing and Sourcing Strategy: Trends and Implications*) Monczka and Trent had published similar figures for earlier research in 1990. In the table below, these 1990 figures are provided for comparison.

Table 13.1 *Forms of supplier development*

Form of supplier development	Percentage of organisations surveyed who practise this form of supplier development	
	1998	*1990*
Enhancing working relationships (eg by improved communication routines)	72.1%	*
Increasing performance goals (eg by reducing waste and speeding up delivery)	68.1%	68%
Requiring supplier capability improvements (eg improvements in quality or in communications)	51.5%	*
Providing support personnel (eg to assist in meeting quality targets)	27.9%	12%
Conducting training programmes (to educate suppliers in latest best practice)	25.3%	47%
Agreeing to contingent liability (eg agreeing to share the cost of failure to achieve predicted sales targets)	17.6%	3%
Providing equipment (eg when outsourcing production previously done in-house)	11.8%	3%
Providing capital (eg to help finance a new development project)	10.3%	6%
Providing progress payments during the development of a project or product	8.8%	3%

* Figures not provided.

1.4 The forms of development are listed in order of how commonly they are adopted, beginning with those that are widely adopted. Not surprisingly, the techniques that cost little in terms of money and management effort are the ones that are practised by most buyers. Relatively few buyers practise techniques that are expensive to implement.

1.5 In the third edition of their text, Monczka, Trent and Handfield provide further ideas on supplier development. In particular, they outline a 'process map' for supplier development. The eight stages of the process are illustrated in Figure 13.1, which is adapted from their text.

1.6 Stage 1 of the map emphasises that not all organisations need to worry about supplier development: their suppliers may already be world class. Even where an organisation does need to embark on this kind of programme, it will not apply to all commodities, only to those that are critical.

1.7 Stage 2 suggests that buyers must identify which suppliers require this kind of programme. The reference to Pareto analysis is a reminder that just a small number of suppliers will account for a very large amount of our critical purchases. It is on these suppliers that we must focus.

Figure 13.1 *A process map for supplier development*

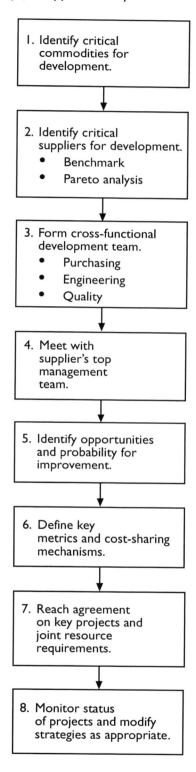

1.8   Stage 3 suggests that buyers must first ensure that they have their own house in order before approaching suppliers with proposals for development.

1.9   At Stage 4 we meet with the supplier's top management. The authors suggest that the buyer should establish three building blocks for further development: strategic alignment, measurement, and professionalism. Alignment refers to the objectives and the technology of buyer and supplier. Measurement means that we must be able to assess objectively the results of development. And naturally a tone of professionalism establishes a solid impetus for progress.

1.10   At Stage 5 we begin on the 'nuts and bolts' of the project: identifying what we can do to improve. Often this is driven by customer expectations.

1.11   At Stage 6 we appraise the proposed development project and assess its feasibility. How can we measure the financial benefits of the expected improvements and how may these be appropriately shared among the parties?

1.12   At Stage 7 we reach agreement on the projects to be implemented.

1.13   Stage 8 emphasises the importance of monitoring the outcomes once the development projects are up and running.

Supplier development in practice

1.14   CIPS guidance for this module cites practical examples of supplier development. Here are some of them.

- A buyer wants to use purchasing cards, but some of his suppliers do not have the capability. The buyer may purchase the electronic terminals for the suppliers concerned. This may be less costly than generating paper-based orders.
- A buyer pays for his supplier's manufacturing processes to be updated, in return for discounted supplies in future. The supplier loses profit on sales to this buyer, but makes significant savings through lower-cost supply to his other customers.
- A buyer outsources production of a particular module, and gives the supplier the machinery previously used in manufacture. Buyer and supplier share in the revenue generated by sales to other customers produced by the machinery.

Why develop suppliers?

1.15   Bearing in mind the expense and effort that may be involved, buyers presumably find a significant value in programmes of supplier development. The gains they expect to make may include any of the following.

- Sharing in the specialist knowledge of the supplier
- Taking advantage of the supplier's capabilities to support a strategy of outsourcing non-core activities
- Improving the supply base so as to achieve better quality, delivery or price

2 *Relationship development*

Benefits of good supplier relations

2.1   Once suppliers are on stream, it is important to manage the relationship carefully. It is not correct to assume that the legal agreement detailing the supply arrangement is sufficient to ensure the required standard of performance. Instead, buyers have a responsibility to motivate suppliers so that maximum value is obtained from the relationship.

2.2   One vital step in the process is to convince the supplier that the benefits are two-way. As a supplier becomes more familiar with the buyer's operations there is less scope for misunderstanding and mistake. There is also less need for direct selling effort on the part of the supplier. This frees up resources to concentrate on areas where cost savings can be achieved to the benefit of both parties.

2.3   From the buyer's point of view the benefits of good supplier relations are very tangible. The need to identify, appraise and train new vendors is avoided if a core group of trusted suppliers can provide most of the firm's materials requirements. Quality problems are ironed out over a period of mutual cooperation. In case of emergency, such as materials shortages or incorrect usage forecasts, suppliers will make every effort to help out if their goodwill has been secured by a systematic policy of maintaining good relations.

2.4   These benefits are most apparent when relationships reflect long-term agreements based on partnership between buyer and supplier. These give suppliers a strong motivation to perform to the best of their ability, because they know that the result will be a reliable stream of work. They also give needed encouragement if the buyer depends on the supplier to invest in research and development in order to provide state-of-the-art solutions to manufacturing problems.

2.5   In purely financial terms there are significant advantages to be derived from good relations with suppliers.

- As mentioned above, motivated suppliers are encouraged to invest in research and development. This frequently leads to lower-cost solutions.

- Use of multiple sourcing and competitive bidding involves the buyer in elaborate and lengthy communications and training with a wide variety of suppliers. The process is much streamlined, and waste is avoided, if just a few reliable suppliers are used instead.

- Long-term agreements mean that the supplier's production costs will fall as a result of the learning effect. This gives scope for price reductions that will benefit the buyer.

Managing supplier relations

2.6   Buyers have often given high priority to identifying and evaluating potential suppliers, while paying less attention to the management of supplier relations once contracts have been awarded. Partly this arose from a climate in which large stockholdings were accepted as an indispensable safety mechanism: if a supplier let you down, it need not be a disaster.

2.7   The discussion above has outlined why such neglect is to be regretted. An active approach to supplier management can bring benefits to both sides. In an era where stockholding is seen as an evil to be avoided, this is even more important because supplier failings have a proportionately greater impact. This section sets out some of the measures that purchasing specialists should take to ensure that such failings do not occur.

2.8   The process should begin as early as possible. From the first stages of evaluating suppliers there should be emphasis on avoiding misunderstandings. Well drafted specifications and constructive face-to-face contact are equally important in this context. In some cases this approach is formalised in a system of early supplier involvement (ESI).

2.9   To minimise the possibility of misunderstandings buyers should adopt a comprehensive approach to the issues for discussion. These should not be confined to the terms and conditions of the agreement. It helps to look behind the agreed terms so that each party knows how the other is operating in order to achieve the requirements. This could involve discussion and clarification of any or all of the following matters.

- Timetable of stages in the operation
- Staff planning: grades of staff, estimated number of hours, arrangements for supervision etc
- Rules and procedures relating to site conditions, operations and safety issues
- Invoicing and payment procedures
- Buyer's responsibilities to provide tools, facilities etc
- Supplier's responsibilities for reporting on progress
- Procedures and timetable for review of progress

2.10   Once these initial procedures have been completed, it remains the buyer's responsibility to motivate the supplier. Of course the supplier should in any case be motivated by the thought of not gaining repeat business if performance is poor, but this is a somewhat negative factor. On a more positive note, many buyers have introduced systems of recognition for suppliers who achieve consistently high performance. This may take the form of private communication with the supplier concerned, or may be a more high-profile exercise involving publishing the names of selected suppliers.

2.11   Another method of smoothing supplier relations involves the provision of training. Dobler and Burt (in *Purchasing and Supply Management*) refer to a number of companies who train their suppliers in techniques of statistical process control, just in time manufacturing and total quality commitment.

2.12   Another area of cooperation is in problem solving when suppliers run into difficulties. Instead of walking away with a shrug of the shoulders, buyers should be ready to accept that their own firm's success depends on the supplier's ability to perform. This should encourage a joint approach to dealing with the difficulties that inevitably arise during complex supply agreements.

2.13   This last issue leads on to another question: how closely should buyers monitor the progress of suppliers to ensure that all is going according to plan? Clearly, it is the supplier's responsibility to ensure that contractual agreements are fulfilled to the desired standard. However, this does not mean that the buyer can simply sit back and hope for the best. Particularly on large-scale one-off projects buyers should take an active interest in the supplier's operations.

2.14 It may be that use of specialised project planning techniques is required, such as network analysis and Gantt charts. If so, then buyers should be encouraged to monitor the output from such systems.

Developing the relationship further

2.15 So far so good, but now suppose we need to develop the relationship further. For example, we may want to move towards a less arm's length relationship because our requirement for a particular supplier's goods is becoming more critical. It could be that over a course of dealing we eventually move closer and closer together through the various stages in the relationship spectrum.

2.16 Ideas for closer links may originate either with the buyer or with the supplier. Buyers must get into the habit of discussing with key suppliers the possible developments that may be appropriate in their relationship. It is always important to emphasise interpersonal relationships.

2.17 One sign of a relationship growing closer is an increase in trust. While written terms and conditions in a detailed contract may be vital in an arm's length relationship, closer links may be formalised in a less weighty document. The personnel most directly involved in the relationship – senior buying staff and senior selling staff – may well prefer to operate on the basis of a short summary of the agreement between the two firms. This does not prevent the legal specialists drawing up a more detailed document containing the strict terms underlying the agreement.

2.18 Another positive sign in a developing relationship is a readiness by both parties to innovate. Once personnel from two organisations are working together they are ready to swap ideas with each other arising out of their frequent contacts. This can lead to benefits for both sides in terms of cost savings and improved efficiencies in processes.

3 Costs and benefits of development activities

The buyer's perspective

3.1 As with all other business activities, it is important to assess the costs and benefits of development activities. Working hard to achieve benefits that are less valuable than they cost is clearly wasteful. So what costs and benefits may a buyer expect to arise if he pursues a policy of supplier and relationship development? See Table 13.2.

Table 13.2 *Costs and benefits of development activities: buyer's perspective*

Costs	Benefits
Management time expended in researching and identifying potential suppliers	Reduction in waste along the supply chain, with favourable impact on the buyer's profits
Management time spent with the supplier discussing the relationship and its possible development	Improvements in products and services, including reduction in time to market and new product development
Cost of equipment and systems designed to run the new relationship successfully	Reduction in production and process costs
Risks involved in sharing information, eg abuse of intellectual property, disclosure of trade secrets	Additional sales arising from improvements to products or reductions in selling prices

The supplier's perspective

3.2 Naturally, the supplier will be conducting a similar assessment of costs and benefits. From his point of view, the balance sheet might look like this.

Table 13.3 *Costs and benefits of development activities: supplier's perspective*

Costs	Benefits
Management time expended in researching and identifying potential customers	Reduction in waste along the supply chain, with favourable impact on the supplier's profits
Management time spent with the customer discussing the relationship and its possible development	Improvements in service to customer arising from greater sharing of information, eg on scheduling
Cost of equipment and systems designed to run the new relationship successfully	Reduction in production and process costs
Risks involved in sharing information, eg abuse of intellectual property, disclosure of trade secrets	Additional sales arising from improvements to customer service which can be used to attract other customers
Restrictions on supplying competitors of the new customer	Longer-term security of business

The costs of quality

3.3 Some of the benefits of development activities are seen clearly when we examine the costs relating to quality.

3.4 The **cost of quality** can be defined as the difference between the actual cost of producing and selling products or services and the costs that would have been incurred if there were no failures during production or usage. By failing to achieve 100 per cent quality, there is a cost to the organisation.

3.5 Quality costs are incurred because the quality of production or a service is not perfect. There are four categories of quality costs.

- **Prevention cost.** This is a cost incurred before a product is made or a service is performed, in order to prevent substandard quality or defective quality being delivered.

- **Appraisal cost or inspection cost.** This is a cost incurred after the product has been made, to ensure that it meets the required quality standard.

- **Internal failure cost.** This is a cost arising from inadequate quality, where the problem is identified before the product is delivered to the customer.

- **External failure cost.** This is a cost arising from inadequate quality, where the problem is identified after the product has been transferred to the customer.

Figure 13.2 *The costs related to quality*

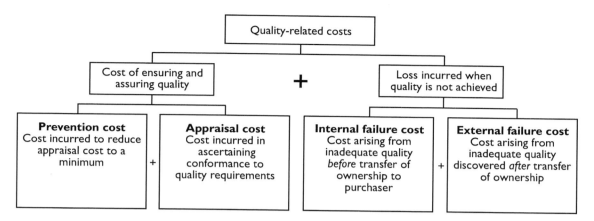

3.6 The different categories of quality cost can be illustrated in the context of a manufacturing operation.

3.7 **Prevention costs** include:

- The cost of building quality into the product design.
- The cost of training staff in error prevention or quality improvement.
- The cost of installing any prevention devices (for example, fail-safe features in the production equipment).

3.8 **Appraisal/inspection costs** include:

- Costs of inspecting finished goods or services.
- Other checking devices such as supplier vetting/due diligence.
- Costs of inspecting goods inwards.

3.9 **Internal failure costs** include:

- Cost of materials scrapped due to failures in the goods received section or inventory control.
- Cost of materials and components lost during the production process.
- Cost of units rejected during the inspection process.
- Cost of any reworking of faulty output.
- Losses due to having to sell faulty output at lower prices.

3.10 **External failure costs** include:

- Cost of warranty claims from customers.
- Cost of repairing products returned by customers.
- Cost of replacing substandard products.
- Delivery costs of handling returned units.
- Cost of the customer services section.
- Loss of customer goodwill and loss of future sales.

3.11   In a traditional approach to quality management, it is argued that there is an optimal level of quality effort, that minimises total quality costs. Beyond this level of quality effort spending more on quality will yield a benefit less than the additional cost incurred. Since diminishing returns set in beyond the optimal quality level, there is no value to be gained by trying to improve the quality further.

3.12   The importance of all this to supplier development and relationship development is that both parties can work cooperatively to reduce quality-related costs in all four areas. This will lead to important benefits for both buyer and supplier.

Chapter summary

*   Supplier development is the process of assisting suppliers (eg with goods, machinery, advice, technology, technical assistance etc) to provide us with something we need.

*   Monczka and others outline an eight-stage 'process map' for supplier development.

*   Reasons for developing suppliers include: sharing in the supplier's specialist knowledge; taking advantage of the supplier's capabilities by outsourcing; improving the supply base generally.

*   Benefits of good supplier relations include a reduction in wasted time and important cost savings.

*   There may come a time when we want to deepen our relationship with a particular supplier. Ideas for development may come from either buyer or supplier.

*   From the perspectives of both buyer and supplier, there are both costs and benefits involved in a programme of supplier development

*   The costs of quality can be categorised as prevention cost, appraisal cost, internal failure cost and external failure cost.

Self-test questions

1   List as many forms of supplier development as you can. (Table 13.1)

2   List as many stages as you can in the eight-stage process map of supplier development. (1.6ff)

3   Give practical examples of supplier development. (1.14)

4   What are the benefits to a buyer of good supplier relations? (2.3)

5   What issues should buyer and supplier discuss in an attempt to improve relations? (2.9)

6   Describe signs that indicate buyer and supplier are moving towards a closer relationship. (2.17, 2.18)

7   List costs and benefits of supplier development activities (a) from the buyer's perspective, and (b) from the supplier's perspective. (Tables 13.2 and 13.3)

8   What are the four categories of quality-related costs? (3.5)

9   List costs arising in each category of quality-related costs. (3.7ff)

CHAPTER 14

Measuring Performance

Learning objectives

4.8   Evaluate a range of measurement tools to assess the performance of suppliers and the strength of relationships between purchasers and suppliers.

- Executive sponsorship
- Account management
- Continuous improvement programmes
- Service level agreements
- Key performance indicators
- Relationship assessment tools
- Feedback mechanisms

Chapter headings

1   Measuring relationship performance

2   Measuring supplier performance

3   Measurement tools

Introduction

We have devoted most of this book to discussions of relations with suppliers and how these may be improved. However, it is not easy to objectively assess how successful our efforts have been unless we have some method of measurement. In this chapter we look at how our suppliers and our relationships with them can be measured.

1   Measuring relationship performance

Introduction

1.1   In a 'traditional' customer-supplier relationship, control is with the customer.

- The customer continually demands improvements from the supplier, and expects to be the beneficiary of any improvements that are made.
- The relationship is characterised by petty disputes and arguments, with poor interpersonal relations between the purchaser and the supplier's representative.
- The customer takes the view that he is never wrong, and whenever any difficulties occur, the problem is passed to the supplier to resolve.

1.2 A more sensible assessment of the customer-supplier relationship should be one where both parties can admit to making mistakes and being capable of improvement. For example, the customer can affect performance by:

- changing delivery schedules and order quantities
- altering order specifications
- poor communication with the supplier
- late payment of invoices
- taking an adversarial attitude to the supplier.

1.3 A customer-supplier relationship should be assessed by an exchange of information, an attitude of wanting to help, and a willingness to make ideas and suggestions. This type of relationship assessment will be more easily achieved where:

- there is a spirit of trust
- the customer and the supplier have a close business relationship and understand each other well
- individuals at various levels in the customer organisation know and get on well with individuals at different levels in the supplier organisation.

The supplier's perspective

1.4 It is not too difficult to imagine how a supplier will rate his relationship with a buyer. He will be concerned with the key variables covered by the supply relationship.

- Adherence to contract terms in relation to volume, required lead times, payment etc
- Operational efficiency in terms of scheduling (and changes to schedules), specifications, communications and reporting, interpersonal relationships etc
- A fair sharing of risks and rewards
- Being given an opportunity to perform well, without every minor problem escalated to the level of a crisis

1.5 The buyer should always bear in mind the supplier preferencing model and attempt to work out how his suppliers regard the buying organisation.

The buyer's perspective

1.6 A buyer must assess whether his current relationship with a supplier is satisfactory. The work of Leenders, Fearon, Flynn and Johnson (*Purchasing and Supply Management*, 12th edition, 2002) is influential in this regard.

1.7 These authors emphasise that different people in the buying organisation may have different perceptions on this point. In simple cases the buyer's impression may depend on an instantaneous reaction to the supplier's sales representative. But in the case of a long-term strategic relationship the assessment will be based on past and current performance, personal relationships and future expectations. Such assessments may change over time.

1.8   Leenders *et al* provide what they describe as 'a simple framework for clarifying the current purchaser-supplier relationship in terms of satisfaction and stability': see Figure 14.1.

Figure 14.1 *A simple purchaser-supplier satisfaction model*

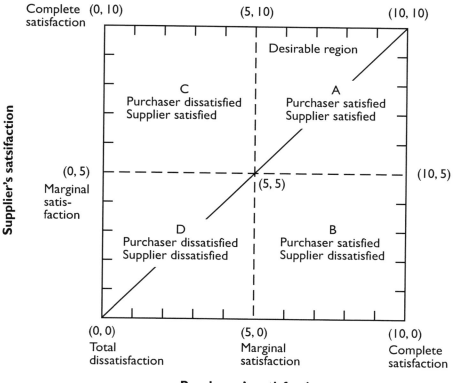

1.9   You may well disagree with the idea that this model is simple, but it is a likely examination topic, so we will press on with it by listing the assumptions on which it is founded.

- We assume that satisfaction with a current supplier relationship can be assessed, however crudely, at least in macro terms, whether it is satisfactory or not.
- We assume that an unsatisfied party (seller or purchaser or both) will attempt to move to a more satisfactory situation.
- We assume that attempts to move may affect the stability of the relationship.
- We assume that attempts to move may fall in the win-lose, as well as the lose-lose, lose-win, and win-win categories.
- We assume that purchaser and seller may well have different perceptions of the same relationship.
- We assume that many tools and techniques and approaches exist that will assist either party in moving positions and improving stability.

1.10 Leenders *et al* proceed by remarking on characteristics of each quadrant in the model.

1.11 In the top right quadrant both parties are satisfied and stability is likely. However, there may still be scope for considerable improvement: for example, a relationship assessed at (5.5, 5.5) falls into this quadrant but is far short of the ideal (10, 10).

1.12 In the bottom right quadrant the buyer is at least marginally satisfied, but the supplier is not. Stability is unlikely, because the supplier will be seeking change. (Another assumption of the model is that bargaining power of buyer and supplier is approximately equal. If one party is dominant, they may be able to resist the other party's efforts to obtain change.)

1.13 The top left quadrant is the mirror image of the bottom right: supplier at least marginally satisfied, buyer not. The buyer will be seeking change.

1.14 In the bottom left quadrant nobody is satisfied. Needless to say, stability will not result from this situation: both parties want change.

1.15 The authors describe the diagonal line as a line of stability or fairness. Movements along this line represent equal improvement (or deterioration) for each party. Both extremes of this line – (0, 0) and (10, 10) are unlikely to exist in practice, the latter because life is never that perfect, the former because no relationship would exist at all if both parties are completely unhappy.

Using the model

1.16 By mapping our relations with suppliers onto the model, we can assess how many of our supplier relationships are satisfactory and how many are not. This can form a starting point for a dialogue with suppliers classified in the unsatisfactory sectors. It also helps in focusing our efforts where they are most needed. For example, we will give higher priority to a (1, 5) relationship than to a (5, 5) relationship of similar monetary value.

1.17 What tools and techniques can we use to bring about change? Leenders et all distinguish between 'crunch' tools – negative measures that may lead to drastic change and possibly severance of the relationship – and 'stroking' tools (more positive, less severe approaches). See Table 14.1 for examples.

Table 14.1 *Tools for moving positions*

The buyer's crunch tools	The buyer's stroking tools
Complete severance of purchases without advance notice	Granting of substantial volumes of business or long-term commitments
Refusal to pay bills	Sharing of internal information, eg on schedules
Refusal to accept shipments	Evidence of willingness to change behaviour
Use or threat of legal action	Rapid positive response to requests from suppliers, eg on discussing price changes

The seller's crunch tools	The seller's stroking tools
Refusal to send shipments as promised	Willingness to make rapid adjustments to price, delivery etc
Unilateral price increase without notice	Inviting the purchaser to discuss areas of difference
Insistence on unreasonable length of contract, onerous escalation clauses etc	Giving ample advance notice of pending changes in price, lead times etc

1.18 According to the authors, stroking techniques are more likely to be used in the A quadrant, further strengthening the stability of the relationship. The use of crunch tools, by contrast, may accomplish short-term objectives, but may damage chances of a stable relationship in the future.

2 *Measuring supplier performance*

Introduction

2.1 When assessing the performance of its suppliers and its own purchasing performance, an organisation is trying to assess whether it is achieving good value. An organisation achieves competitive advantage by meeting the requirements of its own customers better than its rivals. The effectiveness and efficiency of supplier performance and purchasing performance can therefore be considered in terms of:

- the benefits that have been obtained for the customer, and
- whether the customer is aware of those benefits.

2.2 The perceptions of the immediate customer, and the perceptions of the consumer at the end of the supply chain, are worth considering. If the customer and end-consumer are unaware of any noticeable benefit, it would presumably have to be concluded that:

- there has been no improvement in supplier performance and no improvement in purchasing performance, or
- any improvements that have been made have not been passed on to the customer, or
- the customer does not value the improvements that have been made.

The voice of the customer

2.3 The voice of the customer refers to the perceptions held by customers. If the view is taken that the customer is king, listening to the voice of the customer is imperative for suppliers. In other words, a supplier must understand what a customer wants so that he can try to supply a product or service that meets the customer's requirements.

2.4 In some industries, the voice of the customer is not always easy to hear. This is because the customer does not make any comment if the product or service is satisfactory, and only speaks in complaint when the service is sub-standard. An example might be air travel, where most customers are unlikely to make any comment if they are flown to their destination in comfort and on time. They will only speak up if flights are delayed, cancelled or diverted.

2.5 Market research is a well-established technique for finding out the views of consumers, and similar research can be carried out on industrial buyers. Research into industrial customers will have the following features.

- It will seek to obtain a detailed view of the perceptions held by the customer.
- It can allow for a two-way communication between customer and supplier.
- It looks into customer satisfaction and relationship satisfaction issues.

2.6 Research can also obtain answers to questions that are often unasked, such as:

- What really matters to my customer?
- What doesn't matter to my customer?
- In what ways am I meeting, exceeding or missing my customer's expectations?
- Where should I be focusing my attention?

Examples of supplier performance measures

2.7 There are a number of factors in a supplier's performance that a buyer will want to measure.

- Purchase price
- Total cost of ownership
- Quality
- Delivery performance
- Service performance
- Compliance with environmental and CSR standards
- Level of technological capability
- Level of satisfaction among other customers of the supplier

2.8 Each of these can be measured with a number of possible benchmarks.

- An agreed standard, probably laid down in the contract
- An established industry norm
- Past performance
- Performance of other suppliers, including former suppliers of the same product or service

2.9 Once the buyer has settled on appropriate indicators, after consultation with key stakeholders including the supplier, he should implement a system of regular measurement and comparison with benchmarks. Where a shortfall is detected, appropriate management action should be taken to investigate and remedy the problem.

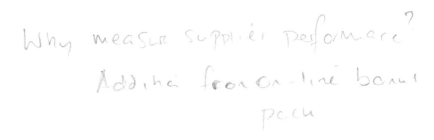

3 Measurement tools

Executive sponsorship

3.1 Topic 4.8 on your syllabus refers to a number of measurement tools used to assess the performance of suppliers and the strength of relationships between purchasers and suppliers. It is not always clear what the author of the syllabus had in mind when referring to these tools, and there is no explanation in the CIPS guidance for this unit. In this section of the chapter we attempt to throw some light on what was intended.

3.2 To begin with, the syllabus refers to 'executive sponsorship'. It is difficult to see how this can refer to any kind of measurement tool, and we interpret the term here as referring to the need for senior management commitment to the idea of performance measurement.

3.3 On this interpretation, we are expected to envisage that a 'sponsor' is chosen from among the senior management team. His task is to support the implementation and operation of the measurement system, using his influence as a senior manager to ensure that it is taken seriously by all parties.

3.4 Typically (but not exclusively), the executive sponsor is a senior executive within the buyer organisation that has overall executive responsibility for the relational development between the organisation and nominated key suppliers.

3.5 The executive sponsor, who is typically from outside the procurement function, will oversee cross-functional activity or simply a targeted key supplier development being managed solely by the procurement function. Commitment to the sponsor project needs to be a two-way affair in order to achieve a strong executive-level alliance between the respective organisations.

3.6 Typically, executive sponsors will meet at least quarterly to review the progress of a key supplier development initiative and its success in achieving the nominated relational objectives. From the supplier's perspective, the sponsors provide a high-level point of contact within the buyer organisation which further demonstrates the commitment of the buyer organisation and the relational value of the supplier.

3.7 The main responsibilities for the executive sponsor's role are as follows.

- Coordinate internal and external interactions with key suppliers and take on responsibility for overall supplier performance and relational development.

- Ensure the alignment of organisational strategic objectives with supplier development objectives across all touch-points. This should introduce business consistency in dealings with key suppliers thereby enhancing trust, and increasing the willingness of suppliers to invest in the relationship.

- Actively promote the relational alliance concept within both buyer and supplier organisations.

- Review achievements related to mutually established key initiatives that are required to bring added value to the relationship and ensure that expectations are being met.

- Resolve relational barriers – conflicting requirements will inevitably arise within such relationships from time to time. When the respective core teams cannot resolve these conflicts, executive sponsors should help reach an acceptable solution.

- Input suggestions and recommendations for future supplier relational enhancements.

3.8 The activities that an executive sponsor might engage in include any or all of the following.

- Attend meetings relating to the measurement of performance, eg meetings in which buyer and supplier debate and eventually agree on key performance indicators (KPIs)

- Track progress of the performance measurement system

- Use his influence within the organisation to remove any barriers or obstacles to the implementation of the system

- Support the buying team in dealing with the supplier if there is failure to meet KPIs

- Report to senior management

3.9 Recent survey findings relative to the use of the executive sponsor's role have revealed some mixed findings.

- Relatively few suppliers surveyed had participated in executive sponsor programmes.

- Key suppliers who had participated in such initiatives viewed the sponsor programme as mainly a 'back door' insurance policy, useful in resolving critical relational problems that the cross-functional or procurement teams can't handle. The key suppliers also see the sponsor facility as an opportunity to further open dialogue about mutual business issues and future opportunities.

- In general, survey respondents from both parties were willing to invest the time necessary to educate respective executive sponsors on their business.

- The frequency of formal executive sponsor reviews was reported to be in the range of 2 to 4 times per year with informal communications used as required.

Account management

3.10 Account management is concerned with ensuring that a contract is performed to the required standard, meeting the specifications, terms and conditions agreed between the buyer and the supplier.

3.11 Aspects of account management include the following.

- Managing all aspects of the relationship between the supplier and the buyer's customers (ie the internal customers in the buyer's organisation).

- Ensuring delivery of the goods or service from the supplier on the agreed terms and to the agreed standard.

- Encouraging the supplier to adhere to agreed standards or key performance indicators (KPIs) and to seek improvements in performance throughout the duration of the relationship.

- Considering future purchasing requirements, and so exploring developments in the supply market so as to achieve improved performance with future purchases.

3.12 The term *account management* suggests that the focus of management attention should be on the performance of particular contracts. The term *relationship management*, on the other hand, can be used to describe the management of the long-term relationship with a supplier, not just the performance of individual transactions.

3.13 The required skills of an account manager are knowledge of the products or services purchased, an understanding of contracts and contractual terms, an ability to write contract specifications, and good interpersonal skills. An account manager must be able to communicate, negotiate, persuade, and listen to the supplier. In other words an account manager will have a large influence on the nature of the relationship with the supplier.

3.14 The benefits of account management are:

- Better control by the buyer over the execution of supply contracts.
- Maintaining communication with the supplier during the course of the relationship, and helping to achieve better performance by the supplier.
- Possibly, improvements in cost and quality, thereby adding value.
- The ability to anticipate and foresee problems early, and deal with them before they become serious.
- Ensuring that the buyer carries out its undertakings properly, so that unnecessary difficulties with the supplier are avoided.

3.15 Effective account management is perhaps most valuable with large and complex contracts, or lengthy contracts, where problems can arise. The effective account manager will seek to resolve potential disputes or difficulties between the buyer and the supplier, and in doing so strengthen the relationship between them. Problems that an account manager might be able to foresee and deal with include the following.

- A lack of communication between the buyer and the supplier, with the result that some unnecessary work is done or some essential work is overlooked.
- The supplier fails to comply with its undertakings, and needs to be notified and asked to rectify the error or omission.
- The contract specifications are incomplete or incorrect, and need to be rectified.
- The buyer and supplier argue about price, or responsibility for unforeseen expenditure.
- The buyer changes the order specifications, and has to renegotiate terms and price.
- The supplier has financial difficulties, and has insufficient cashflow to complete the order without early payment from the buyer. If the supplier becomes insolvent, it will be unable to perform the contract. If the buyer provides financial support, it might be insufficient to save the supplier from insolvency anyway.
- Inflation pushes up the price of materials and labour for the supplier, and the supplier wants to increase prices to allow for this.

Continuous improvement

3.16 The modern total quality management (TQM) perspective does not have a target for achievement. It is an attitude or philosophy. There will always be some other way of doing things better, and an organisation should continually look for ways of achieving further improvement. The search for quality never ends.

3.17 'Kaizen' is a Japanese word meaning gradual and orderly, continuous improvement. A kaizen business strategy involves everyone in the organisation working together to make improvements, without any large capital investment.

3.18 A TQM approach is not to seek major one-off improvements. Small changes can be made, each providing extra value. Small improvements do not need senior management to find them. They can be identified, discussed and agreed at a 'local' level in the organisation.

3.19 Improvements can be achieved by finding better ways of organising work and work flow to add value, so as to improve the quality, speed, flexibility or the dependability or reliability of a product, service or process, or to reduce cost. It is a culture of sustained continuous improvement focusing on eliminating waste in all systems and processes.

3.20 There are two elements to kaizen: improvements and change for the better on the one hand and continuity on the other. The Kaizen Institute, on its website, comments that: 'Business as usual' is not kaizen, because it provides continuity without improvement. 'Breakthrough' is also not kaizen, because this provides improvement but without continuity.

3.21 Although a company can seek continuous improvement within its own operations, it should also consider how improvements can be made further back along the supply chain. Suppliers should be encouraged to adopt a continuous improvement philosophy, and in particular, should consider ways of adding value at the buyer-supplier interface, where the potential for adding value is usually the greatest.

3.22 The implementation of a continuous improvement programme has to be fully supported by senior management. Without the whole-hearted commitment of senior management, it will be too easy for individuals to throw a 'wet blanket' over suggestions for improvements from subordinates or team members, with comments such as 'I'm too busy to look at it', 'It isn't in the budget' or 'Now's not a good time to be trying to change anything'.

Service level agreements

3.23 A crucial element in the success of external service provision is to reach clear agreement on the level of service to be provided. Refer back to Chapter 8, where service level agreements were discussed in detail, and illustrated by reference to a company hiring external contractors to provide office cleaning services.

Key performance indicators

3.24 We have already mentioned the importance of KPIs under the heading of account management above.

3.25 As the specification is developed, each requirement or characteristic of the goods or services must be qualified in terms of how the buying organisation will be able to assess and measure that this particular requirement has been met. These measures may be revisited and refined as the specification is progressed.

3.26   It may be helpful to consider five broad headings or criteria under which these performance measures may be developed.

- Quality
- Cost
- Timeliness
- Quantity
- Compliance

Under each performance criterion a number of key performance indicators (KPIs) may be developed.

3.27   Table 14.2 below suggests how these criteria and indicators may be developed for a particular contract. The example given is for an outsourced vending service.

Table 14.2 *Performance measures for vending services*

Performance criterion	Performance indicator
Quality	Management systems and processes are clear and documented
Cost	Consumable purchasing rates are benchmarked for value for money
Timeliness	Service delivered within the agreed periods of availability
Quantity	Stocks maintained to appropriate levels to ensure continuity of service
Compliance	Corporate policies and procedures adhered to

3.28   It is important to balance both quantitative measures (ie those that can be numerically evaluated, such as costs and quantity), and qualitative measures (ie those that are more subjective and rely on customer feedback, such as quality). The performance management system should be designed to issue an alert if any of these KPIs are not met.

3.29   Before the contract is awarded the buyer will need to ensure that the appropriate systems and procedures are in place to capture the information required to measure performance. For example, costs will need to be captured through an account code or cost centre, and be readily attributable to the contract. It may be possible to extract this information from the existing finance system, but it may involve new codes to be set up for the contract. For the buyer to ensure compliance with corporate policies and procedures it may be necessary to undertake regular audits and visual inspections. The scope and frequency of these will need to be agreed.

Relationship assessment tools

3.30   Refer back to Section 1 of this chapter, and in particular to the purchaser-supplier satisfaction model of Leenders et al.

Feedback mechanisms

3.31   Any measurement tools used will be effective only if their outputs are carefully monitored. This requires systematic feedback mechanisms, providing information for the buyer to assess. Regular reporting (eg of actual cost savings against target savings, actual delivery performance against target performance) must be built into the system.

Chapter summary

- Both buyer and supplier may be at fault if a supply contract is not working. It's not safe to assume that the fault always lies with the supplier.

- The purchaser-supplier satisfaction model developed by Leenders and others indicates how satisfied both buyer and supplier may be within a particular relationship.

- Where both parties are satisfied (the top right quadrant in the Leenders model), stability is likely. In other quadrants, movement is likely.

- Leenders also suggests a number of tools that both buyers and suppliers may use in order to shift their position in the grid.

- There are many factors in a supplier's performance that a buyer will want to measure (purchase price, total cost of ownership etc).

- A buyer can use a number of measurement tools to assess the performance of suppliers and the strength of relationships: executive sponsorship, account management, continuous improvement, service level agreements, key performance indicators etc.

Self-test questions

1   In what ways may a buyer be at fault in a supply contract that is not running smoothly? (1.2)

2   What key variables will a supplier be concerned with when assessing a supply relationship? (1.4)

3   Describe the Leenders model for assessing purchaser and supplier satisfaction. (1.8 and Figure 14.1)

4   What are the assumptions underlying the Leenders model? (1.9)

5   List as many crunch tools and stroking tools as you can for moving a buyer's position on the purchaser-supplier satisfaction matrix. Do the same exercise from the supplier's perspective. (Table 14.1)

6   List factors that a buyer will want to assess in a supplier's performance. (2.7)

7   What benchmarks might the buyer use to measure a supplier's performance? (2.8)

8   What kind of activities might an executive sponsor contribute to? (3.8)

9   List the benefits of account management. (3.14)

10   Under what five broad headings or criteria might supplier performance measures be developed? (3.26)

CHAPTER 15

Mock Exam

THE EXEMPLAR PAPER

The exam paper below was published by CIPS as an illustration of what might be expected under the new syllabus. If you are able to make a good attempt at this you should be very well prepared for the live examination.

Instructions for Candidates:

This examination is in two sections.

Section A has two compulsory questions, worth 25 marks each.

Section B has four questions: answer two. Each question is worth 25 marks.

SECTION A

You are strongly advised to carefully read and analyse the information in the case study before attempting to answer questions 1 and 2.

Background

Albert Blunt is the purchasing manager for a major UK charity which looks at the needs of disabled children. The charity has over 600 high street shops and 15,000 volunteers.

Albert takes pride in his traditional view of supplier relationships which is reflected in his adversarial relationship style with suppliers and the people who work for them. He is often heard to say that you cannot use the words 'trust and supplier' in the same sentence. Albert bargains hard with suppliers and has never accepted so much as a pen from them. Albert also believes that he could make up his mind about a supplier within five seconds of meeting them.

The charity did not have a large purchasing staff and Albert made decisions quickly and without deliberating on strategies and always insisted that his suppliers delivered right first time, on time.

Problems

Albert was having a bad day. He was faced by two problems that related to two contracts he had negotiated recently, both using his preferred style.

1   Firstly, there was the contract for promotional plastic aeroplanes, which were actually marker pens in five different colours – "the kids will love them", one of his colleagues had said. Albert sourced these items internationally, following an internet search and at a fraction of the price that European suppliers wanted to charge.

2   Secondly there was the transport of goods to and from distribution centres and shops where he had used his persuasion skills to develop a partnership with a national electrical goods retailer, FMCG plc, to use its own distribution network to deliver for the charity at a fraction of what it would normally cost, in return for free advertising and the occasional leaflet from FMCG being included within the charity's mailshots.

Albert had just received an email with a scanned copy of an article from a national newspaper where his charity was identified as a major new customer of Kaisler Manufacturing, located 50 miles from the main port of the country and where children working in poor conditions were used to make promotional products in factories with a bad environmental record.

The second email Albert had received was from central administration. It asked him if he had the budget to fund the additional postage costs caused by the substantial and regular distribution of leaflets on behalf of FMCG plc.

Dealing with Kaisler

To resolve the Kaisler problem, Albert decided to telephone the organisation but was annoyed that no one answered the phone, so instead he left a message.

No one returned his call that day but the next morning when he switched on his computer there was an email from Mr Kaisler saying that he would phone Albert at 0700 GMT time that day. The email also said that the first shipment was ready for the charity to collect and a sample of each of the items was being couriered for Albert's personal attention at Kaisler's expense.

As Albert had arrived at work at 0830 he had missed the call but the samples arrived and were excellent. Still concerned that he had not had his questions answered Albert phoned again and then emailed his concerns both about the corporate social responsibility (CSR) issues and the fact that he was expected to collect the goods. Delivery to the charity's distribution centre was, as Albert pointed out, his requirement.

The next day Mr Kaisler replied by email that he had quoted 'excellent quality, at excellent price and ex-works from his excellent factory'. He said he gave excellent employment opportunities to '400 local people of all ages, most of whom provided the main income to the household' and in return he felt that Mr Blunt should send a payment to the Kaisler bank account. Once this was done the goods could be released for collection.

The FMCG issue

To try and resolve the FMCG issue Albert picked up the phone and shouted at Sandra Povey, the marketing manager at FMCG. 'It's got to stop', he said, 'you are costing us far too much in postage, this is not what I had in mind when we agreed the contract'. Sandra replied that, 'while it might be costing you in postage, it was saving the charity a great deal in transport'. Before Sandra ended the call (she said that she had to go to meet an important customer), Sandra advised Albert to 'do a cost/benefit analysis and stop complaining'.

The information in this case study is purely fictitious and has been prepared for assessment purposes only.

Any resemblance to any organisation or person is purely coincidental.

SECTION A

Questions 1 and 2 relate to the case study and should be answered in the context of the information provided.

Question 1

(a) Identify and describe **two** corporate social responsibility (CSR) issues that Albert should have considered before awarding a contract to Kaisler. **(8 marks)**

(b) Describe **five** additional difficulties, in addition to CSR issues, which a purchasing organisation like this charity may find in building up relationships with organisations in distant parts of the world. **(10 marks)**

(c) Identify what Albert should have done to protect the position of his purchasing department when dealing with Kaisler. **(7 marks)**

Question 2

(a) Appraise the business relationship that exists between the charity and FMCG plc, giving examples to support your answer. **(12 marks)**

(b) Define the term reciprocal trading. **(3 marks)**

(c) Identify the advice Albert should have been given regarding reciprocal trading before he did the deal with FMCG plc. **(10 marks)**

SECTION B

Answer **TWO** questions from Section B.

You are strongly advised to carefully read all the questions in Section B before selecting **TWO** questions to answer.

Question 3

(a) Identify and describe a model that may be used by purchasing departments to determine that some purchases they make and some relationships that they enter into are more important than others. **(12 marks)**

(b) Identify and describe how suppliers divide customers into ones which receive different levels of service. **(13 marks)**

Question 4

Identify and describe the benefits of **five** 'e-tools' used in purchasing organisations.

(25 marks)

Question 5

Describe **five** ways in which the public sector supplier selection processes differ from those processes used in the private sector. **(25 marks)**

Question 6

(a)   Define the term 'outsourcing'.   **(5 marks)**

(b)   Describe **five** benefits that a purchasing organisation may seek from outsourcing.

(10 marks)

(c)   Describe how internal relationships change when a part of an organisation is outsourced.

(10 marks)

CHAPTER 16

MOCK EXAM: SUGGESTED SOLUTIONS

THE EXEMPLAR PAPER

Some general observations

Make sure that you have read the 'Instructions for Candidates' section at the front of the Mock Exam, in order to be quite clear as to what is required.

Please bear in mind that our solutions are lengthier than you would attempt in an exam, in order to cover the wide range of points that might be included – and to reflect the suggestions given in the CIPS Answer Guidance.

SUGGESTED SOLUTIONS

SECTION A

Solution 1

Part (a)

A definition of corporate social responsibility (CSR) is as follows.

CSR is concerned with treating the stakeholders of the firm ethically or in a responsible manner. 'Ethically or responsibly' means treating key stakeholders in a manner deemed acceptable in civilised societies. Social includes economic and environmental responsibility. Stakeholders exist both within a firm and outside. The wider aim of social responsibility is to create higher and higher standards of living, while preserving the profitability of the corporation, for peoples both within and outside the corporation

Source: Michael Hopkins: *A Planetary Bargain: Corporate Social Responsibility Comes of Age* (Macmillan, UK, 2005)

In his negotiations with Kaisler two of the CSR issues that Albert should have considered relate to the environment and human rights.

Tutorial note. *For both, a description of the issue was required. Answers may comment upon specific actions that Albert could have taken before he placed the work with Kaisler. Candidates could have answered with the two issues first and then the advice afterwards, but a better structure would be to bring out the issues and then advise Albert of the courses of action he could take on each issue.*

Environmental responsibility

Any purchasing organisation has a responsibility to consider the impact of the negotiated supply on the global environment. For example, is the product being sourced produced from sustainable materials? Is the process of excavation or manufacture having an adverse impact on the local environment (eg harmful emissions)?

In this case Albert's primary motivation was to source the product at the lowest possible cost. The outcome of this was to engage an unknown international supplier Albert had found on the internet.

Given these ambiguous circumstances Albert also needed to verify the environmental stance of the Kaisler organisation. For example. Albert could have requested a copy of Kaisler's environmental policy and checked whether this conformed to local standards. In addition, at the very least, Albert could have conducted some internet research about Kaisler which might have revealed any historical issues relating to the environment. A more costly, but perhaps more substantive, review could have been achieved by hiring a local agent of some repute to review the environmental history of the Kaisler organisation.

Human rights

The International Labour Organisation (ILO) is the United Nations agency devoted to advancing opportunities for women and men to obtain decent and productive work in conditions of freedom, equity, security and human dignity. Its main aims are to promote rights at work, encourage decent employment opportunities, enhance social protection and strengthen dialogue in handling work-related issues.

Source: ILO

The ILO develops and monitors international labour standards. Member states of the organisation agree to and uphold a set of core labour standards regardless of whether they had ratified the relevant conventions. These are basic human rights and a central core of decent work.

The charity, and in particular Albert, needs not only to have an understanding of these core human rights but also how purchasing activities can support them. Typical investigatory actions that Albert could have pursued might have included any or all of the following.

- Request a statement of Kaisler's policy on child labour

- Request a Kaisler customer list and conduct some appropriate research to verify understanding about the Kaisler labour force

- Commission a locally based agent to prepare a report on Kaisler

- Request an age profile of the Kaisler workforce

The media sensitivity to human rights issues receives global exposure and charity activity must be seen to be 'whiter than white' in their related activities. For example, the copy of the article Albert received implicating the charity with Kaisler manufacturing activity using children working in poor conditions could inflict long-term damage on the charity's credibility.

Part (b)

The structure of this question is self-defining as it reasonable to assume that two marks are available for describing each additional difficulty.

In addition to the previously described difficulties relating to ethical and environmental issues there is a wide-range of other issues that will face organisations such as the charity when maintaining purchasing and supply relationships with overseas suppliers. Five typical examples are given below.

Communication

This is not only a problem associated with language differences but also one related to different time zones. For example, in an attempt to resolve the Kaisler problem, Albert decided to telephone the organisation but was annoyed that no one answered the phone, so instead he left a message. No one returned his call that day but the next morning when he switched on his computer there was an email from Kaisler saying that he would phone Albert at 0700 GMT time that day. However, as Albert had arrived at work at 0830 he also missed that call.

Logistics

New entrants to sourcing from international suppliers will often underestimate the logistical problems and costs that are involved. For example, the geographical distances will invariably impact on transport costs, delivery time, packaging requirements etc. In the case concerned the goods needed to be collected from Kaisler's and it is doubtful whether Albert has researched the costs associated with bringing these goods to the UK.

Political and supplier management issues

The political stability of some foreign countries must be fully understood by the purchasing organisation. Whilst some of this information can be researched, site visits are also recommended to get a first hand appreciation of the both the country and the operation. There are cost implications in achieving this but it can often be cost effective in the long run especially where political instability is suspected.

Trading terms

Trading terms and expectations will vary significantly from one country to another and must be clearly understood from the outset of any supply arrangement. For example, dealing with situations where one party does not want to release the goods until they get paid is common as can be seen in this case where Kaisler informed Albert to send a payment to the Kaisler bank account before the goods would be released. Albert's only indication of product quality would have been via the couriered sample which may or may not be representative of the bulk supply.

Duties and taxes

Knowledge and understanding of the local duties and taxes is also important. How and when taxes/duties are imposed must be allowed for in the supplier selection process. Another related problem might be that of fluctuating currency prices where the buyer, or the seller, might be faced with unconsidered costs over the lifetime of the arrangement. Also, the issue of local expectations related to releasing goods across different border controls must be realistically understood and appraised by the purchasing organisation.

Part (c)

From the facts described within the case study Albert acted in a very naïve manner. His naivety has clearly exposed the charity to both adverse publicity and cost situations. However, many of the issues identified above could have been easily avoided by adopting the following actions.

Incoterms – the use of appropriate incoterms would have confirmed the understanding between Albert and Kaisler over any payment issues.

Letter of credit – both parties would have security about payment transactions

Agent – Albert could have commissioned a local agent to purchase the products for him. Part of this commission could also have included the agent providing an ethical and environmental review of the Kaisler organisation.

Research – the use of the internet can often provide valuable information about potential trading partners. And as mentioned previously, Albert could also have requested a customer list from Kaisler and then undertaken some reference checking.

Networking – Albert could have used his existing contacts to provide guidance and direction on dealing with overseas suppliers. In today's global trading environment many organisations have now got well established offices in many parts of the world. It is therefore likely that some appropriate networking would have supplied Albert with useful information.

The techniques listed above are in common use by purchasing departments. The fact that Albert entered into the Kaisler arrangement in the manner he did just further illustrates his naivety when dealing with international issues. It is therefore recommended that such skills are embedded within the charity as a matter of some urgency.

Question 2

Part (a)

The key command word in this part of the question is the word appraise – make a judgement or assessment followed by a justified conclusion. The question theme relates to business relationships and therefore will need to consider appropriate points on a relationship continuum from adversarial to partnership.

The business relationship in question is between the charity and FMCG. In practice the relationship is between Albert Brunt and Sandra Povey, the marketing manager at FMCG.

Albert, albeit perversely, believes the relationship between the charity and FMCG is a 'partnership'. This perception probably stems from Albert's purchasing background being very much steeped in traditional business dealings where adversarial relationships were the norm. It is easy to see how someone from this background might view the arrangements with FMCG as a 'partnership'. However, to support a genuine partnership relationship the following typical characteristics should be present.

- High level of trust between both parties

- High expectation of a long-term relationship

- Loyalty between supplier/buyer

- Both parties are committed to ongoing continuous improvement

- High supplier/buyer willingness to help in difficult situations

- High willingness to handle exceptions by negotiation

- Win-win/risk sharing

- Focus on future business

Evidence from the case study indicates that the relationship that actually exists between the two organisations is highly unlikely to match this description, particularly as regards Albert's behaviour. For example, when Albert tried to tackle the FMCG issue he picked up the phone and shouted at Sandra Povey in an attempt to resolve the problem.

On the other hand, Sandra Povey appears to have a far better understanding and leaning towards a partnering relationship if judged by her retort to Albert's shouting: *'while it might be costing you in postage, it was saving the charity a great deal in transport'*. Before Sandra ended the call she further advised Albert to 'do a cost/benefit analysis and stop complaining'.

The evidence from the case data is that Albert has an apparent preference for 'adversarial' relationships. The relationship will be characterised by a minimal amount of trust, information exchange, and flexibility in dealing with requirements. While each party may assure the other of the importance of the relationship, the reality is different and either buyer or supplier may terminate at short notice if a better opportunity arises elsewhere. Both buyer and supplier will attempt to make the maximum out of the deal and neither will be motivated to 'go the extra mile' or provide additional services.

Evidence from the case data reflects this adversarial preference. For example, Albert is often heard to say that *you cannot use the words 'trust and supplier' in the same sentence*. Also, Albert takes pride in his traditional view of supplier relationships which is reflected in his adversarial relationship style with suppliers and the people who work for them.

Supplier development would appear to be an alien concept to Albert who proudly proclaims that he can make up his mind about a supplier within five seconds of meeting them.

In conclusion, the business relationship between the two organisations will be heavily influenced by Albert and as such will inevitably become adversarial in nature. Modern thinking has moved away from the use of adversarial relationships and much of the academic literature nowadays focuses on alternative approaches. Despite this, most buyers recognise that the adversarial approach still exists and, in the right circumstances, offers the most suitable way of dealing with suppliers. It is suggested that a reciprocal trading arrangement is not an appropriate circumstance in which to apply an adversarial relationship.

Part (b)

Reciprocal trading is an arrangement between two organisations where they both buy and sell from each other. From a business ethics point of view reciprocal trading is acceptable when there is no coercion involved from either of the parties concerned and there is mutual benefit and transparency.

Part (c)

Albert's adversarial negotiation style is often driven by a win-lose mentality. The very essence of a reciprocal trading arrangement is one of a win-win partnership arrangement.

For reciprocal trading to be successful, both Albert and FMCG should have been satisfied about the mutual benefits such an arrangement would achieve.

The following stages would be recommended to Albert (and FMCG) before entering into their reciprocal trading agreement.

Understanding the commitment

It is essential that both parties have a comprehensive understanding of what they are actually giving and getting out of the trading arrangement.

In Albert's case he would have needed to get confirmation from FMCG about the frequency and scope of material to be posted. In addition, Albert should have established, and notified to FMGC, the frequency and location details of charity deliveries.

Having established the details of the commitment Albert should have calculated a cost benefit analysis to ensure that the reciprocal trading proposal was going to deliver a net benefit to the charity. Equally, FMCG should have convinced themselves of their mutual benefit. Without assurance of a win-win scenario there is little chance that the arrangement would survive in the medium to long term.

Stakeholder communication and involvement

Having convinced himself that the arrangement would be in the best interests of the charity, Albert should have then encouraged stakeholder involvement before committing to the deal. For example, Albert could have asked for input from central administration with regard to the financial viability of the proposals and the formulation of associated budgets and cost centres.

Relationship development

Albert should have entered this kind of arrangement on a partnership relationship as opposed to his preferred adversarial approach to suppliers. His frequently used statement *you cannot use the words 'trust and supplier' in the same sentence* reflects an inappropriate attitude for this kind of commercial arrangement.

As with all arrangements problems will inevitably occur and trading circumstances will change. In the spirit of partnership relationships regular review meetings should be held to ensure any issues arising are dealt with in an appropriate and transparent manner.

Question 3

Part (a)

A supply positioning model is a tool for determining what kind of supply relationships we should seek in relation to the various items we purchase for our organisation. The aim is to distinguish between the criticality of the different items purchased and to use this information in establishing suitable relations with the organisations that supply us with each item.

Many academics and consultants have attempted to develop such models. Typical of these is a model developed by the PMMS consultancy. This maps the different items purchased onto a two-dimensional grid. For each item organisations need to determine:

- The level of risk we run in using that item

- The cost of the item

The basic idea is that for items which are critical in terms of their risk, or in terms of the amount of spend, we must adopt a type of relationship that secures supply. By identifying items that are critical we ensure that management time and effort is directed most effectively.

In terms of risk, the following factors might be considered in relation to each item to be purchased.

- Ability of current supplier

- Lead time for delivery

- Technological developments

- Issues of corporate social responsibility

- Complexity of the item (eg in terms of its specification or manufacturing process)

- Competition in the supply market

- Length and complexity of the supply chain

- Length of product lifecyles in the industry sector

- Criticality of the item in terms of our business processes

In terms of the cost of an item, everything is relative: what is a high cost for one organisation may be a trivial amount for a larger organisation.

The model is drawn up in the shape of a two-by-two grid in which each of supply risk and relative cost can be either low or high.

As with many of the theoretical models of this nature this leads to a pattern of four distinct areas in the grid. In the following explanation those purchased items with high supply risk are referred to as strategic; those with low supply risk are referred to as tactical.

Strategic security items are those with high supply risk and relatively low cost. It is vital to ensure security of supply, and the low cost of the items makes it relatively easy to do this. For example, if necessary we can hold large stocks without too damaging an effect on costs. For the medium to long term, our objective should be to reduce the risks relating to supply: finding additional suppliers or developing closer relationships with existing suppliers.

Tactical acquisition items are those with low supply risk and relatively low cost. Often there will be very many items falling into this category, which can become a burden to purchasing staff unless care is taken to streamline purchasing routines. It is likely that there are a large number of suppliers, and at the same time a large number of users within the buying organisation. Typical methods used in dealing effectively with low-value purchases include purchasing cards, call-off orders against a framework agreement, online ordering through approved supplier catalogues etc. In terms of the relationship spectrum we are probably looking at the transactional or competitive end of the spectrum.

For both of the above categories, the low value reduces the buyer's bargaining power. To overcome this, the buyer should aggregate such purchases as much as possible. In the case of strategic security items, it may be possible to tempt the supplier into a better deal if the buyer can offer to increase the range of items he purchases from that supplier.

Tactical profit items are costly but subject only to slight supply risk. Finding a source of supply presents little problem (there are probably many suppliers available), but the opportunity for improving profit must be taken. This arises from the relatively high cost of the items: even a small percentage saving can add significantly to the bottom-line profit. This suggests that buyers should continually shop around among potential suppliers and regularly get quotes before the next purchase. It would be a mistake, for these items, to enter a long-term supply agreement with a single supplier: this would rule out possible savings as factors change in the competitive environment.

Strategic critical items are the most important of all. The supply risk is great, and the cost of these items is high. It is vital to ensure security of supply at a good price, and this suggests a need for long-term collaborative relationships with a very small number of suppliers.

It is a costly and time-consuming exercise to carry out a supply positioning analysis. It can only be justified by the results it delivers. These can be summarised as follows.

- Better understanding of relative importance of items to be bought; the exercise forces buyers to think very carefully about two important aspects of each item they buy: its supply risk and its relative cost.

- Better understanding of required relationship strategies; the nature of the item in terms of its supply risk and its relative cost helps the buyer to determine the most appropriate type of supply relationship.

- Better understanding of stock requirements; items of low cost are relatively inexpensive to hold in stock, and if they are items with high supply risk (ie strategic security items) this suggests a deliberate policy of stockholding (contrary to modern thinking in most cases, but indicated by the results of the analysis).

Part (b)

The supply positioning model as previously discussed illustrates the buyer's perspective on the items to be purchased. This will often differ significantly from the supplier's perspective: what is very important to the buyer may be relatively unimportant to a particular supplier.

The supplier perception is represented by another PMMS model known as the supplier preferencing model. This again is represented by a two-by-two matrix. The vertical axis measures how attractive it is to the supplier to deal with the buyer; while the horizontal axis measures the monetary value of the business that might be available from the buyer.

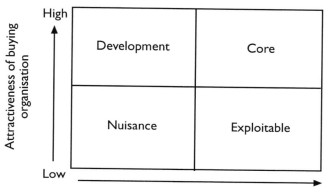

Value of buyer's business

The horizontal axis is self-explanatory, but the attractiveness of the buying organisation (measured on the vertical axis) is less obvious. There are various factors that might make a supplier keen to do business with a buying organisation.

- A buying organisation might be in some way glamorous or high profile. Suppliers will want to deal with such an organisation merely for the sake of boasting to other customers or potential customers about who is on their client list. By contrast, some organisations are inherently unattractive to deal with, and suppliers will give preference to other potential customers unless they are looking to use spare capacity. This might be the case, for example, if the buyer has a poor reputation on corporate social responsibility.

- A buying organisation with a reputation for fair dealing, or with a record of prompt payment to suppliers, will naturally be attractive. Similarly, a buying organisation will be attractive if it has a reputation of engaging closely with suppliers, keeping them well informed, and perhaps working with them on new product development.

In the bottom left quadrant, we have buyers who are neither inherently attractive to the supplier, nor particularly valuable in terms of volume business. The PMMS model labels these unfortunate organisations as nuisance customers. Many suppliers have a policy of reviewing their customer base regularly with a view to terminating contracts with customers who are not 'paying their way'. The situation usually is that the customer takes more effort and cost to service than the value of the business justifies. From the supplier's perspective, the option of termination – or alternatively, hiking prices by a substantial amount – may be the best solution.

The relatively unattractive buying organisations located in the bottom right quadrant of the model contains exploitable customers. They are exploitable in the sense that they offer large volumes of business, which compensates for any lack of inherent attractiveness. It may be this very fact that causes the customer to be unattractive: if the buyers believe they are a major customer, they may exploit this with aggressive behaviour. In such an environment the supplier is grateful enough to do what is required of him under the supply contract, but will not go out of his way to provide extras. And any extras that are demanded will be charged at additional cost.

In the top left quadrant we have development customers. These are customers who do not – or at least do not yet – offer large volumes of business, but who for other reasons are attractive to the supplier. The supplier may see potential for growth in the customer overall, or at least in the volume of business that the customer can offer. It will pay the supplier to court the customer by 'going the extra mile' in fulfilling obligations. This could mean providing extra services for little or no additional cost in order to win favour with the customer, or perhaps accommodating changes in schedules or order levels without complaint. If all goes well, the supplier hopes to push this customer into the top right corner of the grid.

The top right is occupied by core customers. These are the organisations attractive in their own right, and offering valuable levels of business to the supplier. Naturally, the supplier will do all that is possible to stay in favour with these organisations – they are his core business and he will want to maintain close relations. The supplier will want to be aware at the earliest possible stage of any looming threat to the business, and for this reason will keep in regular contact with the customer.

As in the supply positioning model, examined earlier, the supplier preferencing model is not static. The supplier would ideally like to be moving all his customers into the top right quadrant and will work towards doing so. On the other hand, downward progress is possible too. We have already seen that some customers in the bottom left quadrant face possible eviction. Equally, a core customer could move down into the exploitable quadrant if for some reason its inherent attractiveness declined (perhaps because of association with a financial scandal or because of public concerns over corporate social responsibility issues).

Buyers can learn a great deal by trying to view relationships from the perspective of their suppliers. It should not be difficult to guess where in the grid a buyer stands: the general attitude of the supplier's sales staff should give plenty of clues. If the sales staff are helpful, and proactive in involving the buyer closely, the signs are good. On the other hand, if sales staff rarely bother to make contact, or show indifference, then a buyer can conclude that he is in the bottom two quadrants.

It is not necessarily a bad thing for the buyer to be in this situation. For example, a medium-sized firm sourcing its stationery from one of the large number of online catalogues has no particular need to be regarded by the supplier as a core customer. The situation is not particularly sensitive, and the items to be purchased from this supplier are not critical. But if a supplier is the source of critical and valuable items the buyer should work towards becoming a valuable customer. Regular contact with the supplier will be important in establishing what the buyer can do to achieve this.

Question 4

The answer structure for this question is relatively straightforward. It can be assumed that the marks will be awarded equally for each e-tool analysed. The recommended answer structure is as follows:

- ***Introduction***

  Brief definition of e-tools

- ***Main body***

  Identify/discuss five e-tool applications

- ***Conclusions***

  Outline how e-tools have revolutionised the purchasing environment

E-procurement is the general term referring to electronic functionality, mainly internet enabled, to operate the transactional aspects of requisitioning, authorising, ordering, receipting and payment processes for the required services or products. Specifically, e-purchasing is usually the main component of an e-procurement capability. It automates and extends manual buying processes, from the creation of the requisition through to payment of suppliers.

The actual boundaries of an e-purchasing functionality are a debatable issue. However, irrespective of functional boundaries, e-purchasing is enabled by numerous electronic tools, or e-tools, by which organisational benefits can be gained. Five of these available tools are discussed below.

Data warehousing

A data warehouse can be defined as 'an application with a computer database that collects, integrates and stores an organisation's data with the aim of producing accurate and timely management of information and supporting data-analysis'.

The buyer is able to use the database to extract information which will help him in planning a purchase. There are many potential advantages to using a data warehouse.

Data warehouses enhance end-user efficiency in accessing and extracting a wide variety of data. The data warehouse can be further integrated into decision support systems that enable buyers to obtain specified trend reports, eg the items with the most purchase spend by vendor within the last two years. As such data warehouses can be a significant enabler of commercial business applications such as supplier relationship management systems.

The design of any data warehousing system needs to be actively managed to deliver optimum benefits for the organisation. For example, issues such as compatibility, security, storage capacity etc must be carefully considered to ensure a robust data warehousing system.

Electronic reverse auction

This refers to software by which buyers can create an electronic environment in which they can conduct an auction where potential suppliers bid ever lower prices to win a contract. The gradual lowering of bids is what gives the name of reverse auctions. Another aspect of this facility is electronic marketplaces which are websites where buyers can advertise their requirements and sellers their capacity and capabilities.

The auction takes place over a period of time where suppliers can repeatedly enter new, lower bids for the work on offer. These electronic reverse auctions differ from traditional auctions in that suppliers bid against each other to offer the keenest bid for a particular contract.

One particular type of electronic reverse auction is a transparent reverse auction. In this type of auction suppliers know which of the several lines on a visual display is their bid line. In addition they also see the lines of the other competing suppliers but these suppliers remain anonymous. This tool has benefited purchasing organisations by introducing a new form of competition between suppliers and reducing unit costs.

The transparency of these auctions will often remove constraints from suppliers who can put forward their best bids for available business. As a consequence, purchasing staff can undertake faster and more efficient contract negotiations, which is beneficial for suppliers and buyers alike.

Research within the public sector indicates average administrative cost savings from the use of these reverse auctions are in the region of 25% when viewed against traditional paper-based tender processes. This is in addition to the potential unit cost savings.

Electronic tendering

The use of e-tendering replaces traditional manual paper-based tender processes with electronically facilitated processes based on best tendering practices to save time and money. For example, buyers are able to manage the tenders coming in, with all tenders stored in one place. In addition, buyers can cut and paste data from the electronic tender documents for easy comparison in a spreadsheet which also can be automated to further assist the comparison process.

The invitation to tender (ITT) is published via the e-tendering system and is available online for interested suppliers to view. Suppliers would normally access the e-tendering system to view the ITT via the organisation's portal website.

Suppliers respond to the ITT by sending their bids using secure email to the e-tendering system's 'electronic vault'. In-built security features prohibit access to any of the tender responses until a specified time.

Once the tender deadline has been reached the purchasing organisation can view the tenders and collaborate online to evaluate the submitted bids. In the case of e-tendering systems, which include bid evaluation tools, much of the evaluation analysis can be automated. The supplier of the winning bid can be automatically notified of the award via the e-tendering system.

The overall business benefits of e-tendering are many and varied.

- Reduced tendering cycle-time

- Fast and accurate pre-qualification and evaluation, which enables the automatic rejection of suppliers that fail to meet the tender specification

- Faster response to questions and points of clarification during the tender period

- Reduction in the labour intensive tasks and associated paper trail of receipt, recording and distribution of tender submissions

- Improved audit trail increasing integrity and transparency of the tendering process

Extranet/intranet communication

An intranet is an internal network linking computers within the buyer's organisation. This enables staff to access information about many aspects of the organisation, including those related to purchasing.

An extranet extends data availability beyond the boundaries of the purchasing organisation. Subject to password protection, external organisations are allowed to access defined levels of information contained within the intranet system.

This can permit suppliers, for example, to display catalogues tailored for the buying organisation, while staff within the buying organisation can access the catalogues so as to place orders.

The creation of web portals can further enhance the extranet environment. Use of web-based EDI transmissions can permit the rapid exchange of business data between buying and supplying organisations.

Intranet and extranet developments significantly enhance the data transparency and availability both intrinsic and extrinsic to the organisation. This availability can reduce traditional administrative burdens, decrease the time-cycle of many purchasing tasks as well as facilitating supplier development activities such as vendor rating assessment and continuous improvement initiatives.

Electronic tracking systems

Technological advances have led to the development of electronic tracking systems. Often such systems are made possible by the use of barcodes along with radio frequency identification (RFID) and global positioning systems (GPS).

More advanced satellite communications that go beyond GPS technology can also provide information not only about the global location of a container but also about its environmental conditions, whether it has been tampered with, and other useful data.

This kind of advanced tracking information is particularly useful in assisting the management of today's global supply chain applications. For example, the use of inter-modal container solutions is increasingly common in today's global environment. Container tracking can be accomplished relatively easily by associating the container with the carrier whether a cargo vessel, tractor/trailer or rail car.

The key to many of the potential benefits of container tracking and monitoring is sensor technology. Sensors that monitor temperature, humidity, shock, vibration, etc. provide cargo owners with important information about the condition of their goods, whether in real time or displayed as a time-based histogram. Both GPS and RFID systems can be equipped with sensors to collect and report conditions within the container.

These tracking applications can be instrumental in organisations gaining competitive advantage in today's turbulent environments. For example, the ability to have cost effective real time tracking data is fundamental in managing today's lean environments

Conclusion

In recent years the impact of technology on the work of buyers has been dramatic. Specifically, the development of e-purchasing concepts, supported by a myriad of e-tools, has changed the working procedures and routines of purchasing staff forever.

The application of e-purchasing concepts has undoubtedly been instrumental in assisting buyers to gain commercial benefits. However, in the midst of this electronic revolution, traditional purchasing disciplines remain as important as ever. In fact, the applications of e-tools will often remove administrative burdens that actually allow buyers time to focus on the 'real issues' inside and outside of the business.

Question 5

The format of this question significantly assists in planning the answer structure. It can be assumed that each of the five responses will carry equal weighting of awarded marks. Balance is therefore needed within the given responses. A suggested answer plan is as follows.

- **Introduction**

   Outline the growing presence of public sector spend and the associated legislative framework applicable to the public sector supplier selection processes.

- **Main body**

   Discuss five main differences between the public and private supplier selection process

- **Conclusions**

A major classification of buying environment distinguishes between private sector and public sector organisations. Much of the traditional theory and practices were modelled around the private sector. However, changes in much of the European business landscape have put increased focus on the purchasing processes within the public sector.

The spending power of today's UK public sector enterprises is enormous as is the diversity of the public sector service provision. The scope of this provision will need to cover roads, law and order, education, health services, emergency services, and much more.

However, the supplier selection processes that exist within the private and public sector are bound by very different rules of engagement. The following examples compare and contrast these differences, many of which have been influenced by recent EU directives and legislation that needs to be adopted within the public sector.

Official Journal of the European Union

The European procurement directives are having an effect on purchasing in the public sector. Once a buyer has specified the product or service he requires, and has decided to use the tendering method, he must ensure that he complies with European Union directives as specified in the Official Journal of the European Union (OJEU). These do not apply to private sector buying, but do cover purchases by public authorities unless their value is below a certain (low) threshold.

Subject to certain exceptions, the directives require public bodies to use open tendering procedures. They must advertise the invitation to tender according to defined rules designed to secure maximum publicity.

The results of the tendering procedure must be notified to the Office of Official Publications of the European Communities, and will then be made public.

Contract award criteria

Public sector organisations must indicate their award criteria to all bidders before they bid, whereas private sector organisations are not obliged to conform to this requirement. The minimum criteria must be stated in the notice published in the OJEU and/or in the contract documentation. Once selected, the criteria may not be significantly changed.

In general, buyers are obliged to award the contract on the basis of the lowest quoted price, or on the basis of the economically most advantageous tender. If they choose the latter alternative, they must make the fact known to candidates, and must explain by what criteria they mean to assess 'economic advantage'. The purchaser is allowed to exclude firms if they fail to meet defined criteria relating to general suitability, financial and economic standing and technical competence.

Contract duration

Private sector organisations can continue using the same supplier as long as both parties agree that they wish to continue the relationship. In the public sector, contracts cannot normally be extended past their stated duration.

This constraint on public sector contracts gives rise to an important question concerning supplier relations. Modern approaches to supplier relations strongly emphasise the value of long-term partnerships between a buyer and a limited number of suppliers. Competitive tendering retains an important place in the buyer's portfolio of techniques, but is not generally suitable in relation to materials for which long-term partnerships are sought. The public sector buyer, constrained to use competitive tendering in all cases, therefore finds that the benefits of long-term partnership are unattainable.

Competitive tendering

Public sector supplier selection processes need to be transparent and competitive in nature. In contrast the private sector is not bound by this requirement. So, for example, if workload pressures mean that a private sector organisation does not have time for a competitive process they are not obliged to use one. The public sector cannot use this reason for a single supplier selection.

The necessity to conform to this competitive tendering can introduce significant inertia into the supplier selection process. For example, under the negotiated procedure where a contract notice is required, prospective bidders must be given a minimum of 37 days to register their interest to negotiate. In addition, where there are a sufficient number of suppliers who are suitable to be selected to negotiate, the number selected must not be less than three.

Recent recognition of e-purchasing processes has reduced this inertia problem to a certain degree. For example, in the latest EU directive amendments, time reductions can be achieved on the tendering process where:

- Contract notices are drawn up and transmitted by electronic means

- The contracting authority offers unrestricted and full direct access by electronic means to the contract documents and any supplementary documents

Public authorities wishing to take advantage of this opportunity must publish the specifications and the additional documents in their entirety on the internet.

Contract scope

In the private sector, following the award of a contract, it is quite common for the scope of the work within the contract to be extended subject to mutual agreement between both parties. This arrangement is not permissible within public sector organisations as they must promote competition of supply on all occasions.

Again, this public sector selection criterion introduces potential inertia and delays into the procurement cycle. This can be particularly frustrating as often the bidders that will be tendering for the additional work within the authority are the same as those tendering for the original requirement.

Although the ideology of competitive tendering is regarded as good purchasing policy the rigidity of the public sector selection process can also be frustrating in such circumstances of extending contract scope. In contrast, private sector organisations can simply negotiate with one supplier, and ignore others.

In summary, the regime of compulsory competitive tendering in the public sector can be seen as a major potential barrier in adopting and developing modern notions of long-term partnership relations.

The regime that is embodied in European procurement directives clearly encourages equal opportunities within a competitive European trading environment. However, this ideology is not without its downsides. In today's public sector the demand for best value is paramount but this target is not always assisted by the imposed restrictions related to the procurement process, including the supplier selection process.

Question 6

Part (a)

A definition of the term 'outsourcing' is as follows:

Outsourcing is the delegation of work previously carried out in-house to an external service provider. The outsourcer will draw up a contract, typically for the long term, specifying the work to be done, the service levels to be achieved etc. The outsourcer retains responsibility for satisfactory completion of the work, but delegates day-to-day operations to the outsource provider.

Part (b)

Five benefits that a purchasing organisation may seek from outsourcing are as follows.

- Strategically, outsourcing can be used to enable an organisation to focus on its perceived core activities. Core activities can be described as those activities that embody the organisation's key value-adding skills and that confer competitive advantage. Any other activities are often defined as non-core and are frequently regarded as possible candidates for outsourcing.

- A major reason for outsourcing is the possibility that it will be cheaper to buy the services than to provide them in-house. This is not necessarily an easy matter to establish, and assessing value for money in outsourced services is a delicate process. It may not be completely obvious why a third party should be able to carry out the same service more cheaply than can be achieved in-house. However, it is possible that the supplier benefits from economies of scale in the particular activity we are outsourcing. Additionally, they may benefit from greater productivity and efficiency arising from the volume of transactions they handle and the specialist experience they possess.

- In addition to actual cost savings obtained from outsourcing, the organisation can often achieve a leaner balance sheet by divesting itself of assets that would otherwise be required in-house. This can have a favourable impact on the financial stability of the company, and in particular on its return on net assets (RONA) ratio.

- The outsourcer may be unable to keep up with the pace of technological change in a particular activity. Attempting to do so would divert management attention from the more important tasks of running the business effectively. For example, this is often the reason why many companies have outsourced their IT applications.

The outsourcing organisation may simply not be very good at the activity in question. Rather than attempting to improve the in-house performance, especially in an area that is not core to their business, it may be preferable to use the expert services of an organisation specialising in that activity. Both the purchasing organisation and its customers can benefit from this better service.

Part (c)

When one part of an organisation is outsourced this will often lead to reengineering of the business. One of the implications of this activity is that internal responsibilities and relationships are subject to change. These 'softer' people issues need to be carefully considered and subsequently managed appropriately in the event of outsourcing.

In the event of outsourcing it is common for the same personnel to carry out the outsourced tasks, only instead of being employed by the buyer they work for the contractor. There are instances where the original staff remain *in situ*, and even work on the same equipment; the only difference is in the status of the staff (they now work for the contractor, not for the buyer) and the ownership of the equipment (transferred from buyer to contractor). This situation will potentially affect the loyalty of the people concerned. This will probably mean that their loyalty is now firstly to their new employer and not their old employer. As such the purchasing organisation may not get the same level of loyalty from the people who are no longer employees.

The operation of outsourced operations may introduce internal stress and frustration due to the extended speed of response in times of conflict. For example it is easy for the purchasing organisation to complain that the service provider is not reacting quickly enough, but the supplier may retort that constant calls for 'urgent' attention suggest lack of forward planning by the purchaser. Previously, when all the staff worked for the same organisation, and often the same manager, these situations were able to be resolved quickly but now because people from different organisations are involved resolution can be more protracted.

Within any organisation informal processes exist between the user of the service and the internal deliverer of the service. When services are outsourced these informal activities often need to be formalised. This formalisation of processes and relationships can result in increased time to bring about business change. In addition, this scenario may also be accompanied with increased administrative burdens. This formalisation process might also have cost implications as the total task becomes visible to the supplier. In some instances this visibility of total provision and associated costs may jeopardise the outsourcing initiative.

Subject Index